Ten Years of Multinational Business

Ten Years of Multinational Business

by
Malcolm Crawford,
James Poole, editors

Abt Books
Cambridge, Massachusetts
EIU Special Series 5

Library of Congress Cataloging in Publication Data

Ten years of multinational business.

  (Economist Intelligence Unit special series)
  1. International business enterprises—Addresses, essays, lectures. I.
Crawford, Malcolm. II. Poole, James. III. Multinational business. IV. Series.
HD2755.5.T45 1982 388.8'8   82–13821
ISBN 0–89011–580–X

Printed in the United States of America

Contents

Multinational Business

The Economist Intelligence Unit launched Multinational Business in 1971, as a quarterly covering issues related to what is known in academic circles as international direct investment, or more commonly as the phenomenon of the multinational company. The objective was to cover the subject matter in greater depth and with more considered judgment than is possible for writers in newspapers, given the pressures of time upon them, and yet to do so with greater clarity than is usually achieved by articles in academic journals.

The multinational company has been an object of great disputation and sometimes abuse in the 1970s. At one stage it figured in a demonology according to which it loomed as a monstrous threat to the sovereignty of nations. During the decade, informed opinion swung from visions of sovereignty at bay to the spectacle of multinational companies at bay, and in some areas visibly on the retreat. Even so, late in the decade it appeared that the total of international direct investment was still increasing, albeit at a much slower pace than at the beginning.

This EIU Special consists of articles and notes selected to represent the breadth of coverage of the subject matter in the quarterly during the 1970s. While it might have been tempting to call it the best of Multinational Business, the aim has been to publish a text which covers the issues as extensively as possible. Many excellent articles moreover have been excluded because of their topicality when they were published: that which is topical tends to date and be of less enduring relevance. This applies, for example, to the problems of the international petroleum industry and international banking in the mid 1970s.

Authors have been asked to correct errors which could be misleading as to fact, but not to adjust judgments in the light of hindsight. The articles are therefore nearly identical to those published, with two exceptions. In his article in the first section providing an overview of the areas of dispute about multinational companies, Malcolm Crawford, the editor of the quarterly, has synthesised two articles published at different dates, though for the most part what appears here is the second of the two (published in the third quarter of 1976). Also, the same author has inserted into his article on bribery and corruption some amplifying material on American policy contained in a follow up note in the issue immediately after the main article.

The absence of signatures on the shorter notes reflects the practice of the quarterly; in general these are meant to deal more briefly and narrowly with their topics than the articles in depth, and to report rather than assess and evaluate. Most of these notes were written by James Poole, co-editor of the quarterly.

The section headings are self explanatory in the main, but in regard to the company studies it is worth pointing out that these are not simply company profiles, which would be a presumptuous waste of the time of the kind of reader at which Multinational Business has been aimed. Each of them focuses upon a problem or principle of international business operation which is of more or less general application and interest.

The Special thus compiled is, we believe, a useful collection of important articles giving a panoramic as well as penetrating view of the subject.

I. THE INTERNATIONAL POLITICAL ENVIRONMENT

Multinational Business and the Challenge of the 1980s

PROFESSOR J.H. DUNNING●   **No.1 1978**

It was only a decade ago that a learned commentator on multinational enterprises predicted that by the mid 1980s the 300 or 400 super-giant companies in the world would account for 60-70 per cent of the world's industrial output.[1] Many other analysts, economists, politicians, and even businessmen themselves, believed him. At that time, the MNC seemed to be an increasingly powerful force in the world economy, and nothing was expected to stop it in its surge forwards.

Yet in the Fortune magazine, August 1977, there appeared an article by Sanford Rose, one of the more perceptive writers on MNCs, entitled Multinationals in Retreat, the main thrust of which was that, faced with a marked slowing down of world economic growth and increasing hostility, by both home and host governments, to their policies and behaviour, giant companies were cutting back on their international investments, and seeking new directions for their future growth.

The events which caused this dramatic turn-about in the prognosis of the future of MNCs are well known. Almost every week, the press reports some incident typifying the confrontation between MNCs and governments, and of new measures introduced to control or regulate their activities. In international fora, particularly at the UN, demands for stronger international action against the misuse of power by such companies continue to be voiced. In addition to the usually well publicised cases of expropriation of assets of MNCs, there are many more of voluntary or semi-voluntary divestment and refusal on the part of MNCs to accept the demands of host governments - notably in some developing countries. The recent withdrawal of IBM and Coca Cola from India are just two instances of the 'retreat' of MNCs. At both a national and international level, attempts to harmonise the activities of MNCs with the goals of the nation states in which they operate continue unabated. While the OECD has contented itself with the laying down of Guidelines on Behaviour to MNCs - (at the same time accepting that MNCs should not be discriminated against in relation to national firms) - the UN - notably in the guise of Unctad and the Commission on Transnational Corporations (the UN nomenclature for MNCs) - has been pressing for more international controls on the behaviour of such companies. With such attitudes and policies, and within an uncertain and fragile world economic environment, one might be forgiven for believing that these dinosaurs of international business have had their day and must give way to other institutional forms more suited to the needs of the future.

My own reading of the current situation is very different. Just as in 1968 I did not subscribe to the Perlmutter view, so neither do I believe that MNCs are in retreat today. Rather, with one exception to which I will refer later, I believe the peak of the confrontation between MNCs and governments is now passed and that the 1980s will see a more constructive and conciliatory relationship emerging, based on a more intelligent perception of the goals and aspirations of each party; a stronger bargaining capacity of governments; and an acceptance of more involvement by governments in the decision-taking process. In one sense, however, the retreatist view may be correct. That is that the traditional role of MNCs, as providers of entrepreneurial capital, may have passed its zenith. Instead, their future is likely to rest

---

● Professor of International Investment and Business Studies at the University of Reading and consultant on multinational business to the UN Secretariat.

1 H V Perlmutter, "Super-Giant Firms in the Future", Wharton Quarterly, Winter 1968.

in the provision of technical and managerial services bundled together in a variety of ways, the allocation of which will be increasingly determined by contract or by government fiat. In the 1970s, MNCs - particularly smaller MNCs and those from Japan - have shown themselves eminently adaptable to new forms of involvement other than the 100 per cent owned affiliate. At the same time, new opportunities are opening for MNCs, mainly in the form of joint ventures and technical service agreements in the centrally planned economies. In all these cases, although the leopard may have changed its spots, it is still the same beast.

The historical development

In retrospect, the two decades up to 1975 may be regarded as the maturation of one phase in the evolution of international resource transmission. This phase began at the turn of the 20th century, remained inactive in the inter-war years, and blossomed after the second world war in conditions which were ideally suited to the extension of activities of firms across national boundaries, through the medium of equity investment. This particular phase followed a much longer era which dated back to the Industrial Revolution and even before. During this period, capital, labour, and technology and entrepreneurship migrated overseas, largely from Europe to the USA, the Commonwealth and South America. This culminated in the decade before the first world war when Great Britain was investing abroad three times as much as it was investing at home. But it differed from the period which followed it in this fundamental way: although the enterprises were owned and controlled in the capital-exporting country, they were not direct investments as we understand the concept today. The overseas enterprises were at arms length from the owners. Very often, in the case of British investments, they were quoted on the London stock exchange. In an operational sense they were either wholly integral to the host country, as with the various railway investments, or very largely so with a limited degree of British management and operation, as in the case of the Hudson's Bay Company. This characteristic of international investment in the 19th century had three important manifestations.

First, the resources used were transmitted separately and independently of each other; there was no single organisation packaging them together and arranging for their joint shipment. Second, the resources, or the right to their use, were exchanged between independent parties at arms length prices. Thirdly, the exchange was accompanied by a change in the ownership of the use of resources; i e the seller transferred control of the allocation of resources to the buyer.

The contractual method of transferring resources remained the dominant mechanism throughout the 19th century. It was facilitated by an international economic environment in which there were adequate capital markets and few barriers to the international transfer of resources between firms, while there were inadequate mechanisms for transferring resources within firms. Only as transport and communications facilities improved did the territorial expansion of business within particular companies become a feasible proposition. And where it did, it was in the area in which the markets worked the least successfully - e g in the supply of natural resources, where uncertainty over future supplies and terms of transfer led firms to 'internalise' their activities by operating their own mines and plantations.

Events of the 20th century changed this situation dramatically. Analysts suggest there were two main reasons for the growth of the MNC. First, the tremendous improvements in transport and communications technology made it as easy for a New York business to operate a branch plant in Frankfurt or Lagos as in Washington or Los Angeles; the jet aircraft and the computer were the culmination of the trend. Second, the 20th century markets in capital, technology and management failed to provide an adequate mechanism for the efficient transfer of resources, as the equivalent markets of the 19th century had done. In particular, market imperfections, brought about by specialised modern technologies, led to increasing concentration of both capital and knowledge and a powerful advantage for companies first in the field.

The more complex the technology, the larger the size of the firm, the more protection given by the patent systems, and the greater the barriers to trade in goods, the more firms found that the best way to capture the advantages of the technology, capital, and management skills they possessed was by engaging in direct investment overseas.

Until the early 1970s, the growth of MNCs continued unabated. Immediately before the quadrupling of oil prices, the value of international production exceeded that of international trade. Its rate of growth in the 1960s was double that of world output and half as great again as world trade. By 1973, the value of production accounted for by MNCs was put at one third the world's gross output outside the centrally planned economies. Latest figures suggest a slowing down of the rate of growth of foreign direct investment since 1973 to below that of world output. Nevertheless, by the end of 1976, the total stock of foreign direct investment of market economies was estimated at $287.2 bn compared with $158.4 bn five years earlier and $105.3 bn in 1967.

But the point I want to emphasise here is that the non-contractual (i e equity investment) route of transferring resources is very different from the contractual route - or, at least, the contractual route of the 19th century. First, the investing firm organises and transmits a package of resources - such that the contributions (or the costs) of the individual ingredients cannot easily be separately identified. Second, the resources are not exchanged on the open market; rather they are channelled within the same firm, i e they are internal rather than external transmissions. Third, because there is no change in their ownership, control over the allocation of the resources, and local resources used with them, remains with the supplying rather than the receiving firm.

The 1960s saw a very rapid expansion in this method of resource transmission, and with it a changing strategy and organisational structure of MNCs, which resulted in more, rather than less, centralised control over key areas of decision taking. Bretton Woods and Havana provided the economic underpinnings for the pattern of post-war international commerce and resource allocation; yet tariffs and quotas, a shortage of foreign currency in host countries, and a desire of many countries to build up indigenous manufacturing capabilities, forced firms (particularly American ones) to service their foreign markets through local production more than through exports.

At the same time, policies of many host governments were becoming more nationalistic. As part of their search for economic independence and self determination they became aware of the need to ensure that the way resources, whether domestic or imported, were used was consistent with developmental and other goals. Frequently, it appeared that the type of control exercised by MNCs over their affiliates, particularly when they operated a regional or global strategy, clashed with these objectives. Increasingly, too, MNCs were perceived to use their internal transactions to transfer income out of countries, thereby reducing local value added. The smaller and less developed countries found themselves particularly weak in bargaining power against the MNCs, particularly where the latter had a choice of location from which to supply international markets, e g the various manufacturing export platforms of Mexico and South East Asia.

For these and other reasons documented elsewhere[1] the tension between MNCs and governments grew throughout the 1960s and early 1970s. Some issues attracted particular attention. Among these were the control of technology transmission by MNCs, and the continued centralisation by them of technology-creating (i e R and D) activities in the home countries; the

---

1 See for example Multinational Enterprises in World Development, UN 1973 (No. E.73 II A.11).

control over export markets and the sourcing of inputs, which sometimes both had adverse balance of payments consequences and lessened the integration of MNCs with the local economies (this criticism was particularly directed to resource based MNCs that undertook downstream processing operations in developed countries); and transfer price manipulations of MNCs which reduced the local value added by such companies. Added to these concerns were others more to do with the political and cultural impact of MNCs.

In due course, all these concerns were laid at the door of the _form_ of the resource transmission (i e the equity investment or non-contractual route) which allowed the transferor of the resources to retain the right to control the use of them. Attention then focused - and continues to be focused - on (i) ensuring either that the control exercised by the MNC is decentralised or, where this is not possible, that it is used in such a way as is consistent with national goals and policies; and (ii) seeking alternative forms of acquiring foreign resources without foreign control over the use of such resources. In the former case, the methods currently used vary from regulating the conditions of inward direct investment, and/or insisting on certain performance criteria, to laying down a series of guidelines on behaviour to the foreign firms. In the latter, attention has been directed to reducing the equity participation of foreign firms, and to depackaging the resources they provide, with the objective that each resource is bought from a different source on a contractual and arms length basis.

Equity ownership by the resource-exporting firms is not the only mechanism by which international investment can operate. Indeed, a degree of reversion towards the more contractual form which was universal in the 19th century is not inconceivable. Yet to predict or suggest this is not to say that a similar shift in control would accompany it. Control is, as will be shown, to some extent a separate question.

The success which host countries _appear_ to have had in controlling the activities of MNCs and of finding other sources of resources is essentially a reflection of increased bargaining power vis à vis the MNCs. This is due first to their better appreciation of national goals and policies and of the costs and benefits of foreign direct investment and its alternatives - especially by the larger and more prosperous host countries. Second, it reflects the growing competition among MNCs for investment outlets. Particularly significant in this respect has been the growth of 'second league' MNCs and of Japanese MNCs - both of which appear to be more prepared to adapt to the demands of host countries than their predecessors. Third, the alternative sources of capital, technology and management have enormously increased - notably finance and expert advice from international organisations, in some cases technology from the communist bloc, and finance from the international banking system.

The future of MNCs

It is considerations such as these which have led commentators to be pessimistic about the future of MNCs in the world economy. I believe they are wrong, for two main reasons. First, over three quarters of the activities of MNCs are within the developed countries, and while there are concerns about the behaviour and control of such companies, the atmosphere for international direct investment is generally congenial, and likely to continue so in the foreseeable future. Indeed, with the realignment of currencies and the growing technological strength of Europe and Japan there is likely to be a greater symmetry of trans-Atlantic investment flows between OECD countries, and particularly between Europe and the USA, than there has been in the past. In these countries, the main instruments of policy are likely to be Guidelines on Behaviour (such as those accepted by OECD countries) and general regulatory mechanisms of host countries (and of the EEC), e g with respect to new foreign investment and restrictive practices. In the developed world, the main uncertainty about the future of MNCs surrounds the policies of _home_ countries, both towards big business itself (should it be more regulated or broken up?) and to the foreign activities of such companies with respect to their impact on domestic employment, technological capability, and industrial concentration.

Second, although the role of equity capital - certainly the 100 per cent owned affiliate - is likely to become less significant in many developing countries, it will probably not decline as much as was first thought a few years ago. Moreover, even where it does, this does not necessarily mean that the providers of equity capital will cease to provide the other resources needed for development. The reason for the first statement is that the experience of some developing countries - particularly in Africa - in obtaining technology and management skills through the non-equity investment route have not always been as successful as they had hoped. This is mainly because they underestimated the advantages of importing resources as a package or an integrated production and marketing programme, and overestimated their own capabilities to organise and complement the separately imported resources. The reason for the second statement is that, in many cases, the MNC remains a unique source of many of the resources and skills - particularly of organisational skills - required by countries. The main difference is that they are no longer unique in their role as capital suppliers and that, apart from joint ventures, the non-contractual route of supplying intangible assets, including knowledge about, and access to, markets, involves the exchange of services at arms length prices. However, it cannot be presumed that these external prices will be lower than the internal prices charged by MNCs; this will depend on the market conditions for the resources in question. Neither can it be assumed that the control over decision taking will de facto be reduced as a result of a change of the corporate arrangements by which the resources are transmitted.

Indeed, the question 'wherein does control lie' is likely to dominate attitudes of host countries towards the import of resources over the next decade. A lot of preconceptions about control being unique to equity investment have been shattered in recent years. Various studies, inter alia by Unctad, suggest that the extent to which the seller is able to control the use of resources once transferred rests as much on his bargaining power vis à vis the buyer at the time the resources are transmitted, as on any continuing relationship between the two parties. Thus, if the licensor of technology is the sole supplier of that technology he may be able to impose conditons over the use of it (or the marketing of the products it produces) by the licensee. Outside manufacturing industry, one classic example of very extensive and detailed control over day to day resource allocation exercised by a foreign seller of services, without any equity capital being involved, is the international hotel industry. One has only to read the standard contracts and management manuals of the Hilton and Intercontinental chains to appreciate this.[1]

What does this mean for the future of MNCs and attitudes of host countries towards them? I shall draw four principal conclusions.

1. Taken separately, the choice to host countries of obtaining resources, once the exclusive province of MNCs and mainly those of US and UK origin, is widening. In consequence, the opportunities to externalise the import of resources is greater than it has ever been and is likely to continue to increase. On the other hand, MNCs still have, and are likely to continue to have, a competitive edge in supplying - as a package or a system - those types of technology, management, organisational and marketing skills which are unique to running a large and geographically dispersed operation.

---

1   The early concession agreements concluded by foreign mining companies and host governments are another example of 'control without equity investment'.

The terms of the contractual element in any arrangement for the transmission of resources are likely to play a more important role than in the past. This does not only apply to arms length agreements where there is a trend away from concessions to technical service agreements, but also to the contractual (or quasi-contractual) component of an equity investment. Indeed, I would predict that there will be less concern by host countries about the modality of the transmission of resources and more on the conditions attached to the transmission, particularly as to the use made of resources once transmitted. If it is possible to ensure that these are in the host country's interests and that they can be re-negotiated after a period of time long enough to ensure continuity and stability to the company making available the services, then, apart from the purely financial considerations, it may matter little whether the modality takes the form of equity investment or contract.

In this respect, codes of conduct and guidelines may be considered as quasi-contracts in as far as they fulfil two main functions. The first is an informational and a persuasive device, i e to let MNCs know what is desired of them. The second is that they act as a kind of warning signal to potentially offending MNCs. For although, as the situation stands, sanctions may be limited (mainly publicising the "bad boy" and selective action by individual governments with the backing of others), collective agreement has been reached and a machinery established which may be used to consider further steps which could be much less palatable to MNCs. It is for this reason, together with the fact that governments of very different political and other persuasions have found it possible to agree on many issues relating to MNCs, that I would not wish to underestimate the significance of this form of international consensus.

3.   Once the control aspect is settled, the role of MNCs as contractors for governments or consortia of governments opens up tremendously. It is often claimed that MNCs do not meet the basic needs of developing countries. Not only is this a facile statement - MNCs have been directly instrumental in improving agricultural productivity and health, e g by their production of fertilisers, agricultural machinery and drugs, as well as providing transportation and communications equipment; but if they do not do so as much as they might, this is as much the fault of individual governments or international agencies in failing to find the ways and means of harnessing the resources which MNCs do possess to this objective. The exploration of the sea bed, major irrigation schemes, the building of trunk roads, electrification projects, all require the technology and skills which MNCs are particularly well equipped to provide. What is needed is the organisational capacity and entrepreneurial initiative to be directed into ensuring that the MNCs can play a contractual role in doing just this. Here, the future could be very promising for such companies; their role is already seen in major petrochemicals and engineering projects in the Middle East, Latin America and South East Asia.

4.   Both the MNCs and host countries (particularly developing countries) should take note of the Japanese and East European attitudes towards inward direct investment. It is not without relevance that, at the same time as developing countries have been making life more difficult for the MNCs, Japan and East European countries have been opening their borders to foreign direct investment. But observe the differences in the two situations. Both Japan and East European countries outlawed foreign investment and strongly controlled the import of resources through the contractual route, until they felt themselves strong enough to absorb the affiliates of MNCs, without being taken over by them. In both cases, with few exceptions, only minority joint ventures are allowed - the few exceptions

being where the MNC believes that internalised control is essential for the implementation of its global or regional strategy _and_ where the recipient country believes
that being part of that strategy will benefit it more than obtaining the resources
provided by the MNC through an alternative route - or not importing the resources
at all. Observe, too, that in both cases the technological infrastructure is such
that effective use can be made of the resources transferred, i e there is skilled
manpower and supportive technology to know what to do with the resources and
maintain them.

Developing countries

The situation in most developing countries is very different - except that a few countries in the
Far East known collectively as the six Japans are approaching the stage of development of
Japan two decades ago. The rest are in a dilemma: on the one hand if they try and emulate
the policies of Japan in the 1960s they may fail because they lack the indigenous technical
capacity to buy the resources for growth by the contractual route; on the other, if they rely on
MNCs to provide the package of resources they need, they are in danger of being dominated
by and dependent on such companies and tied into their networks. This is precisely the situation from which Brazil and Mexico are trying to extricate themselves at the present time.

The answer is not an easy one, but I believe it lies along the route suggested earlier in this
article. Developing countries should seek to buy resources from the source, by the modality
and in the combination which, taken with their own resources, enable them best to further
their long term objectives. The attainment of control by a country over the direction of resource allocation[1] (as reflected, for example, in its external payments flows or in changes
in the nationality of labour inputs) is not inconsistent with its importing resources with the
assistance of foreign companies, either through direct equity investment or through arms
length contracts. The ability to do just this, together with strengthened bargaining power
coupled with an efficient administrative machinery, is perhaps one of the most useful ways in
which developing countries can help themselves.

Conclusion

The wheel of history is turning full circle regarding the way resources are internationally
transmitted. The MNC is not in retreat or, perhaps one should say, need not be in retreat.
For every door which closes another opens up. The forms of contractual involvement and
the nature of resources provided by MNCs in the last quarter of the 20th century will be very
different from those of the third quarter of the 19th century. Resources may be packaged
together in various ways, and many different institutions may be involved in particular projects. In addition, although I expect the environment for international investment to improve
rather than deteriorate over the next decade or more, the activities of MNCs and other foreign
firms are bound to be circumscribed by guidelines, codes, regulations and laws, many of
these backed by international consensus. But, hopefully, in exchange for these constraints
on behaviour, there will be a greater awareness on the part of governments of their responsibilities to MNCs and a greater perception of their needs, and this may show itself in a more
stable environment in which such business may operate. Within these constraints, and if
governments take advantage of half the opportunities to make proper use of MNCs, the future
for such companies offers both scope and promise.

---

1 NB - This is not the same as controlling the _efficiency_ of resource allocation - which is
more difficult.

The Case Against Multinationals: the Main Criticisms Re-examined

MALCOLM CRAWFORD●   No.3 1977

The intellectual onslaught on multinational companies continues at a level perhaps a little below the almost frenetic peak of 1973 to 1975, but not very much below. In that brief era, the Group of Eminent Persons appointed by the UN Economic and Social Council to study multinationals and their impact on world development reported its findings; the Third World (and much of the other two) was alarmed by the revelations of attempts by ITT some years earlier to persuade the US administration to overthrow the government of Chile; a series of disclosures of bribery and corruption were made involving a variety of American companies, mainly elicited by congressional hearings; and during that time a number of comprehensive if rather emotional attacks on the phenomenon of multinational business as such were published. If the storm has abated since then, it has certainly not ceased.

The term "multinational business", as used by this quarterly since its inception, refers to the activities and problems of companies a substantial proportion of whose assets are located outside the firm's home country. This is also the sense in which it is used in the specialist literature,where the subject developed as an extension of the economics of international investment, married with the economics of technology transfer. The critiques, which are written in a manner such as to have wide public appeal, are however addressed to something much broader than that; they are really complaints about the capitalist system, about the consequences of a system of free (or fairly free) trade subject to the permission of governments, and about the real and sometimes necessarily disappointing effects of the process of international allocation of scarce resources and technical knowhow whether through the channel of non-resident asset ownership or any other. Later in this article it will be suggested that the issues of multinational business as such on which criticism is correctly focused are narrow ones, generally of a technical nature; and that the criticisms related to the broader issues do not really depend on whether assets are owned by residents or non-residents. Finally this article will attempt to assess briefly the practical consequences of the onslaught.

The World Council of Churches is taking a stand

Among the most recent displays of hostility is one which has emerged, odd as it may seem, from the World Council of Churches, which at its annual committee meeting in Geneva in August 1977 considered an internal document accusing multinational companies of acting in a variety of ways against the interest of host countries and indeed of "the vast majority of the world's population", and calling for a programme of action to be devised by its staff. Although the sins of multinational companies are apparently multitudinous, the council appears most concerned about their alleged assistance to evil and racist governments, and about corporate policies which have helped to increase the oppressed state of peoples in those countries. If the concern of the churches is to have any effect, it would appear intended to operate through the consciences of Christian businessmen, ministers and officials in the countries where the firms are owned, controlled, or financed.

Rising to a somewhat higher level of ratiocination, one should cite a study by Sanjaya Lall commissioned and published by the Commonwealth Secretariat (Commonwealth Economic Paper No. 5, Developing Countries and Multinational Corporations) in November 1976. It is not possible to summarise this report briefly. Inter alia, Lall commends host government policies such as those of the Andean Pact members (see Multinational Business No. 4 - 1976) and of the Indian government under Mrs Ghandi; counsels governments to limit the scope and amount of foreign capital and to foster attitudes which reduce the tendency for their economies and societies to become satellites of the developed countries; suggests the restriction of

---

●   Economics editor of the Sunday Times.

foreign enterprise to sectors where local enterprise is lacking or where foreign technology is necessary, and the promotion of joint ventures and the divestiture of existing foreign controlling holdings; warns governments against offering high effective protection for import saving production by foreign owned firms; argues against tax concessions to attract foreign capital except for exporting firms, and outlines a bargaining strategy with regard to those investments which the host government does want to attract. Provided one allows for its favourable assumptions about the potential disruption of welfare and efficiency inherent in such a highly regulated host country environment, there is much that is instructive in this paper.

Perhaps the most celebrated of the books attacking multinational enterprises is Global Reach[1], published first in the USA in 1974 and subsequently in several countries and languages. It may yet prove to be as influential in the developing countries as Servan-Schreiber (Le Défi Américain) was in Western Europe. Its style of argument resembles the latter in some ways, while finding less that is constructive about the multinationals, which Barnet and Müller portray as power wielding, hierarchically organised in ways which suppress national aims and preferences, and as creators rather than satisfiers of people's wants and needs. If J K Galbraith was found less than convincing in his arguments in this vein concerning developed countries, he was (one is asked to believe) absolutely right in regard to less developed ones. Essentially, however, the nub of the Barnet and Müller thesis concerns conflict of interest between multinational firms and nation states, and it is the latter - however autarchic, however chauvinistic, however ill governed - that have the authors' sympathies.

In the UK, a Fabian research paper by Carl Wilms-Wright, secretary of the Economic and Social Committee of the International Confederation of Free Trade Unions, is interesting because of its comprehensive exposition of the alleged malpractices of multinational companies as seen by labour oriented critics in Europe - as distinct from those of Lall and Barnet and Müller, who are concerned primarily with developing countries.

The main charges summarised

While it is not possible to analyse in an article all the criticisms of multinational enterprise contained in these works, the principal charges may be briefly summarised here.

1. Multinational firms invest where they choose, regardless of the wishes and policies of governments. When deciding on a major new investment, they play one government off against another. According to Wilms-Wright, they cut back production or fail to invest at times of low economic growth; equally they cut back production even in a phase of rapid overall growth in response to a longer term policy of disinvestment.

2. Firms move production from one country to another, making employment unstable and putting the unions at a bargaining disadvantage. Integrated production with multiple sourcing may make them immune to collective action by the workforce. They even threaten to move production elsewhere as a collective bargaining tactic.

3. Multinational companies have often been involved in corrupt practices, involving bribery of ministers and officials; and even where this extreme form of improper influence is not alleged, they are said to cooperate with and support power elites in host countries against the interests of the peoples.

4. In many cases multinational enterprises conduct large amounts of international trade within the corporate group, and fix transfer prices in ways that shift profits from one country to another to avoid tax, price controls, or exchange controls.

1 Global Reach: The Power of the Multinational Corporations. R J Barnet and R Müller. Simon and Schuster. New York, 1974.

5. Though firms invest capital in a host country, they often raise as much of it as they can locally, with the result that domestic enterprise may be disadvantaged, given a limited supply of credit, and that the foreign firms' total financial flows, including repatriated profits, fees etc. may be heavily adverse for the host country.

6. Multinational companies have at their disposal vast amounts of liquid capital which they can shift quickly between different currencies, with the result that they have become the world's biggest currency speculators. It is alleged that this causes exchange rate instability.

7. Multinational firms often enjoy product monopolies or, more often, are engaged in highly concentrated oligopolistic competition. As long ago as 1971, the ten biggest multinationals' value added exceeded $3 bn (according to the UN Secretariat report). Such firms, with integrated production and highly developed marketing skills, drive out domestic firms and may thereby reduce competition.

The foregoing relate to the activities of multinational enterprises worldwide. The following criticisms more specifically concern developing countries.

8. Technology made available to the host country is that suitable to the home (or parent) country, and is often highly unsuitable to developing countries. It tends to be too sophis- ticated and too capital intensive, and is therefore too expensive for the host country, while at the same time employing little of its unskilled labour.

9. End products are also frequently too sophisticated and expensive for the host country. Not only do they not give good value for money, they also cater to minorities which are then socially identified and elevated according to the patterns of consumption made possible by what the multinationals supply. Often this elite thinks of itself in Western value terms while the majority of the people retain traditional values.

10. The organisation especially of American multinationals, but also of non-American ones to an increasing extent, has tended to relegate local management to a subordinate role in an integrally managed international group. This has created a neo-colonial relationship in terms of decision making within the firm - a relationship which (it is argued) is reinforced by the effects of (3) and (9) above.

11. Multinationals tend to bring to bear on the host country the political influence of their parent governments, thereby adding an overt neo-colonial element at the level of policy, to the more subtle influences cited above. While this may nowadays only rarely be so overt as that which the United Fruit Company used to exert in Central America or that which the oil companies used to command in the Middle East, it is still said to operate in more subtle ways. One of these is through official export credit agencies of the home government, which deny credit when a regime is considered unsound. US law requires the US to bring its influence to bear in international organisations against countries which expropriate without prompt and adequate compensation and other extraterritorial extensions of US law are often cited, such as antitrust laws and those concerning trading with unfriendly powers.

The key issue is impairment of sovereignty

If there is any single thread to these complaints, it is that multinational enterprise is in these ways a threat to the sovereignty of governments and the economic and social aspirations of people in home and host countries alike. Moreover, according to Wilms-Wright, they com- prise "a vast uncontrolled concentration of economic power which is not subject to the same system of checks and balances that corporations operating at the national level are".

Now, if economic power is the ability to decide the country of location of production and employment, it is certainly central to the issue to ask whether the economic consequences of international investment are different, in a way that is socially harmful, from a system of allocation of resources and production of goods where the agents are entirely uninational. None of the works mentioned above applies this test except in the most casual and intermittent manner.

Let us suppose that there are two countries, A and B, and two firms, one in each, producing similar products. Productivity in country B rises faster (in relation to the cost of labour and materials) than in country A, so that firm B enjoys a gain in comparative advantage over firm A. There is international trade. Firm A gradually declines and becomes insolvent, and the market in country A is supplied by firm B. Does this result occur because firm B has economic power and firm A does not? And how does it differ from a situation in which firms A and B are both part of a multinational company, which responds to the change in comparative advantage by closing the plant in A and "shifting production" to country B? In short, what has the multinational or uninational character of the company to do with the outcome?

There may be a difference if the multinational company, through its internal decision making processes, grasp of market related information, and ready access to capital, is able to react more quickly and increase capacity in country B more quickly than a uninational firm in that country could do. This "internalisation" of factor markets and information by multinational companies is said by some writers to be the principal cause of the rise of the multinational enterprise, being the cause of its advantages over uninationals dependent on outside markets for these requirements. If so, the multinational, in this hypothetical situation, promotes welfare by reacting to change more rapidly.

In this light, the absurdity of charges such as those of the Labour left in Britain that Chrysler "blackmailed" the British government by threatening to pull out, can readily be seen. Had Chrysler been a uninational firm, it would have been bankrupt by the end of 1975 (apart from an infusion of cash of about £20 mn from the parent, it was already technically insolvent). It would have asked to be nationalised - as Chrysler did, and was refused. Chrysler's ability to provide resources from outside the UK, not least a model that was successful in continental markets, provided the basis of a plausible if not wholly convincing rescue operation, which could not otherwise have been mounted.

In regard to employment, leaving aside the bargaining aspects, the conclusions follow readily: multinational firms reduce employment in one country and raise it in another in response to the same economic forces that cause employment in uninational firms to fall in one country and rise in another. The difference is that their reactions in the direction of expansion are sometimes faster; and in so far as their financial resources leave them exposed to government pressures to delay closures (as was the case with Chrysler, and with Litton Industries' Imperial Typewriter subsidiary in the UK) they may, perhaps sometimes unwillingly, sustain employment in a failing affiliate for rather longer than a uninational firm can be obliged to do, because of its lack of external resources on which to draw.

As to the bargaining aspects, those who (like Wilms-Wright) regard powerful trade unions as a benevolent force in today's circumstances will naturally hold the views they do. It may equally be argued that anything which balances the power of unions in regard to upward pressure on money wages and obstacles to efficiency is likely to be a good thing.

Corruption is not a one way flow - nor necessarily to do with foreign investment

With regard to the belief that multinational firms introduce bribery to host countries, and exercise a corrupting influence on them in a more general sense, two observations can be made. One is that it is usually difficult to distinguish from evidence whether a company has bribed ministers or officials, or has been shaken down by them, in effect being sold government services (such as contracts, import licences, etc) by the responsible ministers or officials acting in a personal capacity (or as in the case of the renowned payments to officials of Italy's Christian Democrat Party by oil companies, in a party capacity). In most of the well publicised cases so far there is at least a strong suspicion that the companies did not seek to bribe but were shaken down. It is noteworthy too that in some celebrated cases where the evidence points the other way, such as the systematic payments made by US military aircraft manufacturers more or less globally, these were the actions of exporting firms, which had no tangible investments in the countries concerned. They are not multinational companies. A firm which has no foothold in a potential market may be more tempted to bribe than the one which has; while the latter is also the more exposed to extortion since its investments are in a sense hostages to the host government.

The other point in this connection is that methods and styles of conduct of business vary a great deal among countries, and it appears to make little difference whether the companies involved are domestic or foreign owned. Often the potential sums involved can be larger with multinationals because the firms are usually bigger. In a number of developing countries, it is necessary to gain high level permission for transactions which in most developed ones can be undertaken in a commercially straightforward manner, and such permission acquires a market value. The record of the Nixon years in the USA suggested moreover that such differences in style do not depend entirely on whether the country is developed or underdeveloped.

Transfer pricing is a multinational phenomenon

Transfer pricing is undoubtedly a phenomenon of multinational enterprise. It has become incumbent upon the revenue authorities of governments to assess the values of international transactions, and if necessary determine or negotiate the equivalent of arms length prices where these are not transparent. Gradually, governments are acquiring the necessary legislation and technical prowess to do this. It is not easy.

Financing in host countries: a technical decision for governments

The implications of the raising of finance in host countries present a difficult technical issue. It is not difficult for a government to limit the extent to which multinationals may raise finance within its frontiers. This has been the practice of the UK government for many years; in general, foreign controlled enterprises are required to maintain equity or loan finance raised from outside the UK at least equal to their fixed assets.[1] This causes them to finance a greater proportion of their investment internally (according to an earlier Fabian research pamphlet by Kennet, Whitty, and Holland, Sovereignty and Multinational Companies. 1971, foreign subsidiaries in the UK raised 75 per cent of their finance requirements from internal cash flow, compared with 66 per cent in the case of British manufacturing firms) and this in turn raises the cost of capital to the multinational firm. Whether the consequent reduction in welfare is borne wholly by the shareholders or is shared by consumers in the host country is not a matter that has been investigated, to the present author's knowledge. On the other hand, total absence of any government control would reduce welfare (if only by reducing competition) in the host country if the foreign owned firms gained, on the strength of their international prestige, a disproportionate share of available domestic credit.

1　Following the lifting of UK exchange controls in 1979, this requirement no longer applies.

As to whether the foreign currency transactions of multinational firms have adverse implications for welfare, it would be necessary first to show that foreign exchange speculation, conducted rationally with good information and reasonably long time horizons, is itself damaging. (We need not be concerned here with the semantic distinction between hedging and speculation, so beloved of corporate public relations officers - a hedging policy which is intermittent and discretionary is speculation; and no company of any size hedges all transactions at all times.) A good deal of empirical work on international monetary economics which has emerged in recent years tends to show that the major movements in exchange rates can be accounted for by non-speculative factors, mostly in the realm of monetary policy. Specialist research on the effects of speculation have generally shown speculative movements in exchange rates to be of very short duration. In theory, the effects should be stabilising in a free market (i e without fixed exchange rates - in which context speculation is destabilising) provided the speculators act rationally and on good information. On the whole, the treasurers of multinational companies fulfil this desideratum rather better than wealthy individuals and exchange dealers, who operate (when taking open positions) by extrapolating very short run movements in rates.

More knowledge of the monopoly aspects would be useful

Monopoly and concentration in an international setting comprise perhaps the most seriously under researched aspects of the multinational enterprise phenomenon. It is easy enough to establish the amount of capital, capacity, and value added created by international investment but much harder to assess the extent to which the effects have displaced competitors and (possibly) thereby reduced competition, or have prevented the entry of competitors to markets. As a number of large scale studies have shown (e g the UN Secretariat's 1973 report, 'Multinational Corporations in World Development'; and the Steuer report on the UK situation, 'The Impact of Foreign Direct Investment on the United Kingdom') multinational companies tend to operate in product markets which are highly concentrated.

Even where host governments have taken over the parts of a business which lie within their territories, concentration in the international marketing and processing stages may be relatively unaffected. This has been the case in the oil industry, but it may be so to an even greater degree in less well publicised cases. Tea plantations in the Indian sub continent have been nationalised or subjected to obligatory divestment to local interests, but this was in any case the less concentrated part of the business; the concentrated part was (and is) the wholesale marketing of tea in the developed countries. Yet, suppose these companies imported and marketed only in their home countries, i e were not multinational. Would there then be any reason to expect that competition would be thereby enhanced?

The Steuer report[1] concluded that foreign investment in the UK had increased the extent of competition, in spite of the fact that the firms were mainly found in highly concentrated industries. In other words, the industries would probably be less competitive were the multinationals confined to their home countries. This is likely to be true of most developed countries which permit foreign investment. But it could well be untrue of countries where foreign investment is so dominant that it may have stunted the growth of domestic enterprise. In the case of many developing countries, however, monopoly profits have been created or encouraged by governments which have sought investment in particular projects, and attracted them with fiscal subsidies and high tariff protection. The Commonwealth Secretariat paper by Lall, cited above, contains a good deal that is interesting and critical about such policies and their adverse effects on the welfare of host countries.

---

1 The Impact of Foreign Direct Investment on the United Kingdom. M D Steuer et al. HMSO 1973.

There are moreover some special aspects of international monopoly or oligopoly, such as that arising from patents. Pharmaceuticals are a much studied industry in this connection, and some spectacular examples of huge international price differentials and monopoly profits, notably those enjoyed by Hoffman La Roche in the UK and elsewhere, have been uncovered. This is a special area which the study of the international pharmaceuticals industry, now being conducted by the UN Commission on Transnational Corporations, will explore more extensively than hitherto, and some general observations about optimal patent lives, not necessarily confined to the pharmaceutical industry, might be worth developing. It is perhaps unfortunate that the subject of monopoly and oligopoly, and the extent to which multinational enterprise increases or diminishes such tendencies, is not being studied by the UN, at least at this stage, for it is an aspect to which a good deal of emotion but little analysis has yet been devoted.

UN role at present is to demythologise

Sotiris Mousouris, senior transnational corporations officer with the UN Secretariat, and assigned to work with the commission, said in a speech in New York in March that the primary role of the secretariat's work with the commission at this stage, next to preparing the code of conduct (which he said had been given "top priority"), was to demythologise the subject of multinational enterprise. This approach is very much to be commended, not least because the secretariat's 1973 report, though largely descriptive rather than analytical, was capable of being construed in ways that tended to support many of the most popular myths.

The impact of research on ministers of state, and on politically influential pressure groups, is of course difficult to assess, and is often slight. More important are the proliferating codes of conduct. A tendency has developed to regard codes of conduct as unimportant, so long as they are voluntary. Governments have generally resisted mandatory codes, because these would limit their powers of decision, and thereby would impair their sovereignty - even if multinational companies did not. The tendency of voluntary codes to proliferate has also devalued them in the minds of some business and trade union observers. This attitude may be mistaken.

The difference between a voluntary and a mandatory code of conduct may in practice prove slight, if the provisions of the code reflect a consensus attitude among governments which in turn becomes embodied in national legislation. If codes of conduct proliferate on the basis of principles held in common among them, these must become the minimum conditions which governments can assume in framing legislation unless they see strong practical reasons for doing otherwise. Although most governments in host countries continue to welcome foreign investment, and expect it to need to pay a return to its providers, their attitudes turn sour rather easily when an investment has outlived its usefulness or becomes unexpectedly profitable. In the home countries, the unions usually see it as in their interests to oppose outward investment, and can use principles enshrined in international codes of conduct, agreed to by their governments to press their case. It is a weak defence for a government to say, in such a situation, that the code is not mandatory.

It is difficult, moreover, for the drafters of a code, in the prevailing intellectual climate, to make it more favourable to multinational firms than the existing codes. The developed countries represented on the UN Commission thought at first of proposing the OECD code as a starting point, but (according to Mousouris) abandoned that idea when it became clear that to do so would divide the commission between the developed and the developing. Even the OECD code, while in general a sensible document, somehow emerged containing a highly dubious and potentially dangerous clause which declared that companies should not shift production to another country during an industrial dispute (so to prevent such a shift, the unions would need only to raise a dispute - were the code not voluntary). Managements of multinational firms would do well to pay close attention to the drafting of international codes, and should not assume that because they are so far largely voluntary they will in practice always remain so.

In respects other than those concerning codes of conduct, multinational enterprise faces some difficult challenges in coming years, for which public opinion and employee opinion needs to be prepared. To cite only one, the large build up of investment abroad since 1960 must increasingly necessitate some weeding out of the less successful undertakings. Disinvestment must therefore become commoner even among firms that continue to expand globally. In this as in other ways, it must become clear that multinational enterprises are subject to essentially the same economic disciplines as uninational firms. That truth has been heavily befogged in much of the debate so far.

In the capital exporting countries, the climate may be becoming less hostile

In the USA, the climate has been affected in an interesting way by the presence of a new administration which (unlike its predecessor) is not committed to the support of American business abroad. The area of political controversy has shifted somewhat from the US multinational as a powerful force for doing good or harm to American interests, to the activities of foreign multinationals, and to investment related trade issues. In this setting, the US multinational is apt to appear not so much like an evil grand master as one of the knights (if not exactly a pawn) on the board.

Increased fear of and respect for big foreign enterprises, especially Japanese ones, among labour and business alike, has become a strong element in the climate of opinion in the USA. A number of American unions have been pressing for protection against imports to the USA of goods produced by US firms abroad; these pressures are reflected in union lobbying for abolition of the generalised preferences for goods from underdeveloped countries, goods which are often produced by US multinationals, and against possible joint ventures abroad by US firms in civil aviation. So far they show no sign of being successful. Companies and unions have formed common cause in pressing for controls upon imports from Japan, but unions have noted that such controls have sometimes diverted trade to other sources of supply where US firms have investments. The unions dislike this, but have not convinced opinion in Washington that counteracting measures would be desirable. The legislation prohibiting compliance with the Arab boycott has caused firms some difficulties, not least in competition with foreign firms – a situation which has attracted some sympathy in Congress. Increased suspicion of foreign multinationals has been enhanced too by the prosecution of the uranium cartel, in the course of which Westinghouse appeared to some as the victim of foreign economic powers. These developments, particularly the latter, inspired the US attorney general, Griffin Bell, to issue a call for "comity" on the part of foreign governments – a statement which was generally construed abroad as an appeal for universal acceptance of the extraterritoriality of American law.

In short, the political climate in the USA is on the whole less hostile to American multinational business than it was under an administration that openly sponsored it. In serious published writing, there is now a good deal of sober reappraisal of the role and prospects of American multinational enterprise. It is no longer argued that US multinational business can develop the world, or establish an optimal (or seriously non-optimal, as per Barnet and Müller) allocation of the world's supply of capital and technology, as was commonly argued in the past. Various academic studies have moreover reported on disinvestment abroad by US firms, and identified the sectors where their foreign operations are (or are likely to be) decreasingly competitive.

The notion that the impetus behind foreign direct investment may be waning has however made no discernible impression on intellectual opinion in Europe. On the other hand, foreign investment is itself no longer a live political issue in the principal European capital exporting countries, as it was in the 1960s.

Technological bias may also be a misconception

The charge that multinational companies are inimical to the welfare of developing countries because they use excessively capital intensive or skill intensive technologies has been subjected to considerable research, and the results are extremely uneven. The hypothesis tends to be confirmed in respect of some countries and some industries, and to be reversed in others. On the whole, the evidence suggests that there is little difference between foreign owned and domestic enterprises in respect of capital intensities. Those studies that found for the hypothesis have concentrated on US multinationals, which tends to suggest that American firms may on the whole export higher technology than those of some other capital exporting countries. Some multinational companies actively seek out second hand machinery from developed countries to install in their establishments in the third world. This would of course benefit the host country only if the custom was sufficiently general that competitive output prices were influenced by the low cost capital inputs. Lack of competition, aggravated by high protection, may remove any penalty to profit that would in a large developed economy result from use of uneconomic capital equipment or technology by the firm. Not uncommonly, host governments have encouraged the use of excessively high technology for the sake of prestige, or the employment of host country technology graduates, and the establishment of an industry called for on national economic planning considerations (i e political ones) has on occasion led to uneconomic local manufacture of technological products, often requiring very high tariff protection.

End products are also too sophisticated

The arguments that end products, as well as technology, are too sophisticated, and warp consumption patterns in less developed countries, relate to brand name products in the food and drink sector, household durable goods, passenger cars, hotels and restaurants. Conceivably one should add the numbered Swiss bank account, though that form of consumption is neither ostentatious nor supplied by multinational companies. This is far from being the whole spread of multinational business. Moreover, much of the ostentatious consumption of the elite classes is imported from abroad - and would be even if there were no foreign direct investment. In any case, foreign investors have to take the class structure of the host country as they find it - which is not to deny that they may alter it unknowingly. Yet where an elite class exists, it will find its own way of expressing its role in society, without needing to rely on foreign firms.

That being said, it must be conceded that successful brand marketing of consumer goods at high prices, and the general absence of regulatory supervision of advertising and consumer product safety pose welfare problems for developing countries. Foreign owned companies are not however wholly responsible though, again, it must be conceded that they dominate consumer advertising in some LDCs.

Problem of centralised control has serious political implications

The trend towards more centralised control of multinationals has implications for the host country which cannot be easily discounted. Where local management is simply a cog in a larger wheel, this can be a matter of legitimate concern for the host country, if it is associated with the use of the multinational as a vehicle for the political influence of the parent country on the host country. Even apart from extreme cases of dispute where export credits are withdrawn or other overt sanctions are applied by the parent country government, it will usually be difficult for the multinational's head office management to decide in favour of the host country, where strong political pressure is applied from both ends. This is especially likely to be the case if the unions in the parent country are involved. For example, if a multinational is pressed politically at home to expand production there rather than in a foreign country, such pressure is hard to resist, even if yielding to it may expose the firm to risks in the foreign (host) country. Where the local management is given overall managerial authority, subject to good profitability, such pressures are easier to resist.

The extraterritorial effect of some American legislation is also cited as a problem whereby multinationals may be the vehicles of infringement of sovereignty. Some forms of extraterritorial application of law are not necessarily against the host country's interests. For example, US antitrust law has limited the involvement of American multinationals in international cartels.

In this area of political influence, multinationals are not so much agents of political pressure on the host country, as placed in double (or even multiple) jeopardy by conflicts of interest which can bring conflicting political pressures upon them. The multinational as a transmitter of political pressure is a problem which international organisations could fruitfully study and, hopefully, produce solutions. It would be very much in the interests of multinational companies to assist them in doing so. This is, it must be stressed, essentially a problem of relations between governments, not between companies and governments.

After a year and a half of negotiation among the organisation's 24 member governments, the OECD Guidelines for Multinational Enterprises has been agreed. It is not a treaty, nor even explicitly a legislative programme, but rather a series of recommendations on good practice both for governments and companies. One consequence of this is that it is almost wholly devoid of definitions: the term multinational enterprise is taken as self explanatory, but the context indicates that all firms with direct investments or even "significant influence" outside their home countries are meant to be covered. Operational terms, such as "bribe", are also not defined, so that in many of the more contentious clauses a good deal of scope for difference of interpretation exists.

Discrimination against foreign controlled companies is to be notified

As expected, the main thrust of the guidelines is aimed at limiting the alleged powers of multinational companies and increasing their responsiveness to government policies. For the most part these exhortations are unexceptionable, though there are two or three potentially awkard clauses, in our view, which we note below. One section however comes as a bonus to companies: the Decision on National Treatment. Measures taken by a member country, or a subdivision of such a country, which cause foreign controlled enterprises to be treated differently from domestic ones, are to be notified to the OECD promptly (within 30 days). The OECD's Committee on International Investment and Multinational Enterprises, founded in January 1975, is to receive such notifications and act as forum for consultations. Measures of this kind would include investment incentives or state procurement policies which discriminate against foreign controlled firms. The British government, for example, expects that it will have to notify its policy on computers, which favours International Computers Ltd over foreign firms (a live issue just now, as Honeywell is taking court action against the Anglian Water Authority over its preference for an ICL model following the technical recommendation for the order to go to Honeywell).

The disclosure issue is the most contentious

The guidelines are headed by a set of 'general policies' which are at least as important as any of the more specific clauses, and we quote the former here in full.

"Enterprises should:

1.   take fully into account established general policy objectives of the member countries in which they operate;

2.   in particular, give due consideration to those countries' aims and priorities with regard to economic and social progress, including industrial and regional development, the protection of the environment, the creation of employment opportunities, the promotion of innovation and the transfer of technology;

3.   while observing their legal obligations concerning information, supply their entities with supplementary information the latter may need in order to meet requests by the authorities of the countries in which those entities are located for information relevant to the activities of those entities, taking into account legitimate requirements of business confidentiality;

4.   favour close cooperation with the local community and business interests;

5. allow their component entities freedom to develop their activities and to exploit their competitive advantage in domestic and foreign markets, consistent with the need for specialisation and sound commercial practice;

6. when filling responsible posts in each country of operation, take due account of individual qualifications without discrimination as to nationality, subject to particular national requirements in this respect;

7. not render - and they should not be solicited or expected to render - any bribe or other improper benefit, direct or indirect, to any public servant or holder of public office;

8. unless legally permissible, not make contributions to candidates for public office or to political parties or other political organisations;

9. abstain from any improper involvement in local political activities.

Beyond that, there are five subject headings: disclosure of information, competition, financing, taxation, science and technology, and employment and industrial relations. Probably the most contentious issue was disclosure. The section on disclosure states that information on the structure of the firm, its operating results, sales, capital investment, sources and uses of funds, numbers employed, etc, should be published periodically not just for the reporting unit but also for the multinational enterprise as a whole, and by geographical areas. For this latter purpose countries may be grouped together, e g continents, or on some other basis to be chosen by the firm. Countries such as Japan which do not require consolidated accounts to be published were unhappy about this, but most member countries regarded this as desirable disclosure. On the whole, this seems right, for many multinational companies have done multinational business in general no good by enhancing the aura of mystery about the subject by indulging in a certain coyness about the international ramifications of their businesses. Publication of information of this kind can only improve the state of knowledge of the business world, and managements (not just academic analysts and officials) need information about other companies.

Rather more sensitive perhaps are two other recommendations about disclosure. One is under taxation, and states that enterprises should supply tax authorities in the countries in which they operate with the information necessary to determine taxes correctly. Generally speaking, tax authorities have no extraterritorial powers to obtain information, for example from a foreign parent company (though the US authorities do in fact exercise powers of this kind) and companies are not usually eager to help the taxman to increase their tax burdens. In the long run, however, such powers are bound to come, one way or another. Revenue authorities can exchange information with their foreign counterparts, where double taxation agreements provide for this, and increasingly they do. The world is gradually approaching the situation where only limits upon the time and staffing of the revenue authorities limit their ability to prevent the shifting of profits to tax havens. So companies might as well provide the information. Not surprisingly, the second clause under taxation says that companies should not shift profits by transfer pricing or similar techniques.

The other, perhaps more dangerous, clause concerning disclosure is the third under the 'general policies' quoted above. It says that parent companies should provide their affiliates with all the information which host governments want, subject to "business confidentiality". This proviso is vague, and companies could perhaps interpret it widely, but in practice, when a government department wants information from a company it usually handles the confidentiality problem by promising to keep the information secret. So long as the guidelines remain purely hortatory, current practice in these matters will probably change little as a result of this clause. But as the years go by, these guidelines, and others to be produced by the UN (which may well take the OECD ones for a model - or so some officials thought during the deliberations in Paris) will become enshrined in national legislation. If host and home governments alike legislate along these lines. the business knowledge of companies may well gradually become world wide public property. It has been suggested to us that neither the USA nor the UK is likely to legislate to this effect. The right of the parent company to with-hold information from an affiliate so that it cannot pass it on to government departments or agencies in the host country. possibly for use against the company's interests. is one which multinational firms properly value. Obviously the importance of this right would be greater where the host government is actively interventionist and makes wide use of state industries whose interests could conflict with those of a foreign owned company. Under the OECD regime. we are told by way of guidance. the proviso about "business confidentiality" is generally to be taken as construed by the firm.

The sections on competition. technology. and financing present little difficulty. except for a firm which deliberately seeks to frustrate known public policies in these areas.

The clauses on employment and industrial relations stretch to nine in number, largely as a result of avid lobbying by the international trade union organisations. In general they are fairly anodyne. except for one. This says that "in the context of bona fide negotiations" (and this is defined to include a strike) firms are not to threaten to use any capability of trans-ferring production to another country in order to influence the negotiations "unfairly" (whatever that word means). Difficulty could arise over this. If a company does choose to shift production. would an announcement to this effect be a threat? This clause is an attempt to swing bargaining power in favour of unions.

The bribery issue remains undefined

The issue of bribery is treated only in the clause quoted above under 'general policies'. The USA wanted something stronger. and indeed this clause is stronger than the one in the ori-ginal draft, which we reported last year (Multinational Business No. 4 - 1975) which said that companies should conform to the practices generally observed in the host country. International business organisations such as the Business and Industry Advisory Committee to the OECD wanted something tougher. too. especially on shakedown operations conducted by ministers and officials. It is unfortunate that the word "bribe" is not defined. for there are massive grey areas attached to multinational bribery and corruption.

A useful basis for the eventual UN document

As the powers of governments in relation to multinational companies are often ill understood. and those of the companies often exaggerated, an exercise of this kind is likely to be helpful, in general, apart from those points on which we have cast doubt. Despite occasional pro-testations to the contrary from their managements, multinational companies are different from uninational ones in certain important ways. and sometimes problems with governments genuinely arise from this fact. It is meant to apply only in the OECD area. As suggested above, however, there is a strong possibility that the document will influence the one which will eventually emerge from the UN, and on the whole that will be helpful.

II. MULTINATIONALS IN THE THIRD WORLD

Restrictions on Multinationals in the Developing World

DAVID J.C. FORSYTH •

No.4 1977

In recent years multinational companies (MNCs) have been the focus of great attention in the developing world and in the international institutions which provide a forum for the discussion of the interests and policies of the less developed countries (LDCs). The general tone of official comment has been critical - the unfavourable views of the Committee of Eminent Persons[1] proving both influential in directing subsequent comment and fairly characteristic of the genre. The most important effect of the debate from the point of view of MNCs is the spill-over into new restrictive - sometimes punitive - legislation which is either threatened or already actually in force in many host countries. Given the large stake that MNCs already have in manufacturing and raw material production in the Third World, and the high probability that direct investment there will continue to grow in importance, accurate evaluation of the operations of MNCs in these areas should be an essential prerequisite for the formulation of these policies. It is the contention of this article that, in certain crucial areas of "anti MNC" policy, restrictive measures are being introduced largely in the absence of reliable information and on the basis of a vague conventional wisdom as to what MNCs are doing. Moreover, such hard evidence as has (very recently) been put together suggests that present and prospective legislation in this area may, in fact, be inimical to the interests not only of the MNCs, but also of the developing countries which seek to enforce it.

The case against the multinationals

Multinationals operating in LDCs have been subject to a wide range of criticisms, most of which are well known, and which can only be summarised here. It is alleged, for instance, that MNCs use their considerable market power to make excessive profits; that they avoid local taxation by manipulating import/export prices (especially where intra-company transactions are involved)by remitting fees for the administration/accounting/management/R & D services provided by the parent company; that they produce goods suitable for the elite, and are in this respect irrelevant to the needs of the masses; that they worsen inflation by putting heavy pressure on limited local supplies of certain material inputs and grades of labour; that they destroy, through intense competition, long established local craft or workshop industry - and the traditional way of life that went with it; that they erode local sovereignty; and finally - but very significantly - that they frequently install the "wrong" technology - a characteristic now regarded by many observers as the most important single source of a wide range of the costs which MNCs are said to inflict on their hosts. This last problem has far reaching implications - and it is on this "technology issue" that attention is focused in what follows.[2]

The technology issue

The technology issue comes in a variety of forms, but the criticism is generally that the methods of production used by MNCs in LDCs tend to be too capital-intensive and, as a result, inflict a whole range of additional costs on the host economy. This contention has its origins in a standard piece of production theory familiar to any second year student of economics. The elementary theory postulates the existence of a wide range of possible capital-intensities in the production of any commodity, and demonstrates the commonsense conclusion that the lower the wage rate and the higher the cost of capital, the more labour-intensive will be the technology selected from the range by the omniscient profit-maximising entrepreneur. Translated into advanced country/developing country terms, what this means is that when

• Senior Lecturer, Department of Economics, Strathclyde University, Glasgow.

1 UN. The Impact of Multinational Corporations on Development and International Relations, New York, 1974. 2 Many of the other lines of criticism were discussed by Malcolm Crawford in "The Intellectual Attack on Multinationals" in Multinational Business, No. 3, 1977.

moving from the former to the latter, firms will substitute labour for capital in order to take advantage of cheaper labour and avoid increased capital costs; any firm failing to do this, the theory runs, will get its input mix wrong and will consequently incur unnecessary costs.

This is, of course, only the bare bones of a theoretical structure which in its more advanced form reaches a very high level of sophistication and is hedged around with all sorts of qualifications. So restrictive are the assumptions under which the mechanism operates, however, that few economists would regard it as an adequate guide to investment behaviour. Nevertheless, as an a priori "insight" into the principles guiding the optimal choice of technology it has had a powerful influence on current thinking of opinion formers.[1] It is not going too far to apply here Keynes's famous dictum that ".. the ideas of economists ... both when they are right and when they are wrong, are more powerful than is commonly understood... Practical men, who believe themselves to be quite exempt from any intellectual influences, are usually the slave of some defunct economist"..[2]

The current interest in the "technology issue" is the result of a shift in the emphasis placed by development economists on the various problems faced by LDCs. The traditional belief in accelerated growth of GNP as the principal aim of development policy was the natural result of the identifying of poverty as the key problem in these countries. In recent years rapid increases in population together with massive migration from the country to the towns have led to greatly increased open unemployment, especially in the urban areas. Here the unemployed are much more of a social liability than is the case in the countryside where the extended family and work-sharing provide a cushion. In LDCs, rates of urban unemployment now often exceed 30 per cent and many national governments are uneasy about the long term economic and political consequences of this problem. Development economists now frequently cite relieving unemployment and improving income distribution (rather than promoting growth) as the main priorities for LDCs. The "technology issue" fits neatly into this pattern, for if labour-intensive technologies could be found which were more profitable than those currently in use, then at one stroke the near miracle could be performed of simultaneously increasing efficiency, creating additional employment, economising on scarce capital, and improving the distribution of income (by expanding the wage-earning segment of the population).

MNCs are believed to introduce less appropriate technology –

What has all this to do with MNCs? Certainly they are not the only targets for attack in the present context, but the current emphasis on the "dependent" nature of LDCs coupled with the inevitable prominence of MNCs in backward economies, tends to earn them a disproportionate amount of attention. It is argued that MNCs have a built-in tendency to opt for high technology partly because they are not compelled to borrow at high cost in local capital markets as are indigenous firms, and partly because it is not in their commercial interest to try to develop new or modified technology when they already have access through their affiliates to a proven package of hardware and operating know-how. Furthermore, the technological dominance of the MNCs either batters down pre-existing local competition in the traditional, small scale, labour-intensive sector (in which case more jobs are destroyed than are created by the advent of the MNCs) or forces a small number of local survivors into using very similar technology. Either way, the monopoly/oligopoly position created by the MNC will remove any pressures generated by market forces for the move towards more labour-intensive technology indicated by the elementary economic theory outlined earlier. Competitive disciplining of technology choice may also be by-passed if the MNC simply uses its bargaining strength to persuade the host government to grant it special privileges such as

---

1   See 'Appropriate Technology in Civil Construction in Developing Countries', page 34 below.   2   J M Keynes, The General Theory of Employment, Interest and Money, page 383.

high tariff protection. And where MNCs do finance their operations locally, they will be able to borrow at the very lowest rates available, thus draining away one of the scarce resources of the LDC - capital; this may be seen as both a cause and an effect of high capital intensity in the foreign owned sector.

The supposed predilection of MNCs for high technology has. it is said, other unfortunate effects. As these technologies are often skill-intensive, there is a tendency for MNCs to put heavy pressure on the strictly limited supply of skilled labour. Again, the fact that the sophisticated technology of the MNC (and of those indigenous firms that imitate it) has to be imported not only increases foreign exchange requirements. but also deprives the machinery-producing sector of the economy of the stimulus of local demand that is essential for organic growth. Finally, it is suggested that high technology and sophisticated variants of products go together. and that MNCs often provide only for the special tastes of a small elite whose local power and influence they help to confirm by concentrating. rather than broadening. the economic base of the LDC and, therefore, further concentrating the distribution of income.

This, in brief. is the technology-based case against MNCs in LDCs. In its extreme form it is carried to the point where MNCs are accused of "immiserising" the bulk of the population rather than conferring on them the benefits long supposed to accompany direct foreign investment in poor countries.

The arguments set out above are worthy of careful attention as they have proved sufficiently persuasive to induce several LDCs to adopt an objective "appropriate technology" policy designed to foster the use of labour-intensive technologies in new manufacturing projects and curtail the use of capital-intensive methods. (The case of Mexico is an interesting example here.) They have also formed part of the increasingly widespread and perhaps more significant policies of "indigenisation" (or sometimes outright nationalisation) of manufacturing - which aims to bring a greater proportion of manufacturing under local control. partly because locals are believed to make more "appropriate" choices of technology.

Not all LDCs. it is true. favour such policies. but where they do the implications can be considerable. Thus, in India, the "Indianisation" programme is estimated to jeopardise the existence of around 40 per cent of all foreign owned subsidiaries.[1] And while a few countries are actually liberalising their regulations regarding inward investment (Egypt. Chile and South Korea are prominent examples) the overall trend is very obviously running strongly in the opposite direction. It is not possible to provide a comprehensive account of such legislation. but a quick review of the case of Ghana gives the flavour. Under the terms of the Investment Policy Decree no person other than a Ghanaian may own or be part owner of a firm manufacturing one of a list of seven product groups (the "reserved enterprises"). while in a very much broader range of product groups (over 40 in number) foreign participation is limited to 40 per cent to 60 per cent. Multinationals operating the latter type of enterprise are required to sell an appropriate amount of share capital to locals, and to institute training schemes for Ghanaian employees designed to equip them with all the skills required for the operation of the enterprise. and for the assumption of supervisory and managerial positions. This group of industries includes the manufacture of soap and detergents. beer. sugar. pharmaceuticals. motor vehicles, domestic electrical goods, textiles and footwear, in all of which MNCs are well established in Ghana. as well as a wide range of goods in which MNCs are heavily involved elsewhere.

---

1 OECD. Development Cooperation. Paris. 1975.

The further proliferation of such measures designed to exclude, encroach on, or regulate MNCs may confidently be expected, and there is little doubt that the growing clamour of concern over the "inappropriateness" of technology choices made by MNCs in the past has provided an important rationale for such intervention. Indeed, it is to be expected that the technology issue will <u>grow</u> rather than diminish in importance in the near future as it has now been adopted by a number of important international agencies, and is to be the subject of a major conference on Science and Technology for Development to be mounted by the UN in 1979 (and already one year in preparation).

- but there is little evidence to this effect -

We have seen that the issue of the choice of technology by MNCs in LDCs has assumed major importance in recent years, that MNCs attract considerable criticism because of their supposed preference for high technology, and that this has been wholly responsible for new LDC legislation seeking to influence their choice of technology - and partly responsible for a battery of indigenisation measures. The widespread adoption of, or, at least, sympathy towards, the "appropriate technology" cause is reflected in recent publications by such influential international bodies as the OECD and the ILO[1], and academic interest in the issue may be measured by the weight of citations in this area made in a review of the problems of industrialisation published in the <u>Economic Journal</u>.[2]

And yet, curiously, a detailed sifting of this voluminous literature discloses the singular fact that until very recently hard evidence was almost totally lacking. It is, of course, accepted research procedure that hypothesis formulation precedes empirical testing, but it is perhaps surprising that, in this case, so much significance should have been attached to the hypothesis <u>prior</u> to testing. Thus the view that labour-intensive technologies are in general most desirable in developing country manufacturing has been examined with respect to only a very tiny sample of industries, and that very recently. The more specified allegation that MNCs are a vehicle for the introduction of "wrong" choices of technology is only now coming under review. The results of investigation into these interconnected issues are surprising.

Looking first at the latter issue we find that research results in general fail to confirm, and in some cases directly refute, the conventional wisdom. In an important article on the Kenyan experience[3], Howard Pack notes that "...many widely accepted views of the output-employment relation are erroneous in a number of dimensions" and that "...perhaps surprisingly, in view of the conventional wisdom that foreign owned firms (or those employing Western trained technicians) will duplicate Western methods, it was typically a subsidiary of a foreign firm which carried out labour-intensive adaptations and was more willing to use older equipment".

Turning to the situation in Ghana, a study by the present author[4] suggests a somewhat more ambiguous answer, but one which still invalidates any broad critical generalisation regarding MNC behaviour. The figures in column (i) of Table 1 indicate the relative capital-intensity (value of plant and machinery per operative) of foreign owned and indigenous firms[5] in nine industries. It will be seen that in five of the nine industries covered, the foreign firms are

1 See e g A S Bhalla (ed), <u>Technology & Employment in Industry</u>, ILO, Geneva, 1975.
2 D Morawetz, "Employment implications of industrialisation in developing countries", <u>Economic Journal</u>, September 1974. 3 H Pack, "The Substitution of Labour for Capital in Kenyan Manufacturing", <u>Economic Journal</u>, March 1976. 4 David J C Forsyth and Robert F Solomon, "Nationality of Ownership and Choice of Technology in a Developing Country", <u>Oxford Economic Papers,</u> June 1977. 5 This group includes a number of firms owned by resident aliens, as opposed to MNCs - but the characteristics of these two groups were found to be substantially similar.

clearly the more capital-intensive. In four industries, however, the difference between the two groups is either insignificant (sawn timber and concrete blocks) or is, in fact, such that local firms are relatively capital intensive (wooden furniture and bread, biscuits, etc). Moreover, in no fewer than seven of the nine industries the foreign firms required relatively fewer skilled men than did the Ghanaian firms – a convincing rebuttal of the claim that MNCs make particularly heavy demands on the limited supplies of skilled labour.

Finally, studies for the Philippines and Mexico find that the technologies used by MNCs and indigenous firms are difficult to separate in terms of capital intensity.

Table 1

Capital Intensity and Skill Intensity in Foreign and Indigenous Firms in Ghana

Industry	Capital (plant & mach)[a] per operative		Ratio of skilled employees/ total employees	
	Foreign	Ghanaian	Foreign	Ghanaian
Footwear	3,129	625	0.15	0.21
Sawn timber	1,142	1,121	0.17	0.14
Bread, biscuits, etc	442	1,183	0.16	0.33
Wooden furniture	507	1,062	0.13	0.22
Small metal fabrications	1,672	775	0.20	0.31
Small plastic fabrications	2,237	1,327	0.16	0.19
Concrete blocks	776	772	0.13	0.22
Shirts	633	552	0.14	0.17
Blouses	797	405	0.14	0.14

a Measured in Ghanaian cedis (¢) per operative.

Source: David J C Forsyth and Robert F Solomon, op cit.

What are we to make of such conclusions, all reached through detailed analysis of the characteristics of individual firms? In evaluating them it is important to recall that the arguments put forward in support of the view that MNCs are likely to be excessively capital intensive in LDCs are a priori arguments, and on further consideration it becomes clear that equally plausible counter hypotheses can be set up. Thus we can argue, with Pack, that while the more sophisticated managers and engineers will "understand why operations are performed the way they are and the possibility of using ... adaptations which allow a more labour intensive process to function properly" the less expert ones will "lack the ability (and will) often duplicate the Western process in toto". The greater technical expertise of the MNC may be used not to confirm its faith in sophisticated technology, but rather to generate a more "appropriate" labour intensive technology than is accessible to indigenous firms whose relative lack of expertise forces them to buy Western plant and machinery "off the peg".

– and is labour intensive technology always the most appropriate?

Our discussion of relative capital intensity has, hitherto, been conducted – as is the general custom – on the assumption that the more labour intensive the technology the better it is for the LDC. But what if, on closer examination, a labour intensive technology turns out to be hopelessly inefficient (even when assessed in terms of "shadow prices" in order to measure the social rate of return) relative to the capital intensive one? Then, surely, labour intensity would be no virtue and capital intensity no vice. Once again, hard information on what constitutes the most "appropriate" technology in given industries is virtually non-existent.

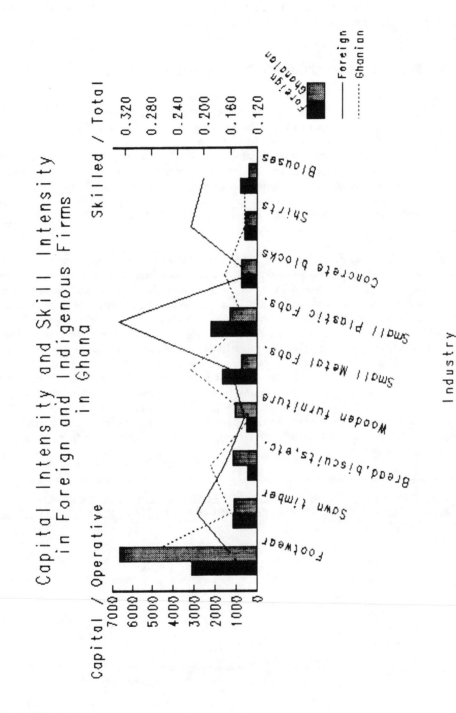

Capital Intensity and Skill Intensity
in Foreign and Indigenous Firms
in Ghana

27

The very few detailed studies thus far undertaken come to ambivalent conclusions in the sense that some industries appear suitable for labour intensive operation while others are not[1]. Without a detailed investigation of the economics of the technology alternatives in each industry only guesses can be made at the way in which the pattern of relative efficiencies will lie. But the argument that the greater technological expertise of MNCs will enable them to identify optimal technologies more easily than can indigenous firms is certainly persuasive.

The MNCs need to provide the evidence from their experience

The immediate conclusions to be drawn from the above analysis are fairly obvious. It seems that the widespread view that MNCs are generally more capital intensive than indigenous firms in LDCs and are thus less desirable is itself based on very shaky logical and empirical foundations. The few hard facts available in this context show clearly that MNCs are by no means always more capital intensive than local firms and, moreover, tend to undermine faith in labour intensity as an adequate criterion. An examination of available data suggests, indeed, that indigenisation aimed at helping local firms at the expense of MNCs could have the apparently unexpected effects in certain industries of _increasing_ capital intensity and _increasing_ the demands on the small pool of skilled labour - so harming both MNCs _and_ the LDC economy.

Two recommendations emerge from this. The first is that LDC governments proceed carefully with legislation of the type discussed above, and ensure that the implications of altering the investment rules for any given industry are examined in the light of an adequate knowledge of the relevant technological considerations. Second, and equally important, is the need for MNCs themselves to contribute to the growing public debate on "appropriate technology". By and large, discussion is carried on between social scientists, public officials and others, at a high degree of abstraction and involving very little hard information as to the available alternative technologies for producing particular products, or their consequences for employment, consumption patterns, etc. By far the best placed institutions to provide information on the "flexibility" of technologies, on the way in which they can and have been modified to suit LDC circumstances, and on the relative merits of the variants used by MNCs and local firms, are the multinationals themselves. There is a growing danger that, if some way of conveying this information to opinion formers and decision makers is not found, their case - which is very probably a strong one - may soon go by default.

---

1 See e g Norman C McBain, _The Choice of Technique in Footwear Manufacturing in Developing Countries_, HMSO, London, 1977; David J C Forsyth, _Appropriate Technology in Sugar Manufacture_, HMSO.

Has Multinational Corporate Foreign Investment Been Oversold?

Egypt as a Case Study

LAWRENCE B. FRANKO●   **No.2 1977**

What can multinational companies do for a developing country with virtually no natural resources, but plenty of cheap labour and proximity to markets of developed countries? Many
ideologues of international business, particularly in America, have been inclined to assume
that a great deal can be accomplished by the multinational company, if only the legal and
political environment is favourable.

Egypt appears as a test bed for this proposition, which was advocated to President Sadat by
senior US administration officials during the negotiations which followed the severance of
economic support of the country by the USSR, and which led to closer relations with the USA.
Egypt immediately established a tax free zone on the Suez Canal for foreign firms, subject
to a range of conditions concerning exports, engagement of Egyptian labour and expertise,
etc. Subsequently further zones of this kind have been established inland, near Cairo and
Alexandria.

Dr Franko, who until July 1977 has been deputy assistant director for international affairs
of the Congressional Budget Office in Washington, and who has been a widely published
author on multinational companies and the economics of international investment, analyses
the case of Egypt in this context. (The Editors).

The hopes placed in multinational investment –

It has been ten years since J J Servan-Schreiber's influential book The American Challenge
was first published. During the ensuing decade, it has been followed by books with awe-
inspiring titles such as Invisible Empires, Sovereignty at Bay, and Global Reach: The Power
of the Multinational Corporations. These works, while making widely different value judgments on multinational enterprise, conveyed an image of multinational corporate omnipotence
which has led to a widely held belief that the multinationals could develop the world, if they
only tried (or were forced to). Such hyperbole has led to much suspicion, and to many
attacks on the multinationals. But equally it has reinforced some policymakers' tendencies
to expect too much from them. Awesome as they may appear from a distance, it is not clear
that multinationals can make a significant contribution to development in the third world or
even to the development of one of its medium size members such as Egypt.

Multinationals have been looked upon as purveyors of capital. Egypt in particular has looked
to multinationals to help finance the more than $1 bn foreign exchange component of the nearly
$3 bn per year of investment inscribed in Egypt's plan. Multinationals have rarely been great
foreign investors of their own capital in developing countries, however, except in petroleum
and some other extractive industries. The US Treasury has estimated that total net US and
non-US foreign direct investment flows to non-oil LDCs in 1975 totalled some $4 bn. On past
form, it is probable that between one third and one half of that sum was invested in petroleum
exploration, extraction, transport and refining. If Egypt were to discover large quantities
of petroleum, the oil majors might oblige by investing and developing in a way that could lift
Egypt out of its present poverty. But geologists are pessimistic. The question remains: can
Egypt divert the rather small stream of MNCs' non-oil investment in developing countries
toward itself?

● At the time of writing, Lawrence Franko was deputy assistant director for international
affairs, Congressional Budget Office. The views expressed in this paper are solely the
author's responsibility. They may or may not be shared by other employees of the CBO.

- led to Egypt's open door policy

Egypt has predicated much of the solution to its grave economic difficulties on the success of its "open door policy". Egypt's severe external debt service burden (32 per cent of exports in 1974), and its lack of agricultural and industrial products exportable for hard currency, have obliged the country to seek foreign financing both of its current budget and trade deficits and of its longer term development. Foreign aid has been sought for both of these purposes from the US government and from the wealthy Arab oil exporting states. But President Sadat's government considered that aid would not be enough: foreign investment was to play an important role as well. In 1974 the Egyptian legal framework was altered to indicate that foreign private investment was no longer the pariah of the Nasser years, but, on the contrary, was to be courted and protected.[1]

During the two years the Open Door Policy has been in effect its results have been disappointing. Compared to trade balance deficits of $1.7 bn in 1974 and an estimated $2.2 bn in 1975, foreign direct investment in Egypt has been tiny: despite many announcements of project approvals by the Egyptian government, industry sources speak of US private direct investments (outside of the oil sector) totalling less than $10 mn, and non-US investment of not much more, during the past two years. The press speaks of the Open Door Policy "in disarray", and notes that there has been little in the way of follow-through to the well publicised pilgrimages Western businessmen have made to the Nile.

But expectations are unrealistic

Many reasons have been adduced for the reluctance of foreign investors to walk through the open door. Foremost among these have been the obviously overvalued rate of exchange at which investors are being asked to convert their capital, and the oft noted shortcomings of Egypt's slow moving bureaucracy, which have caused some companies to give up after lengthy negotiations with the Egyptian authorities. The country's lack of an adequate hotel, telecommunications, rail and airport infrastructure are also cited as difficulties, if not actual barriers. Frequently thought, but usually unmentioned, are investors' concerns with the possibility of another war with Israel, troubles with Libya, or - after Cairo's January riots - internal instability. And press reports of Arab official aid falling in 1976 to roughly half of the $2 bn it reached in 1975[2] led to dark rumours of a "loss of confidence" by the oil exporting states, rumours which do nothing to reassure would-be private investors.

---

1 See: The Arab Republic of Egypt, "Law No. 43 of 1974 concerning the investment of Arab and foreign funds in the free zones." The US government apparently played some role in persuading Egypt to extend a renewed welcome to foreign investors. President Nixon, during his trip to Cairo, spoke of a potential $2 bn US investment. (Cited in Waterbury, "Egypt 1976," American Universities Field Staff Reports, North East Africa Series, v 21, no 3, 1976 p 5.) The then secretary of the Treasury also seems to have played a role in raising Egyptian hopes concerning the policy's likely success   (see, Forbes August 1, 1974, p 24). 2 Middle East Economic Digest, January 28, 1977, p 5.

As is often the case, however, hope springs eternal; hope on the part of the Egyptian govern-ment - too committed to the Open Door to downplay it lightly - and on the part of some senior US officials of the former (Republican) administration, who instinctively believed that foreign capital would fly to Egypt, if Egypt would only put its own house in order.

It is perhaps possible that these optimistic hopes will be borne out. Indeed, every sympathetic observer of Egypt's overpopulated, subsidy dependent, foreign exchange-short economy would wish such to be the case. The chances for the realisation of such hopes, however, are slim indeed. There are more obstacles to foreign investment in Egypt, and especially to the export oriented foreign investment for which Egypt hopes, than those usually listed. Worse, if the obstacles under Egypt's control were to disappear overnight, foreign investment would still be able to make only a marginal contribution to Egyptian development.

Multinationals as providers of employment

Multinationals have also been looked to as providers of employment. The 400 largest US and non-US MNCs included in the Harvard Business School-Ford Foundation project on compara-tive multinational enterprise employed a maximum of 30 mn people worldwide in 1971[1]. 30 mn people is a number which includes the people employed by multinationals in developed countries. It is a number somewhat less than twice the total employable male population of Egypt. And it is a number which is consistent with the capital intensive, not labour intensive, nature of the vast proportion of MNC activity.[2]

If one assumes, consistent with the distribution of MNCs' assets and sales, that some 60 per cent of MNC employment is in the home country and some 60 per cent of the remainder is in other developed countries, then the total number of people employed in LDCs by MNCs is less than five million, a number not even twice as large as the employable population of Cairo. To be sure, such numbers concern only direct employment effects, and not indirect job creation by local supplier or customer industries. Even here, however, the outlook is hardly hopeful. A recent series of studies undertaken by the World Employment Programme of the International Labour Office suggests that the maximum indirect employment effects, such as those observed in the export oriented economy of South Korea, are equal to about 60 per cent of the direct effects. In other words, the employment creation effect of all MNC activity in the less developed world might reach a total of some eight million people.

MNCs have also been looked to as providers of non-traditional exports, and hence as providers of foreign exchange. However, total sales outside of home countries of manufacturing affi-liates of US and non-US multinationals in 1970 probably did not exceed $150 bn[3]. Almost certainly no more than 40 per cent, or $56 bn, of those sales were produced by LDC based affiliates, probably 5 to 10 per cent ($2-$5 bn) were exported, and two thirds of these exports were concentrated among six countries - Hong Kong, India, Brazil, Mexico, South Korea and Taiwan. Moreover, despite the myth of the "run away" offshore export plant of multinationals flying to seek low wage production sites, it appears that only some 2 per cent of the foreign manufacturing subsidiaries of multinational firms are both in less developed countries and are primarily oriented toward export markets[4]. Even if Egypt were to become another South

---

1 The author was director of the Continental European part of this project from 1971 to 1975.
2 See, for example, L G Franko, "Multinational Enterprise: The International Division of Labour and the Developing Countries," International Labour Office, Geneva, 1975.
3 Estimated for the Comparative Multinational Enterprise Project by Prof Robert Stobaugh of the Harvard Business School. 4 L G Franko, The European Multinationals, Greylock Press, Stamford, Connecticut, 1976, p 126.

Korea or Taiwan, such a development would take place only over several years; it would be far too late to solve Egypt's current difficulties. Moreover, as we shall see, there are many reasons for thinking that it is quite unlikely that the export oriented manufacturing for which Egypt hopes will be forthcoming in the near future.

MNCs could help (and historically probably have helped) a developing country such as Egypt most by undertaking import substituting investment which would save scarce foreign exchange. Egypt has been reluctant to encourage such investment, however, primarily out of fear that MNCs might come to dominate a local industry which is both competitively weak and largely Egyptian government owned. Moreover, without a realignment of Egypt's many artificially administered internal prices with world prices, it is conceivable that MNC investment predicated on current artificial prices could, if aimed at import substitution, do harm as well as good.

Barriers to export oriented foreign investment

Egypt's own bureaucracy and poor infrastructure are, to be sure, barriers to the attraction of the kind of foreign exchange earning multinational investment which Egypt seeks. Foreign investment oriented toward producing to far away markets is dependent on adequate port, rail, mail, telex, telephone, and air coordination. The export oriented foreign subsidiary is, in a sense, only part of a factory: it lives by schedules, quality standards, designs, and quantity requirements set in another country - or in several other countries. Similarly, little foreign investment is so dependent on the cooperation, sympathy, and knowledge of government administrations as is export oriented investment. Customs officials, fiscal authorities, and transport and utilities services are not so much barriers to production as to export marketing: the bureaucratic mechanism is apt to set a pace too slow to be consistent with the survival of the enterprise in competitive markets.

Other barriers to export oriented investment are, however, not internal to Egypt. Egypt has often been spoken of, or has presented itself, as a potential gateway to other Middle Eastern markets. But in export oriented manufacturing, not only does the production site require political and social stability, but so do the lines of transit. Traditionally, many of the lines of transit to the Middle East's most populous markets have passed through the ports of Lebanon. In recent times, at least, few investors would have been comfortable with the risk inherent in investing in Egypt in order to depend primarily on such a volatile route to market.

Multinationals have yet other sources of hesitation in siting production in Egypt for export to the European market. Europe is currently in recession, and faces unemployment problems which make European countries little inclined to be liberal with respect to importing the labour intensive sorts of goods Egypt can produce. European plants are operating far under capacity in shoes, textiles, electro-mechanical products, food processing, furniture, and similar industries, and tend to react fiercely to new foreign competition. Egypt would have to compete not only with existing production sites in the more developed EEC countries, but also with plants in the heavily subsidised less developed regions of those countries, with the less developed countries of Europe such as Portugal, Spain, Greece, and Turkey (most of which have association agreements with the EEC), with the LDCs which are members of the Lomé convention and therefore have preferential access to the EEC, with all other LDCs which are included in the Generalised System of Preferences, and last - but very far from least - with the attraction that low wage production has been exercising on European (and some US) firms to source from affiliated plants in Eastern Europe. (Business International estimated Egypt's average hourly wage in manufacturing in 1974 at some 54¢, that of

Bulgaria as some 50¢, and of Rumania - a country with numerous East-West joint venture and coproduction arrangements - as 66¢. Hourly wage costs were estimated for Hong Kong at 52¢; Malaysia, 52¢; India, 19¢; Pakistan, 13¢; Morocco, 51¢; Senegal, 28¢; and Ghana, 48¢.[1])

More bureaucratic simplification would help, but the MNC contribution will still be small

If Egypt were able to obtain direct investments in 1977 of an amount equivalent to 5 per cent of total net US manufacturing and service investments in LDCs in 1975, the amount involved would equal some $90.5 mn[2]. 5 per cent of MNC related exports of manufactures from LDCs would equal some $100-$200 mn, a moderate amount that - even were Egypt to be able to capture it - would in any case be unobtainable during a three to four year period during which plants and marketing networks were being put into place.

What could Egypt do in order to attempt to obtain what in any case would be relatively small contributions to the financing of its trade deficit and its investment needs? Egypt has recently improved its competitive position relative to EEC linked LDCs by negotiating a similar link[3]. Egypt has also moved to allow firms to invest and to repatriate profits at a realistic exchange rate. Perhaps Egypt could further improve - or at least simplify - the incentives it offers to foreign investors, incentives which some MNC executives regard as so complex as to discourage investment. Another change might be to allow more import substituting investment - at least in sectors where internal prices are not excessively distorted and where the risk of domination of local enterprise would be small. Egypt could also attempt to reform its bureaucracy so that policies adopted at the top were more forthrightly implemented at the bottom. But all of these steps take time to produce results, and none are likely to have a payoff which will provide a significant financial substitute for public foreign aid in the foreseeable future.

---

1 "Indicators of Market Size for 132 Countries," Business International, December 3, 1976, p 390. 2 Net US capital outflows for direct investment in developing countries equalled $3.7 bn. Of this amount $1.9 bn was undertaken in the petroleum sector. Manufacturing accounted for $0.4 bn, and service for $1.4 bn, for a non-oil total of $1.8 bn. See Survey of Current Business, August 1976, p 47. 3 See IMF Survey, February 7, 1977, p 7 for details.

Indigenisation in India

Taking on IBM and Coca Cola

No.3 1977

The Coca Cola colony view of the impact on the third world of US multinationals is far from uncommon. No other international product has the same symbolic power. Couple the dominance of the brown brew from Atlanta, Georgia, with the feared technological supremacy of IBM in the computer and electronics age and you produce the multinational bogey. This seems to be the view of the new government in India, which is currently engaged in turning the screw on all foreign owned business.

Both Coca Cola and IBM have refused to hand over 60 per cent of their Indian subsidiaries to local investors. Neither wishes to contravene the 1976 foreign exchange regulation act, and both had hoped to negotiate exemptions. But neither will relinquish control, Coca Cola of its secret formula and IBM its 100 per cent rule for key subsidiaries. The disputes with these MNCs seem arcane, but it is precisely the issues represented by these two very different concerns that are most representative of the problems of international business for developing nations. In the case of Coca Cola it is access to a formidable potential market of 600 mn that is the point at issue with the government. IBM for its part represents the cost of technology which the developing nations find an increasing financial burden.

In a recent review; 'Multinational Companies and Developing Countries; negotiating positions and conflicts of interest' – part of the useful series of research papers from the Hamburg Institute of Economic Research – the authors find that transfers of profits out of developing countries are a multiple of their net capital accrual from international investment (262 per cent in 1970-72). MNC transactions taken as a whole lead to considerable losses of foreign exchange for the developing nations. In this analysis the high technology companies are a particularly heavy cost for these states. Moreover it seems probable that such imported technologies do not usually fit into the factor scarcity profile of the host countries. This could be labelled the IBM problem for the developing nations. The problem is that there is little they can do about it; Indianisation of IBM could possibly be harmful when it comes to terms of acquisition of future IBM products.

Luxury imports could become a local product

The Coca Cola problem is probably more simple. The company takes its worldwide profit out of the carbonated drink by supplying concentrate to bottlers. In India this means that the local subsidiary imports concentrate from its parent at a price which reflects the royalty element in the brand name. The first aim of the government has been to replace the import with local made concentrate. This would present no problem except that Coca Cola will not put its formula into the hands of anything other than a 100 per cent controlled subsidiary. The government responded to the dispute by suspending import licences, which forced the Indian Coca Cola factory to shut down this summer. In a clumsy attempt to dislodge the company the authorities first threatened to have the product designated a drug and registerable as a medicine. More recently government response to Coca Cola's threat to pull out has been to warn the company that the state will appropriate the brand name and go into the manufacture of a local drink using the label. The consequences of that in a country the size of India would be very serious for the company, which prides itself on quality control, international standardisation of product and maintaining the uniqueness of the multinational brand. Compared to this the actual loss of the market is of secondary importance.

The Coca Cola case exemplifies what the Hamburg study describes as an increasing power of third world governments vis à vis MNCs, arising from the growing size of markets. Coca Cola is a particular example of a multinational product which figures early on in the development process. Coke may not be development as bankers and politicians see it but to many ordinary people it ranks with bicycles, wristwatches, and radios as among the most desirable early signs of developing affluence. Whether that would be the case in India if the product was Indian coke is a matter for conjecture.

The battle firmly illustrates the new government's desire to control the foreign sector, some would say to eliminate it. In theory MNCs with high priority exports as the predominant part of their production can retain up to three quarters of the equity in local operations. But in practice it rarely works out. IBM has offered to Indianise its local service bureaux operations according to the 40 per cent decree if it can set up a separate 100 per cent subsidiary which will make data processors and export the lot, at least $10 mn worth a year. But it wants the wholly owned subsidiary to service all imports. The Indian government has rejected the ploy despite the 'export' carrot attached, on the grounds that an unrestricted right to service should belong to the Indianised company. As we go to press talks are still proceeding.

The Indian government appears unconcerned that its policies have cut off Indian subsidiaries of MNCs from overseas organisational and technical inputs. For a number of years the extremely tight profit repatriation and foreign currency controls have been diverting MNCs' resources from India anyway. A number of subsidiaries now bear little or no relation to the businesses of their parents. Since export earnings were the only qualification for repatriation of funds there are now Indian paper and tobacco companies whose main activity appears to be fishing for exportable foodstuffs.

In fact foreign exchange reserves are high. The need for foreign investment is low. India has adopted the indigenisation tricks demonstrated in Nigeria and other developing nations. Share issues to the public to implement indigenisation are at prices controlled by a capital issues commission which sets very low values. It is then almost impossible for the companies to challenge this market mechanism as expropriation. The process has been employed for some time before the new government took over. Last year the Central Bank, which administers the Foreign Exchange Act, forced 19 mostly service and trading operations to shut down, a process which astonishingly included operations whose main raison d'être was to act as buying offices for the export of Indian textiles and other goods. In addition to such operations there are 138 foreign owned manufacturing enterprises in India which have been told to cut back to 40 per cent foreign equity ownership. It all goes to demonstrate the danger of passing draconian laws the worst effects of which will need special government dispensation often in exchange for political favours - the system operated by the Ghandi regime. In comes a new government dedicated to cleaning up such 'abuses' and the law is applied even where it may not be in the national interest.

Growing Exports of Manufactures
by Multinationals from LDCs

No.1 1978

Whereas foreign direct investment was once aimed largely at the securing of supplies of raw materials and the winning of protected markets, in recent years it has been increasingly aimed at production of manufactured goods for export. In an article in the current issue of the Economic Journal, Deepak Nayyar attempts to measure the scale of such exporting and analyse its characteristics.[1]

In at least one respect, his conclusions are surprising. The proportion of total exports of manufactures by less developed countries accounted for by multinational companies, which he estimates to be about 15 per cent or slightly over (in about 1974), has not increased significantly since 1966. The reason for this is not, it would appear, that the pace of investment in such undertakings has fallen, but rather that the rate of increase of total LDC exports of manufactures to developed countries has been very high indeed. From 1962 to 1973, in terms of US dollar value, it averaged 18.7 per cent a year. The rate of increase was particularly high in engineering products, exports of which totalled less than $100 mn in 1962 yet by 1973 were second only to clothing.

Table 1

Imports of Manufactured Goods from LDCs by the Industrialised Countries, 1962-73

Product group	Imports 1962 $ mn	1973 $ mn	Average annual percentage growth 1962-73	Composition of imports %	%
Clothing	233	3,003	26.2	9.6	18.7
Engineering products	93	2,820	36.3	3.8	17.7
Textiles	552	2,386	14.2	22.8	15.0
Wood products	252	1,788	19.3	10.4	11.2
Food products	409	1,383	11.7	16.9	8.7
Miscellaneous light manufactures	124	1,348	24.3	5.1	8.5
Leather & footwear	96	886	22.4	4.0	5.7
Chemicals	223	740	11.5	9.2	4.6
Iron & Steel	50	649	26.3	2.1	4.1
Drink & tobacco products	305	246	-2.0	12.6	1.5
Others	84	672	20.8	3.5	4.1
Total	2,240	15,920	18.7	100.0	100.0

Source: Unctad, Trade in Manufactures of Developing Countries, 1973 Review, Geneva, 1974, p 41 and 1974 Review, New York, 1976, p 13.
Note: (i) The percentages have been calculated. (ii) Petroleum products and unwrought non-ferrous metals are excluded from the classification of manufactures.

1 Transnational Corporations and Manufactured Exports from Poor Countries.

The share of foreign owned (or controlled) companies in total exports of manufactures was found to be highest in Latin America; in Brazil it is estimated at 43 per cent, in Mexico 25 to 30 per cent, and in Colombia and Argentina at least 30 per cent. The four largest exporters of manufactured goods (to all markets) were Hong Kong, Taiwan, South Korea, and India, in that order, and although for this observation the data are rather old, these four were so far ahead of the rest (and the first two so far ahead of the third and fourth) the ranking is unlikely to have changed much. Among these four countries multinationals accounted for the highest share in Taiwan (about 20 per cent or more) with South Korea second (at least 15 per cent).

The importance of partial manufacturing, as part of a multinational production process, is illustrated with regard to exports to the USA in the figures for US imports from LDCs under tariff headings 807 and 806.3, which relate to goods processed partly in LDCs and partly in the USA.

Table 2

US Imports from LDCs under Tariff Items 807.00 and 806.30

Year	(i) Gross value $ mn	(ii) Dutiable value $ mn	Gross value as a % value of manu- factured exports from LDCs (iii)	Share of US- controlled affiliates in manu- factured exports from LDCs (%)
1966	60.7	31.4	1.1	10.6
1967	99.0	42.8	1.6	11.5
1968	221.7	97.7	2.9	11.0
1969	394.8	177.3	4.3	9.2
1970	541.5	245.9	5.8	10.8
1971	652.5	314.1	5.9	9.5
1972	1,031.7	531.2	6.6	8.5
1973	1,522.9	827.0	6.3	8.1
1974	2,328.8	1,289.4	7.2	8.7

Source: For columns (i) and (ii), US Tariff Commission.

Alongside this table is also shown a column giving the share of US companies' majority owned affiliates in exports of manufactures from developing countries. It would appear, comparing this column with column iii (gross value of tariff 807 and 806.3 items as a percent of manufactured exports from LDCs) that partly processed imports to the USA have risen nearly to equality with total exports of manufactures by US controlled enterprises in LDCs to all markets (which in turn account for at least half of all exports of manufactures from foreign controlled enterprises in the Third World). It should be noted that not all imports in column iii are from US affiliate firms: imports by affiliates of non American companies located in the USA are included, as are those of US companies which have no direct investments abroad. However, this category of exports of manufactured goods from developing countries is now clearly very important. There are no data for similar exports to other countries but in principle the scope would appear to be very great, to the extent that tariff rates and "orderly marketing" arrangements permit it.

Partial manufacture is efficient because it permits the most labour intensive part of a manufacturing process to be conducted in a low wage country. Nayyar notes that while wage differences are very great, differences in productivity for identical operations do not differ so significantly between developed and developing countries. Moreover, if one may add a point he does not make, partial manufacture for export also offers a form of operation which

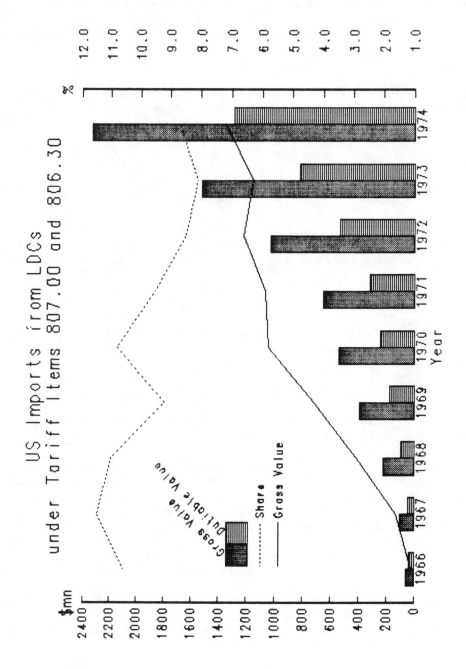

US Imports from LDCs
under Tariff Items 807.00 and 806.30

Imports of Manufactured Goods
from LDCs by the
Industrialised Countries

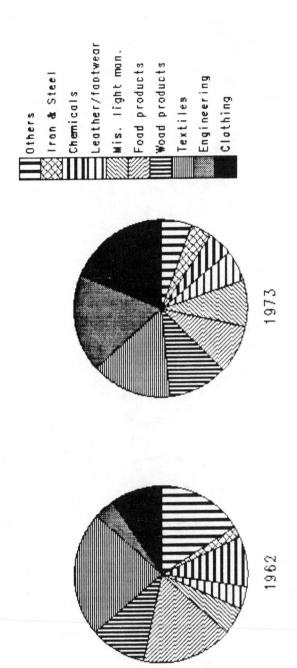

Others
Iron & Steel
Chemicals
Leather/footwear
Mis. light man.
Food products
Wood products
Textiles
Engineering
Clothing

1973

1962

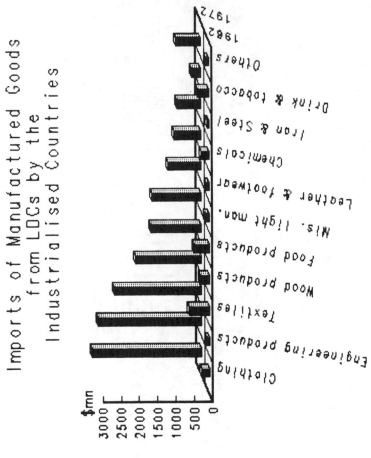

Imports of Manufactured Goods
from the
Industrialised Countries

$mn

3000
2500
2000
1500
1000
500
0

Clothing
Engineering products
Textiles
Wood products
Food products
Mis. light man.
Leather & footwear
Chemicals
Iron & Steel
Drink & tobacco
Others

1982
1972

Product Group

is highly resistant to political influence, expropriation, or control by host governments – unless of course they conclude that such an enterprise provides no net benefit.

Also noteworthy is the declining share of American controlled affiliates in the total of manufactured exports from LDCs. This is accounted for by an increasing share of domestic enterprise in exports, and in the (roughly constant) multinational portion, by non-US firms, in which Nayyar emphasises the growing importance of Japanese companies.

He also stresses the importance of what he calls "buying groups" – meaning trading companies and distributors which are not investors (and whose transactions are therefore not included in the data relating to foreign controlled exports). There appear to be no data on these but they appear to be a growth element in exports of manufactures from LDCs, especially in simple labour intensive products. Partial manufacture would appear to predominate in products where technology is involved (though not exclusively in these). As the degree to which domestic firms in LDCs can assess consumer tastes and quality requirements in advanced countries, and design products in accord with them, varies a great deal, the scope for commercial relationships between LDC manufacturers and "buying groups" in developed countries is considerable – and entails rather more than the sending of telex messages.

Third World Multinationals

LOUIS WELLS JR.●   No.1 1980

Before the 1960s, only a tiny trickle of foreign subsidiaries emanated from third world companies. The pre-depression foreign operations of Argentina's Bunge y Born, Siam di Tella, and Alpargatas were indeed unusual cases. But the trickle has now turned into a steady stream. In South East Asia, it is closer to a flood. Hong Kong (even excluding British owned firms and the registry-of-convenience cases) seems to account for the second largest number of non-mineral foreign investments in Indonesia. Malaysia has approved some 400 investment projects originating in Singapore. And it is an unusual large Taiwan firm that does not nave at least two or three foreign manufacturing subsidiaries; many have several licensing arrangements as well. Hong Kong firms have ventured outside South East Asia as far as Ghana and Nigeria to produce textiles and other goods; Taiwanese firms are beginning to explore manufacturing opportunities in Latin America; and companies from the Indian subcontinent have projects in African nations such as Zambia, Somalia, and Tanzania.

Third world multinationals certainly do not yet account for a volume of investment comparable to that associated with the multinationals from the USA, Europe, and Japan. Nevertheless, their rapid spread has significant implications for managers of the traditional multinationals and for the governments of the countries involved. Third world multinationals have their own peculiar strengths, and consequently offer special opportunities as well as threats.

Third world MNCs have learnt how to supply small markets –

In theory and, in most cases, in practice, to operate successfully abroad a firm must have some kind of special skill that is not easily supplied by local competitors, and will offset its higher overhead costs, lack of familiarity with local markets and institutions, and the penalties imposed by governments which prefer national investors. Multinationals have usually derived their original strengths from innovations that were undertaken at home in response to the conditions in domestic markets. For the US based firms, it was the high income, labour scarce US market that led to the sewing machine, mass production of automobiles, and, later, computers and so on. European and Japanese enterprises have developed skills based on the home markets with which they were familiar. Similarly, third world companies have also been influenced by the peculiarities of their own national markets.

In many cases the skills of third world multinationals have been generated in response to the relatively small size of markets in the developing countries for manufactured products. To survive, firms have had to develop ways of manufacturing efficiently on a small scale. A second stimulus for innovation has been the difficulty of access to specialised materials, parts, and components that would be readily available in the industralised countries.

Innovation to supply small scale markets can take several forms. In some cases, adaptation requires no more of the firm than access to secondhand machinery used in the USA or Europe at an earlier stage of development when volumes there were smaller. But even successful acquisition of secondhand machinery requires certain skills. The market for used equipment

---

●   Professor at the Harvard Graduate School of Business Administration. Professor Wells's material is based upon work supported by the National Science Foundation under Grant No.PRA78-10238. Any opinions, findings, and conclusions or recommendations expressed in this publication are those of the author and do not necessarily reflect the views of the National Science Foundation.

is poorly developed; machinery is difficult to locate and even more difficult to evaluate, once located. Managers must learn sources, relative prices, reliability, availability of spares, ways of assessing condition, and so on. In some cases, mastery of this market provides a firm with a rather special skill.

In many cases, the critical element in small scale manufacture is flexibility of plant design. Machinery is selected or constructed in such a way that various models of a product or various products can be produced with the same equipment. Hong Kong firms use simple sheet metal working tools to produce cabinets for both refrigerators and stoves. A Pakistani firm selects printing, cutting, and folding equipment that can be used for cigarette packages or candy boxes with a minimum of set-up time in a change over.

In some cases, the adaptation of technology to small scale manufacture consists largely of selecting just the right new equipment from the industrialised countries. A packaging plant may be made up of a few German machines, some from Scandinavia, and a number from Italy. A few manufacturers have built up the experience with suppliers that enables the efficient design of such a plant. Once the experience is acquired, it can be used elsewhere.

- to reduce imported inputs -

In other cases, the developing country firm manufactures its own machinery for small scale production. Many such firms have begun machinery production as a sideline, to utilise shop capacity created for repair work to imported machines. As the need for adaptation becomes apparent, spare capacity in the machine shop is used for modifications to existing machinery and, eventually, for the manufacture of complete pieces of equipment.

In response to the difficulties found in importing inputs, developing country firms have designed their products and processes to reduce the need for foreign materials, components, and parts. In South East Asia, a paint manufacturer based in a developing country uses local clays, which are somewhat different from those specified by the originators of the paint technology. In India, the restrictions on imports of vegetable oils and on the use of edible oils for soap manufacture has led Indian firms to develop skills in the processing of oils available at home. Indian firms have carried the resulting skills to other developing countries.

- and adapt products to environments

In a few cases, developing countries have modified or innovated products in response to their environment. An Indian firm has developed sun fast dyes which it now produces elsewhere for tropical markets. Brazilians have marketed appliances in Africa based on the claim that they are especially designed for tropical conditions - resistant to corrosion from high humidity and not easily damaged by fluctuations in voltage. They appear to be ready to start manufacturing abroad as the governments of the countries in which they sell begin to restrict imports.

The vast majority of manufacturing investments by third world multinationals are "downstream", from the more industrialised to the less industrialised developing countries. This is hardly surprising. It is the firms of the more industrialised countries that first face the problems that appear later in the less industrialised countries. Having found ways to respond to small markets and to the scarcity of materials and components, the innovating firms take their skills to the next tier of countries as industries there begin to encounter similar problems. Thus, Indian firms can set up textile plants in Indonesia drawing on their skills at designing plants for short runs of individual products. The Pakistani firm mentioned earlier can design a flexible paper packaging plant for Zambia. And a Brazilian firm remembers how to manufacture bicycles at a scale appropriate for Bolivia, because it has not been too long since its home operations were of a similar size.

Operating costs are kept low, though expatriates are numerous

To keep costs down, most developing country investors try hard to keep overheads low. Offices are usually not as plush as those of the multinationals from the industrialised countries. Expatriates are on a starvation budget compared to those employed by the traditional multinationals (but not usually compared to what they would earn in their home developing country!). Families may not be sent along. Housing is simple.

Although the cost of a foreign manager or technician is held low, the number of expatriates assigned to the overseas operations is typically greater than the number one finds in comparable firms from the advanced countries. But that seems to be the result of the technology itself. It takes more people and a longer time to transfer technology that borders on the job shop kind required for a flexible, small scale plant. In contrast, substantial parts of the large scale technology provided by many traditional multinationals can be reduced to a manual. Technology for a plant that shifts lines frequently is harder to codify. Moreover, third world firms have not usually felt the need to codify their technology at home. No branch plants and little turnover of personnel mean that knowhow can be kept in the heads of managers and technicians. There is little pressure to write it down or to find other ways to simplify passing it on to others.

For the typical third world multinational, headquarters control over subsidiaries is rather lax. Indeed, in many cases foreign ventures are managed by relatives of the firm's owners. Trust, rather than formal mechanisms, provides the principal tool for control in most such cases.

Flexibility is a characteristic of relations with governments

With the lack of an equivalent of the US Securities and Exchange Commission or, in many cases, outside owners, third world multinationals are often very "flexible" in dealing with governments. That term, when used by managers of such firms, implies not only that they are willing to accept joint venture partners, but also that they are good at working around exchange controls at home. One Latin American firm, for example, pays royalties to a Panamanian shell company for its trade name and technology. That company is, of course, owned by the same family that owns the national company. The circuitous route for money means that currency can be made available for other operations abroad in spite of exchange controls. "Flexibility" also means that such firms are able to deal with host governments in ways that are difficult for the traditional multinationals. Questionable payments can be handled easily in the relaxed accounting systems. And "informal joint ventures" are easily arranged. Thus, one finds in Indonesia, for example, projects that have foreign ownership but which are not registered as such. They consist of joint ventures between Hong Kong or Singapore firms and local businesses, often with no formal joint venture agreement at all.

Strong brand names are not a characteristic

Few of the developing country multinationals have strong brand names, and in most cases they seem not to have the skills to develop them. There are of course a few exceptions. The Philippine producer of San Miguel beer, for example, has conquered the Hong Kong beer market with its promotion (and good product!). It is increasing its share of the Indonesian market. Singapore firms have established strong positions in soft drinks and cigarettes in Indonesia, based on heavily promoted brands. In Ecuador, Inca Kola, a Peruvian firm, seems to have done well in the tough soft drink industry, but its record in Bolivia and Puerto Rico is less enviable. In California and New York, it seems to have had some success in appealing largely to the local immigrant Latin market.

In most cases, brand name is not the preferred competitive weapon of the third world multi-national. Price is the usual fighting tool. Even in product lines dominated by heavy advertising in the industrialised countries, there seems to be a corner for a price fighter in the developing countries. Firms have succeeded by relying on price rather than brand in such traditionally brand oriented products as detergents, cosmetics, and flashlight batteries.

Cooperative arrangements with industrialised MNCs are sometimes made

In some cases, the new third world multinationals are in direct competition with multinationals from the industrialised countries. Cigarettes, flashlight batteries, textile weaving, and radios are examples of markets in which such competition is evident. In other cases, third world multinationals are engaged in activities of little interest to the multinationals of the industrialised world. Plastic dishware, aluminium pots, and umbrella assembly have little appeal to the older multinationals. But there are still other cases in which multinationals from developed countries and third world multinationals have found it useful to form some sort of cooperative arrangements.

For some projects, the older multinationals have turned to third world firms to take up an opportunity that, for some reason, does not attract direct action by the advanced country firm. For example, a European firm that supplied paper packaging technology to other countries was approached by a firm in a country in which it was not active. Perhaps because of the small size of the market, the shortage of technicians for overseas assignment, or the high cost of such personnel, the firm recommended a company in another developing country in its place. The European company had previously supplied that firm with knowhow. More-over, it retained a small equity holding and received some income from licence fees. Responding in some way to the initial request might well result in sales of equipment and materials. Using a previous recipient of its technology in another developing country could lower costs, result in some slight increase in dividends and licence receipts, and still pro-vide the desired tie to the supplies of the European company.

In some projects, the eventual ties between an older and a third world multinational may be very close. A common situation is between firms that have a buying-selling arrangement. For example, an investor from an industrialised country required cartons for exports of agricultural products that it was growing in Africa. To obtain a reliable supplier, it sought out an Asian firm with which it had maintained a satisfactory supply relationship in its (Asian) market. In Africa they established a joint venture. Separate investments appeared unsuitable, given the fact that the Asian owned firm (with import protection) would probably be the only box supplier, and the user would be the only customer.

In other cases, the relationships are less intimate. For example, parts suppliers to automobile multinationals in one Latin American country have followed (or been pulled) by the multinationals to other markets, when a small volume, reliable parts supplier was required to serve affiliates there. Since problems of price and reliability had long been worked out in the old relationship, joint ownership was not required, although mutual dependency would be very high. In still other cases, the relationship has been very intimate indeed. A Japanese multinational acquired a major interest in a Hong Kong textile firm. Jointly they have begun the process of building and modifying a vertically integrated textile system in South East Asia. The Japanese firm supplies synthetic fibres and its technology. The Hong Kong firm supplies spinning and weaving skills and, especially, garment making knowhow. In third countries, operations usually begin with garment making, eventually include spinning and weaving, and finally incorporate fibre manufacture. Ultimately, the Hong Kong and Japanese firms own the integrated system.

In still other cases, the complementary skills that lead to joint ventures may not involve vertical integration, but rather they may be skills that can be combined effectively for one particular product. Most commonly, the multinational from the advanced country provides a trade name and the marketing knowhow. The third world partner provides cheap management, small scale technology, and an ability to operate smoothly in a developing country. A paint manufacturing operation in one South East Asian country provides an example. Equity was shared between a well known US company and a firm from another Asian country. The brand name was American; most of the expatriates were Asian.

The export incentive

The third world multinationals discussed thus far have built their overseas nets to manufacture for the markets where their subsidiaries are located. But there is another group of firms that have set up foreign operations for a different purpose: to supply export markets in the industrialised countries. In the vanguard were the Hong Kong textile firms that, faced with restrictive export quotas at home, started in the mid 1960s an international expansion that seems not yet to have ended. When "voluntary export quotas" were established in Hong Kong, firms went to Singapore, carrying with them access to their export customers who had learned to count on their record for reliable delivery and predictable quality. As Singapore fell under quota restrictions, the same firms added subsidiaries in Malaysia and Thailand. Recently, such firms have established facilities in Mauritius, to take advantage of that country's favoured access to the EEC market. Footwear and television manufacturers from Korea and Taiwan have spread their operations for reasons similar to those that influenced the textile firms.

Quotas were not the only incentive for the internationalisation of exporting firms. In some cases, production costs at home grew prohibitive. Having built up goodwill with customers abroad, the firms had an asset to exploit in lower cost countries. Thus, a Taiwanese pineapple grower began production in Thailand and the Ivory Coast, as wage rates in Taiwan increased so much that pineapple growing there was becoming unattractive.

Tariff or transport costs have provided additional incentives for foreign ventures by exporters. Duties and shipping could, in many cases, be saved by assembling the final product in the destination market. Thus, Asian firms began to assemble furniture and electric fans in the USA, using parts made at home. Such facilities have turned out to be useful sources of market information, according to managers of the parent enterprises.

Non-manufacturing third world MNCs

Like the multinationals from the industrialised countries, many of the third world multinationals are in the service industries. A few extract raw materials.

The internationalisation of banks from the developing countries began long ago. The initial motivation for venturing abroad was usually that of servicing customers at home who were exporting. To keep exporting firms loyal to the bank, a presence in the major export markets was often required. Correspondent relationships seemed to provide only an inadequate substitute for branches and subsidiaries. They seem not to be able to provide the intimate institutional knowledge required for credit analysis and market information or the required assurance that an important customer's business would be handled promptly and correctly. As the banks from the advanced countries arrived in the developing countries, the incentive for developing country banks to move abroad was particularly great. If the home bank could not provide the international network, the industrialised country's would.

More recently, there have been other reasons for the internationalisation of banks from the third world. As the subsidiaries of multinational entrepreneurs from the industrialised countries became important potential customers of banks in the developing countries, local banks wanted their business. To gain it, they have had to supply international services. Additionally, banks have found a presence in the major money centres (London and New York) essential for satisfactory handling of their foreign currency assets and liabilities.

Construction and engineering consulting firms from Korea, India, Brazil and elsewhere have rapidly spread their interests to other countries. But this is a rather different story from that of the banks. Where firms have had experience with projects at home similar to what is being considered in other developing countries, some have mastered the technology as well as firms from the industrialised countries. In fact, they may be better at operating in the difficult conditions of developing countries. However, their principal advantage seems not to be knowhow, but rather their ability to supply cheap human resources. In some cases they simply supply technical personnel; Brazilian and Indian engineers cost less than European and North American ones and, for many jobs, are as good. In other cases, the firms supply not only engineers, but even the low skill construction labour to labour-scarce developing countries, largely in the Middle East. Thus, Pakistani and Philippine workers are moved in large numbers to complete construction projects in the Persian Gulf countries.

There are still only a few extractive multinationals from the developing countries. Where they exist, they have usually sought raw materials abroad for use at home. The imperfect South East Asian markets for timber have led Hong Kong furniture manufacturers to seek to tie up wood suppliers in Borneo, for example. Oil-scarce developing countries have sent their state owned firms abroad to try to find reliable sources of petroleum, and also to participate in ventures with advanced country firms in the hope of learning technology that could help in finding oil at home. Argentina's YPF has been involved in concessions in Bolivia and Ecuador. Brazil's Petrobrás has had petroleum concessions in seven countries.

The NICs can be expected to produce an increasing number of MNCs

There seems to be little reason to expect a slowdown in the growth of multinationals from the third world. Indeed, the growth is likely to accelerate. The newly industrialised developing countries (NICs) have provided an increasing number of firms experienced in meeting the peculiar needs of third world markets. As a result, third world investment in Asia has come largely from Hong Kong, Singapore, Taiwan, and India. Argentina and Mexico seem to stand at the head of the list in Latin America.

The careful reader might be struck by the absence of Korea and Brazil among the countries principally responsible for third world multinationals. The explanation seems to lie in the fact that, in contrast to the other principal source countries, these nations have begun only in recent years to export significant quantities of manufactured goods to other developing countries. Like other multinationals, firms from the developing countries gain their familiarity with foreign markets first by exporting. India, Hong Kong, Singapore, and Taiwan were early exporters to other developing countries. Their exports were followed by investments. Until recently, Korea and Brazil have aimed their exports primarily at the industrialised countries. In fact, in Latin America, overall regional trade has, until the past few years, been small. As a result, the development of Latin American multinationals has lagged far behind that of Asian multinationals. Investment, if not nowadays the flag, follows trade.

More recent data suggest a promising future for Korean, Brazilian, and other developing countries' multinationals. Latin American trade in manufactures has been growing rapidly; no doubt, investment will follow. Indeed, there are many examples. The Brazilian bicycle manufacturer, mentioned earlier, followed exports to Bolivia and Colombia with investment. The efforts of Korea's Hyundai to sell its automobiles in West Africa will, if successful, almost certainly be followed by the construction of local assembly plants as African countries try to encourage local manufacture.

Indeed, all the evidence points to a continued rapid growth in third world multinationals. The experience of the firms from the more advanced developing countries will be relevant in the next tier of countries. Third world multinationals may well provide one of the few significant instruments for cooperation among the developing countries.

III. THE ETHICAL ENVIRONMENT: Bribery and Corruption

Bribery, Corruption, or Necessary Fees and Charges?

MALCOLM CRAWFORD   No. 3 1975

American multinational corporations have not been highly successful in keeping their images shining brightly in Washington this year. The oil companies have been in more trouble than most, and for more reasons than most. Many of the reasons arise from the Church sub-committee's marathon investigations into their international activities. Firms in numerous other industries too, however, have been finding it necessary to "come clean" about various aspects of their business which they have hitherto managed to keep secret. Those aspects with which this article are concerned are the ones that are popularly referred to as bribery and corruption. Whether that is a proper description is a matter we shall discuss. We shall also consider the strategies open to companies in this area, the likely policy implications, and larger implications for US multinational enterprise and its worldwide relations with governments.

Senator Church's subcommittee on multinational corporations has probably uncovered more information about the oil companies than any other body. But the newspapers, the Securities and Exchange Commission (SEC), and lawyers and auditors representing shareholders and third party interests, have been busy too. There has also been some backwash from the Office of the Special Prosecutor set up during the Watergate hearings.

<u>Questions of definition</u>

Perhaps the most interesting and instructive single case history that has come to light through these events is that of Exxon's record of political contributions in Italy. For this reason the two principal documents on that case are included as appendices to this article, and are highly recommended as worth reading in their own right, in portraying what should not be allowed to happen in any business organisation, however large and difficult for top management to monitor in detail it may be.

The words "bribery" and "corruption" are strongly loaded, ethically and politically. "Corruption" is essentially a subjective judgment – it is what the beholder judges to be rotten or corrupt. Bribery can be defined as payment in expectation of favours or services which ought not be rendered, i e which are either illegal or contrary to regulation or policy. That is not a definition which would embrace cases where official services should be offered, or would be expected as part of the normal functions of government, but are forthcoming only against special payment. Most people would call such a payment extortion or protection money – or in American slang, a "shakedown". Whether such payments are demanded by the potential recipient, or are offered by the one seeking the favour, is an important distinction. On the basis of the information available to us, our conclusion is that such payments are far more often asked of than offered by multinational companies. And yet, if one looks at such practices in any particular country in their totality – as distinct from the decision framework which will normally confront any one firm – the distinction between bribery and protection or shakedown is often much less clear cut than it will appear to the firm.

The outright, barefaced bribe is comparatively rare. More commonly there are essentially three types of payment which may relate either closely or loosely to this broad class of transaction:

1.   Political contributions.
2.   Agents' fees.
3.   Consultants' (legal, economic etc) fees.

49

Bribes themselves may take the form of direct payments in cash or kind to government officials, indirect payments through over invoicing of goods and services supplied to a government agency, the excess payment being credited to an account in a foreign country, or gifts to charities fronting for ministers etc.

The SEC takes action

Senator Church's committee is a subcommittee of the Senate Foreign Relations Committee, and its prime purpose has been to allow Congress to form views as to what if any further legislation is needed on this subject. Moral indignation has tended to run high, and the present mood seems to point to legislation. The SEC's interest in the matter primarily concerns disclosure. Public companies are required to disclose more information in accounts in the US than in any other country, and for obvious reasons many of these payments have been either wrongly accounted for or else inadequately designated. Fraud and occasionally outright bribery are also being prosecuted by the SEC. Among the cases now in hand, the SEC has charged United Brands (formerly the United Fruit Company) with bribery of officials of foreign governments, and also with violations of the reporting and anti-fraud provisions of the 1934 Securities Exchange Act. Ashland Oil and some of its executives are charged with failure to disclose large sums of money handled "without proper accounting procedures or controls". Gulf Oil and its former vice president for government relations are charged with diverting over $10 mn in corporate funds to a foreign subsidiary, much of it via false entries in the books. Of that sum, over half was (by admission of the chairman) returned to the USA for illegal political contributions. Phillips Petroleum and four executives are charged with diverting $2.8 mn to Switzerland by means of false entries on Phillips's books. Of that amount, over $1.3 mn was allegedly returned in cash to the US, about $600,000 being spent on political contributions "some of which were unlawful". The American Ship Building Company and its chairman are charged with using corporate funds for political campaign contributions (which is illegal in the US). The Minnesota Mining and Manufacturing Company, its chairman, and two other executives, have been convicted of similar charges, and of falsely recording such funds as insurance and legal expenses.

In another case, involving General Refractories, the Swiss bank involved, the Swiss Bank Corporation, is a codefendant. This extends the question of extraterritoriality to the problem and must raise the level of concern among non-US banks dealing with American clients. It is difficult however to see how they could be guilty of an offence under these laws if they did no more than receive deposits from the companies and pay out moneys in accord with normal banking practice.

Exxon's financial entanglement with Italian politics –

In the case of Exxon, the salient feature is the way relatively small political contributions in Italy in the early 1960s grew, in the absence of financial control, to such large sums as to alarm regional and then head office – and eventually to create political scandals in both Italy and the USA. A figure of $763,000 is given by the company as the total payments in 1963. Over the period from then until 1971, the total came to $27 mn in payments authorised from regional head office (London) and a further $19 mn in unauthorised payments which were discovered only after an audit had been ordered from New York. According to Exxon's controller, the company had no way of verifying either the purposes or the recipients of these latter payments. Even in the case of the authorised ones, for which receipts were obtained, the actual destinations were unclear. Newspapers and other publications acted as a conduit for some of the money. And although it is clear that requests for campaign funds by the Christian Democratic Party started the whole thing, and that much if not most of the money went to it or persons connected with it, one newspaper report said that the Communist Party received at least one payment via an affiliated publication. The party denied the allegation. During the time of the centre left coalition in the early 1970s, the Socialist and Social Democrat parties also received authorised contributions from the oil companies.

50

Political contributions were and are legal in Italy, and until 1974, were not publicly disclosed. The oil industry's trade association, the Unione Petrolifera, acted as consultant and as conduit for some of the payments to the CDP. It would "advise" the oil companies how much they should pay in each year. All or nearly all oil companies operating in Italy made such payments, and it is far from clear whether any special favours were bought yielding advantage to any particular oil company, or even whether the industry gained any net advantage. The industry has never been satisfied with its treatment under the informal price control system in Italy - indeed British Petroleum pulled out in 1974 because of low profitability attributed to this cause. On the other hand, certain fiscal concessions were made to the industry during the period, though at least one of them was fairly minor, another was apparently in lieu of price increases, and it is doubtful if in total they were worth as much as the sums contributed over the years. The US oil companies involved claim that their impression was that they were paying to ensure no more than a generally favourable economic environment. It is unclear from the documentation whether the initiative emanated mainly from the CDP or mainly from the oil industry.

- was less controlled or open than that of Mobil

Mobil Oil appears to have gone to greater pains than Exxon in creating internal accountability for its political contributions in Italy. Not only were receipts obtained for all payments, the amounts were entered as costs both for corporate income tax and also as part of the base on which turnover tax was charged. Exxon's payments, in contrast, were disguised in various ways, for example by the issue of vouchers for goods or services that were never purchased. Mobil, moreover, managed to resist pressures for political contributions until 1970. It seems that in Italy, if not elsewhere, it was possible for foreign companies to say "no" at least for some considerable time, without disastrous consequences.

Last year, Italy passed a law requiring companies to disclose their political contributions. This puts Italy roughly in line with the United Kingdom, Canada, and West Germany, in this respect. In the USA, the law not only requires disclosure but also makes payments to party funds, officials, or politicians illegal in the USA - though it permits them to be made abroad. [1]

Wrath of host governments falls on Gulf

Gulf Oil, in easily the most spectacular set of admissions in these hearings, was found not only to have made payments to several foreign countries, but also to have routed some of the money back to the USA, via a Bahamian subsidiary, for the purpose of making politically related payments which it admits were illegal. Gulf's admissions were initially made in camera before the SEC. Word was leaked, however, that at least $5 mn had been given by the company in political contributions in foreign countries, $4 mn of it in one country. Immediately a wave of righteous indignation went up from the host country governments. Venezuela threatened shutdown if that country was not exonerated within 48 hours. Peru expropriated Gulf's assets. Ecuador launched an investigation. In public testimony before the Church subcommittee, Gulf's chairman, Robert Dorsey, felt compelled to disclose that the recipient of the $4 mn had been South Korea's ruling Democratic Republican Party. According to Dorsey, senior officials of President Park's party first demanded $1 mn during the election campaign which began in 1966. This was paid, under severe threat. Four years later, before the next presidential campaign, $10 mn was demanded. Dorsey became personally involved in a negotiation during which (he says) he beat the Koreans down to $3 mn. He added, in testimony, that American firms including his own had been cajoled by the US State Department to invest in South Korea, to underwrite the reconstruction of that country after

---

1 Author's note (1980): The latter is no longer true, following enactment of the Foreign Corrupt Practices Act of 1977.

the war with North Korea. It is highly unlikely that State Department did not know of the contributions since managements of multinational firms everywhere know South Korea as a country where politically related payments of one kind or another are the rule, not the exception. However, Dorsey said he did not consider there to have been any possibility that the US government would help Gulf in that situation.

Gulf is also in difficulty over payments in Bolivia, including $350,000 to the ruling party and $110,000 for a helicopter for the late President Barrientos - who was killed when the same helicopter crashed. Gulf's senior executive in Bolivia has been arrested and compensation for $70 mn worth of assets, which were being nationalised, is in doubt. Another payment by Gulf of $50,000 in Beirut is interesting, in that it was to finance a public relations campaign to assist with better understanding of the Arabs in the United States.

Expectation concerning payments varies greatly from one host country to another

Much the greater part of the political payments made by multinational companies are more in the nature of protection money than bribery, if only because companies rarely want to spend money which may or may not yield a return. A bribe,by its very nature, is likely to be a risky investment. It is especially unwise for a company not familiar in considerable detail with practices in any particular country to go waving money about in a manner that could be construed as bribery. The testimony before the Church committee, despite that senator's ready use of the words "corrupt" and "obscene", is consistent with these evaluations.

When asked, the companies generally pay - at least in less developed countries. In Europe company management may more readily doubt whether the political processes really tolerate such payments even if a particular request may have been received. Such doubts are less often felt in the third world. Not all underdeveloped countries tolerate bribery or political protection rackets, however. One needs to be very careful about offering bribes in Tanzania, for example. And in Latin America, rising suspicion of foreign business has made such transactions much more sensitive than they used to be. Peru is fairly puritanical in this respect. Left shaded governments tend to be more so than those which support capitalism with enthusiasm. It is always best to use agents or consultants, or better still to work through the local joint venture partner who is becoming an almost universal feature of direct investment in developing countries.

Agents can prove a handicap sometimes

This raises the question of choosing the right agent, consultant, or partner. At least one British firm in India fell foul of officialdom through having an Indian director who was persona non grata in official quarters handle its government relations. The same happened to a large American multinational in Kenya - where, unlike in India, the traffic is fairly open and standard rates for deals assisted by ministers and senior officials can be ascertained upon enquiry. Even an agent who has proved himself highly useful may have diminishing value. Northrop documents prepared for the SEC reveal that executives of that company which had used an agent called Adnan Kashoggi in Saudi Arabia to profitable effect considered that in future his usefulness would diminish because an increasing number of officials in Riyadh were coming to feel that he was getting too big a share of this trade.

Firms unfamiliar with the ground rules in a particular country can usually gain helpful advice from embassy officials of their own nationality in that country. The latter can sometimes be helpful too in advising on the choice of agents or joint venture partners. This is true for European companies, though the present uproar in Washington is likely to make US officials less helpful to American firms on matters with uncertain ethical overtones. This would naturally tend to give a slight advantage to the Europeans. But it is doubtful whether the US commercial attaches were ever as useful to American firms in these matters as some of their European counterparts.

The importance of not being a multinational with a permanent presence

The Northrop documents suggest that US officials were not able to offer that firm any significant help in government relations questions. (Yet some American armaments makers, such as General Dynamics, are known to have received help from successive administrations in dealings with foreign governments. Partly this is a question of getting the hardware included in the Pentagon's official defence sales programme.) Northrop, like most defence equipment makers, is not really multinational. Such firms must go into a country without having any permanent stake in it, and are therefore much more dependent upon agents or consultants for guidance as to how to oil the wheels of government. This is especially important in military sales because governments are the only significant buyers of defence equipment. For years, Northrop had suffered from inadequate entrée to higher levels of officialdom in Western Europe, and around 1968 it began studying how Lockheed handled these matters. It engaged a consultant, Frank DeFrancis, once the legal representative in Washington for the Bonn government, on a contract modelled on those used by Lockheed, to act as lobbyist for them in Germany and to assist indirectly in improving access to appropriate levels of government in other countries. There is neither evidence nor testimony that DeFrancis bribed anyone. He did, however, assist in setting up a Swiss company, headed by a Dr Froriep, which for one purpose or another received over $3 mn from Northrop in connection with military sales in Brazil, Taiwan, Iran, Malaysia, and Saudi Arabia. Northrop management do not appear ever to have dealt directly with Froriep, and only one other Northrop executive apart from the chairman ever dealt with DeFrancis. Written records concerning this connection were kept to a minimum.

This method of tackling relations with governments is characteristically not that of a multinational company; it is rather that of a supplier of government procurement goods, of a kind that encourages more than the usual degree of secrecy in the attendant transactions; and where the supplier lacks a foothold in the foreign countries concerned, apart from agency representation.

Payments to unfreeze a bureaucracy

Northrop was involved in another type of transaction in Iran, again not of a kind that involved any long term investment. This was its part in a consortium which also included Siemens, Nippon Electric, and General Telephone and Telegraph (of Italy), in building a $225 mn telecommunications system in that country. Owing to Siemens' greater experience in the Middle East, the German company was elected custodian of funds to finance fees and other payments in Iran. Somewhat over $1 mn was agreed to be deposited by each member in a Swiss bank account designated by Siemens. Again, there is no evidence that the funds were used to bribe any public officials. The Northrop subsidiary involved did however find it necessary to make a direct payment to an Iranian tax official to prevent him from deducting withholding tax from salaries paid in the United States on behalf of Northrop staff working on the project (tax was paid on the portion of salaries paid in Iran - and from then on, Northrop paid on the portion paid in the US too, so as to avoid further pay offs). According to the report of the working group examining the case for the SEC, Siemens did not reply to their request for information about how the money was spent. Northrop's assistant controller "does not assume that Siemens did anything other than pocket the money, but the implication (he) drew from his understanding is that the money was probably, in part at least, used to pay off some mid level Iranian officials".

"The implication drawn" (the report goes on) "is rooted in his (the assistant controller's) belief that there is a need to make such payments in Iran. The way in which the bureaucracy operates makes it almost impossible to get the necessary approvals on schedule, if at all, unless there is a special effort. All members of the bureaucracy operate on the understanding that a mistake can put them and their families in jail or worse; the best way to avoid a mistake is not to make a decision. Another way is to submerge their responsibility for any decision by having other people share (in it). We were told... that as many as 46 signatures were required for payments under the contract. And even when you got the signatures, payment was not necessarily forthcoming. Other legitimate explanations for the Siemens type payments are to secure for the consortium members   logistical information they would otherwise not have respecting reliable sources of supply, or subcontractors..."

The Northrop officer interviewed tried to deduct the payments from US taxes, but the firm's tax director did not see his way clear to doing this, since he knew that documentation was inadequate. This meant placing the items under "Schedule M" - non-deductible expenses. However, the Revenue officials still wanted to know details about them, in case any of the money had been paid to US nationals. Generally speaking, revenue regulations in European countries are more permissive. Nevertheless there is still a need to produce evidence that payments, unless trivially small, represent a necessary business expense. This, quite apart from the consideration of keeping a low profile in the host country, is another reason for channelling payments via agents or consultants as fees.

Can shakedowns by officials be resisted?

It is clearly almost impossible for firms in a competitive situation to resist demands for payoffs when an essential service or function would otherwise be withdrawn or if payments owing to the company would be stopped - provided, of course, appeal to a higher level does not solve the problem. Failing that, the payment must be made. An example is the inability of customs officials in certain West African countries to clear goods through the docks in less than a matter of months, unless quicker procedures are made worthwhile.

A firm which enjoys a degree of monopoly is in a stronger position. But even then, the brazen courage (or avarice) of some officials can exceed normal expectations. A local affiliate of British American Tobacco(BAT)[1] operating in a West African country last year received a request from the head of state for a substantial contribution to a worthy cause dear to his heart. After a little thought, the head of the affiliate refused. The company enjoyed a monopoly, using locally produced raw materials, much of them bought from a state monopoly. Very soon, a foreign company was allowed into the market - importing its products from South Africa. As the South African product is widely known to be better than that manufactured from the locally grown produce, there is every likelihood that it will gain a substantial share of the market, at least in the principal city. Elsewhere, it may encounter distribution problems. BAT may well consider that it has a sufficiently strong hold on the retailers in the towns and villages to make it less than worthwhile for the newcomer to penetrate outside the principal city.

The local executive may also have calculated that it would be better to lose his monopoly of this market rather than expose his firm to repeated and possibly escalating demands. A somewhat similar case was publicised some years ago, concerning a Canadian Bank in Haiti, where the head of state demanded gifts to a hospital charity. Several gifts were made, until eventually the bank refused one, in the amount of $100,000. One night, the bank's vaults were broken into, and exactly $100,000 was removed.

---

1 A pseudonym was used in the original article but owing to a coup in the meantime in the country in question the issue is no longer sensitive.

Clean companies and clean countries

If a firm is going to resist demands in order to prevent them from continuing and perhaps escalating, the strategy would gain from giving it publicity, for it is in a stronger position if governments know that a firm has an adamant, unshakeable position on politically related payments. Among American firms, Xerox, IBM and RCA all claim to be totally and immovably "clean" in these matters.

To adopt a strong moral position at the highest levels is a straighforward (if not exactly riskless) senior executive decision. To refuse to make payments to lower officials, where this is necessary to oil the wheels (as in the case mentioned where payments are necessary to move goods through the ports) is another and more difficult problem. For a firm that is well established in the host country, it may be worthwhile to press, at high levels, to have the situation cleaned up, rather than make payments. Otherwise it can always get worse. The difficulty is, however, that such a firm will be embarrassed to admit the payments it has already made.

Although most firms affected by what they see as systematic shakedowns may feel that they are victims of a corrupt administration, it is likely that, where the existing practices in the host country are "clean", the initiative may have come from a company. It is not diffi-cult for a company to refuse to make a payment of this kind where existing practices in that country are reputable, and indeed it would be very risky for a low or middle grade official to make the first demand.

Nevertheless, the present situation is that in a great many countries there is a long tra-dition of payments for official services which would be illegal in the USA, the UK, or most other parent countries of multinational firms. It appears that in the great majority of cases, at the higher levels of corruption at least, they arise from "suggestions" from ministers or officials of host governments. Yet high level bribery by multinational firms is not unknown. The celebrated payment of $1,250,000 by United Brands to a Swiss bank account in favour of a member of the Honduran government, which coincided with efforts of that company to reduce that country's export tax on bananas (and indirectly those of other Central American governments) would appear to have been a case of outright bribery at the highest levels. The tax was reduced from $1 per 40 lb box to 30 cents. Both the ministers who were named in SEC hearings - President López Arellano and Economics Minister Bennaton Ramos - have denied the allegations. Nevertheless, after the news broke, López Arellano was removed from office and Bennaton Ramos was charged in a Honduran criminal court.

Repercussions on firms do not stop with prosecution and embarrassment

For the corporations involved in the present scandals in the USA, the difficulties do not stop with prosecution by the SEC and embarrassment before congressional committees. The 3M Company was fined $3,000 and its former chairman $500, on federal misdemeanour charges. The state of Minnesota convicted them of similar charges and levied fines of $5,000 and $3,000 respectively. The company and two executives have also been charged with tax fraud, for which the trial has yet to be held. And shareholder actions have been brought, and settled out of court, with the effect that the former chairman and executives are to pay a total of $475,000 to the company by way of reimbursement. Civil action is also being taken by shareholders against the estate of the late chairman of United Brands, who committed suicide after the alleged bribery became public knowledge.

The adverse effects upon the company abroad can be devastating too, as Gulf Oil found. In this area however the consequences of such payments (or of refusing to make them) are most difficult to predict. Some executives, testifying before Senator Church's subcommittee, urged that legislation be passed prohibiting politically related payments overseas, just as they are now prohibited in the USA. This, it was said, would make it easier for firms to resist extortion. One company chairman suggested that disclosure rules be tightened to require more detail, e g to name all recipients of certain kinds of services.

The Senate Finance Committee has drafted a resolution urging the administration to initiate, in the multinational trade negotiations at Geneva, and in other negotiations and "appropriate international fora", a code of conduct and of "specific trading obligations among governments", designed to eliminate "such practices". It urges the administration to negotiate a code with governments, which those governments might (hopefully) then enact and enforce accordingly. For this reason (and also the fact that it made no mention of obligatory disclosure of agents' fees to foreign governments) the draft resolution won the unequivocal support of no less a body than the Machinery and Allied Products Institute, which includes some armaments exporting firms among its membership. The resolution recently passed the Senate by a 93-0 vote. The administration could not totally ignore such a result, even if it wanted to.

The question of extraterritoriality is likely to arise if and when this approach is not seen to be working effectively. The resolution, in a "whereas" clause, reminded the president of his responsibility, under section 301 of the new trade act, to "take all possible and feasible steps within his power" to eliminate discriminatory or otherwise unreasonable policies or acts by foreign governments, which burden or restrict American business. What the senators have in mind here is that if US legislation makes it more difficult for American firms to compete with foreign firms in dirty business in lands where ethics are unknown (or at least unamerican) the administration must try to do all it can to redress any such disadvantage. The senators are not so wet behind the ears as to think that a code of conduct, however high principled, will ever erase the sins of the world. Section 301 empowers the president to take almost any retaliatory act short (apparently) of war.

If this clause in the resolution means anything, therefore, it means that the Senate wants American business protected and encouraged unto righteousness abroad by more than just a code of conduct. There are, in short, hidden teeth.

At this stage, however, a code of conduct is the first priority. The US tried to insert into the OECD code of conduct on international investment, which coincidentally was also drafted last summer, a clause consistent with the Senate draft resolution. This was received stonily by other OECD countries, on the grounds that such things do not happen in our countries, and if our companies have to indulge in unusual payments in order to compete in certain foreign countries, it is the responsibility of those host governments to do something about it. Some felt it was a problem for the UN, if it was one for international organisations at all. In the end, a clause appeared in the OECD code to the effect that companies should "adapt to best local practices". In Washington this is regarded as quite meaningless.

Nobody in Washington appears to expect any code of conduct (if one is agreed internationally) to have any enforcement mechanism. The Senate resolution mentions procedures for settlement of disputes, but even that would appear doubtful. Basically, senators feel that once the matter does achieve high level public debate, no government will stand openly opposed to honesty; and while practice will often depart from pledged principles, at least the pledges can be used to embarrass those who can be shown to have departed from them.

It is difficult to see how the present US approach would be of much help to the established multinational firm, frequently and heavily "shaken down". Clearly, however, unilateral action by the US against offending governments would be even less helpful. Concerted pressures by the leading OECD governments on the host countries which carry such practices to the greatest extremes could probably be effective - but to precisely what effect? If for example they caused the downfall of President Park's regime in South Korea, what other regime would be expected to replace it? Would it be possible to mount pressures selectively, i e concentrating on regimes which, in the opinion of the capital exporting countries' foreign ministries, could be improved by such pressures? If so, this would be not merely extraterritoriality, it would be neo-colonialism in a more active form than the non-communist world has yet seen.

A change in US official attitude to its multinationals?

It appears certain that the present wave of actions, both civil and criminal, will exert a considerable discipline on American companies in future. New legislation will almost surely appear. It is entirely possible that direct payments by US corporations to ministers and officials could be effectively banned, in this way. It is unlikely however that even the most detailed disclosure requirements, or proscriptions of political payments, could abolish transactions made via agents, consultants, and the favourite "charities" of ministers. The most that could thus be achieved would be to reduce the amounts paid for dubious purposes. However, in the case of contracts on investments running into hundreds of millions, a few thousand or even hundred thousand in fees might not appear excessive. A ban on such payments by American companies would moreover award a competitive advantage to non-American multinationals, and indeed uninationals, selling in countries where payments of dubious kinds are expected. Any reduction of competitive pressures in this area which American law might bring about would however tend to reduce the scale of such traffic as a whole, if only by reducing the bargaining power of the recipients.

There is a wider sense in which the recent scandals may affect multinational firms, especially American ones. There has been an increasing tendency in the US administration to question whether multinational corporations are in fact useful to the USA. They are no longer an extension of US foreign policy, as they used to be. Even their use to cloak CIA agents has been made more difficult by recent exposures. And as C Fred Bergsten remarks in a recent article in Foreign Policy (Coming Investment Wars?), "Sovereignty is no longer at bay in the host countries". He concludes that US administration policy will not only become less helpful to US multinationals, but will actively discourage them more and more, due to a variety of emerging conflicts of interest associated with their activities abroad. Bribery and corruption are not among those he cites and analyses, but could easily be added to the list.

Where host governments should take a stand

As to whether multinational companies corrupt governments of host countries by such disreputable activities, no honest and well informed observer can possibly give a clear cut answer. Leaving aside cases of outright bribery, where payment is neither solicited nor expected (which would appear to be relatively few), any company looking at the matter from its individual standpoint must usually take the ethics and administrative standards of the host country as it finds them. In some countries, especially in Africa, the governmental system depends on sub rosa payments, nobody wants the system changed, and it might even be impossible to change it.

It has been traditional for centuries in much of Africa and Asia that merchants from outside a kingdom honour the ruler with gifts, and the tradition lives on, despite alterations in the form of government. Yet in many other countries, where the political system is more developed, it is undeniable that regular payoffs to ministers and officials tend to support the kind of government that needs companies which will help to corrupt them. As we have seen, these are not necessarily multinational companies, for the newcomer, or a firm like Northrop selling without a foothold in the country concerned, is likely to be in a weaker position to resist pressures to pay. A further major difficulty for multinational companies, faced with corrupt government, is that they do not want to do anything that would tend to threaten the stability of the regime. Multinationals can do business in democratic countries, in right wing dictatorships, and in Communist countries, albeit in different ways. What they want most of all is continuity of administration so that their plans, contracts, taxes and tariffs, etc are not disrupted or varied unfavourably. They will therefore generally do what is required to achieve this end. The onus must, accordingly, lie mainly with host governments to correct corrupt practices - if that is really what they want to do.

APPENDIX I

TESTIMONY OF A L MONROE ON ITALIAN MATTERS.
SENATE SUB-COMMITTEE ON MULTINATIONAL CORPORATIONS JULY 16, 1975
(Controller of Exxon since 1973)

Before going into detail, I will summarise the facts vital to an understanding of the Esso Italiana problem.

The Esso Italiana problem resulted essentially from a failure of management and financial controls to detect promptly abuses by the country manager at that time. As chief executive of Esso Italiana for about twenty years, he was admired and respected not only by Exxon but throughout Italian industry and government. Exxon's trust was misplaced, as I will describe.

When the abuses were discovered in early 1972, they were cured quickly and decisively and they were cured before anyone heard of Watergate, and long before the Italian government or our own government began investigations of political contributions.

Until mid 1971, Esso Italiana was authorised to make political contributions, which were then and still are lawful by corporations in Italy. All the political parties have large administrative staffs and subsidise newspapers and other publications. Major non-Communist parties depended almost entirely upon business support until mid 1974 when a law on political contributions introduced government subsidies of about $75 mn per year.

The country manager maintained it was necessary for Esso Italiana, as an Italian corporation, to make substantial contributions to the major non-Communist political parties and candidates. At no time did Exxon management approve any contributions to the Communist Party. Moreover, he maintained, the political parties did not want the details of the business support they were receiving to be revealed. Accordingly, company management was persuaded that it was necessary to make authorised contributions without disclosing the recipient, as indeed it appears was the custom. This meant handling the payments so that they could not be identified as political contributions on the books of Esso Italiana. This was a mistake.

Now, for the events which took place in Italy up to 1972 and the findings of our Italian investigation.

Authorised political contributions in Italy grew from $760,000 in 1963, the earliest year covered by our investigation, to over $5 mn in 1968, by which time Esso Europe headquarters in London - the regional management to which Esso Italiana reported - had become very concerned at the size and control of these expenditures. They instructed the country

58

manager both to reduce the amount of the contributions and to agree in advance with his Esso Europe contact vice president the amount of such payments each year. The country manager began submitting estimated expenditures and the authorised contributions were reduced to $3.5 mn in 1970. Finally, in mid 1971 regional management,which had become increasingly concerned about lack of control and possible abuse, ordered these payments stopped completely. From 1963-71 the contributions authorised averaged $3 mn per year. Although I express money amounts in dollars, all contributions were made in lire from general funds by Esso Italiana.

Because of rumours of possible conflicts of interest, Esso Europe began a special audit of the country manager's activities in January 1972. While this was in its initial stages, it was learned that the country manager had made unauthorised secret commercial commitments and payments.

When this came to light in mid March 1972, the special audit was immediately intensified into a full scale investigation. An executive vice president of Exxon was placed in charge of the investigation. Shortly thereafter, the country manager was terminated, by which time other unauthorised activities had come to light. Among these were secret purchases of real estate, secret guarantees to banks in favour of other companies, and abuses of the capital budget procedure.

These secret and unauthorised activities also included about $19 mn of payments made over many years. The country manager claimed these were political contributions in addition to those authorised but, as we will explain, we have no way of verifying the actual purposes or recipients of these payments.

The investigators reported in 1972 the methods of making and booking the authorised and the unauthorised payments. They were always approved by the country manager and were often made against invoices for goods and services not actually received, or by cash disbursements with no supporting documentation. The country manager generated funds by rebates from suppliers, customers, and banks. Most of the funds from these sources were channelled into secret bank accounts known only to him and his personal assistants and not recorded on Esso Italiana books. He also made payments by opening overdraft accounts, and frequently transferred funds between accounts which made subsequent tracing of these funds almost impossible. He controlled all deposits and withdrawals from these accounts, and had all bank records channelled to him personally. This tight personal control that he had over the bank accounts prevented the auditors from detecting these secret accounts through normal bank confirmation procedures, since the banks, at his request, did not reveal the existence of the accounts to our auditors.

As a result, despite the subsequent exhaustive investigations, we do not know to this day with any certainty where the money went, except for certain commercial payments. This is true both for authorised political contributions as well as unauthorised payments he claims were political. In fact, even in the case of payments booked and supported by invoices from politically related organisations, at least half of the funds were recycled into bank accounts known only to the manager or his personal assistants. Of the cash withdrawn, allegedly to make political contributions, verification of final recipients is practically impossible.

We are reasonably certain that large amounts did reach political parties, in part because after contributions were stopped in 1972, the new Esso Italiana management had to resist party pressure to resume on a large scale.

In 1968, as I stated previously, our regional management were concerned not only about the size of the political contributions in Italy but also about the lack of control and reasons for such large contributions. In the procedure introduced to effect better control and a clearer understanding of why these large contributions were necessary, the country manager allocated the total amount to categories relating to business objectives. This procedure itself raises the question as to whether these objectives were special favours so tied to the contributions as to make them improper, as opposed to being simply business objectives which could best be achieved in a favourable business environment. The vice president of Esso Europe, who annually reviewed this allocation, says that he was told repeatedly and understood that all payments were lawfully made to political parties. The country manager stated that these were only a list of the objectives that justified Esso Italiana's making expenditures to support the parties - and not a list of specific favours to be obtained by agreement.

It is important to an understanding to know whether we are looking at this problem in the light of hindsight or in the light of facts known in the period before 1972. It was in 1971 that regional management became sufficiently concerned about improper tie-ins that they ordered all political contributions stopped.

An Italian parliamentary commission and the Italian prosecutor's office have been investigating political payments by the Italian oil industry for the past year and a half. Many people, including our ex country manager and two Esso Italiana employees, have been under investigation. We understand that he had denied any impropriety, and has insisted that all payments made were political contributions not related to any special favours. We know that our employees under investigation have denied any wrong doing.

When confronted with the findings of the Italian investigation in 1972, Exxon management moved promptly and decisively. The major actions taken to establish proper controls over Esso Italiana operations were:

1. Termination of the country manager, and installation of new management.

2. Termination of all political contributions in Italy by the new management - as instructed by Esso Europe in 1971.

3. Strengthening financial and management controls in Esso Italiana.

4. Instituting arbitration proceedings to recover payments made relating to certain unauthorised commercial transactions.

5. Reviewing the findings of our investigation to determine whether there is sufficient basis for a lawsuit against the country manager. This matter is still under consideration.

In addition to corrective actions in Esso Italiana, Exxon management, determined to see that what happened in Italy would not occur anywhere else, took further steps in 1972-74 affecting worldwide operations. New financial controls were implemented and a strong policy statement was issued by the chairman of the board emphasising strict observance of laws, and directing that transactions must be properly booked and information not withheld from auditors.

In mid 1973, Exxon's internal audit organisation was strengthened. Our auditors, as a fundamental part of their audit programmes, evaluate compliance with this policy and are instructed to report any violations directly to New York. Some few minor violations have occurred since then and been corrected, but none of these involved political contributions.

While the concealed expenditures were large, they were not material in the context of Exxon's worldwide operations. However, our management has considered it desirable to review again the 1972 investigation and the corrective actions taken at that time, to determine whether any additional action should be taken. This review is presently in progress and is expected to be completed within several weeks.

In summary: Exxon has run its business throughout the world on the principle of compliance not only with local laws but with basic standards of honesty and candour. The Italian situation was a unique aberration.

The investigation disclosed errors of judgment at various times in the past by members of Esso Europe, and New York general management, the controller's function, the internal audit staff and others. With the advantage of hindsight, it was a mistake to authorise the country manager to handle political contributions in the manner agreed. However, the principal cause of our difficulties was clearly the country manager's own breach of the trust placed in him.

We are concerned and embarrassed by the fact that these irregularities occurred on such a scale and for several years in one of our affiliates. This is particularly distressing because we believe we have built a reputation for lawful and ethical conduct worldwide. However, I hope you will keep in mind that when the full situation was disclosed by our own investigators we stopped all questionable activities promptly and decisively, on our own initiative, over three years ago.

Gentlemen, that concludes my prepared remarks. I've mentioned the basic policy statement of our chairman, which I would be glad to read.

APPENDIX II

STATEMENT BY J K JAMIESON, CHAIRMAN
OF THE BOARD EXXON CORPORATION, OCTOBER 1972

The policy of this company, as stated by the Board of Directors years ago, is one of strict observance of all laws which may be applicable to its business.

Our policy does not stop there. Even where the law is permissive, Jersey chooses the course of the highest integrity. Local customs, traditions, and mores differ from place to place, and this must be allowed for. But honesty is not subject to criticism in any culture. Shades of dishonesty simply invite demoralising and reprehensible judgments. A well founded reputation for scrupulous dealing is itself a priceless company asset.

An overly ambitious manager, who is not aware of our policy and our views, might have the mistaken idea that we do not care how results are obtained, as long as he gets results. He might think it best not to tell higher management all that he is doing, not to record all transactions accurately in his books and records and to deceive the company's internal and external auditors. He would be wrong on all counts.

First, we do care how we get results. We expect compliance with our standard of integrity throughout the organisation. We will not reward a manager who achieves results at the cost of violation of laws or unscrupulous dealing. By the same token, we will support, and we expect you to support, a manager who passes up an opportunity or advantage which can only be secured at the sacrifice of principle.

Second, and equally important, we expect candour from managers at all levels, and compliance with accounting rules and controls. Our system of management will not work without honest bookkeeping, honest budget proposals, honest economic evaluation of projects. We don't want liars for managers, whether they are lying in a mistaken effort to protect us or to make themselves look good.

One of the kinds of harm which results when a manager conceals information from higher management is that subordinates within his organisation think they are being given a signal that company policies and rules, including accounting and control rules, can be ignored whenever inconvenient. The result can be fast spreading corruption and demoralisation of an entire organisation.

I am aware that there can be exceptional cases where we may want to conceal from third parties a transaction which, while lawful and ethical, is sensitive in the local context. But we do not want such matters concealed from us or our internal or external auditors. If information is sensitive, it is in order for management to bring this sensitivity to the attention of our auditors, so that the auditors can take appropriate measures to see that it is not disclosed outside of company channels.

The ICC Crusades Against Bribery and Corruption

When the International Chamber of Commerce announced two years ago that it was about to set up a commission to devise a code of conduct on unethical business practices, the onslaught against multinational companies and armaments contractors was at its height. Revelations about the activities of Lockheed, ITT, and the American oil companies appeared with sensational frequency in the press. The US Senate committee chaired by Frank Church, uncovering large scale undeclared payments by American multinationals around the world, stirred antipathy towards multinational enterprise which has produced a continuing train of legislative and administrative activity in the USA in this area. This has in turn produced echoes in several international organisations, and, to a far lesser extent, in other countries in which multinational companies are based.

The commission was appointed by the ICC in March 1976, under Lord Shawcross, a former UK attorney general. Its early crusading momentum has been heavily impaired, if not dissipated, largely as a result of opposition from companies' organisations in those countries where the reactions of the media and governments to such scandals cause the least inhibition. Representatives of these countries have been able to point to serious practical difficulties entailed in promulgating a code with quasi legislative force.

It was surely necessary for the international business community (if there is such a thing) to react, however. Quite apart from the antipathy to large scale international business activity that was generated by the scandals, there was a danger, in the minds of some large multinational managements, that the huge post 1974 Opec revenues would give rise to further escalation in fees, kickbacks, and shakedowns of legitimate foreign businesses - as well as ordinary bribery which (most multinational company managements claim) is much less common than the public has come to believe. They also feared that political stability in a number of lucrative markets could be threatened, and local agents as well as rulers' families brought into disrepute, if not worse.

An executive of British American Tobacco - a company which had been faced with extortion in one of its African markets, and had suffered for refusing to pay - went to the UN conference on "transnationals" in Lima in the spring of 1976 and declared that the ICC would take it upon itself to investigate the extent of bribery and corruption in the awarding of international contracts, and draw up a code of conduct to which the international business community could voluntarily subscribe. Though the BAT executive was not on Shawcross's commission, his presence in Lima was seen as a warning shot from that group.

The intention of those involved was to anticipate further criticism of the business community, and to have ready when asked a well thought out document which could serve as a draft for possible UN and OECD action with respect to corruption. The ICC had already performed in a somewhat similar consultative role with respect to the OECD guidelines for MNCs. Lord Shawcross's own aims, however, appear to have been slightly more ambitious.

The other members of the commission included Jean Rey, once president of the EEC Commission; Subramanya Bhoothalingam, former secretary of the Indian Ministry of Commerce; Rudolph Peterson, retired president of the Bank of America; and Shaikh Yamani of Saudi Arabia.

When Shawcross announced his appointment, he went straight to the point, with a candour that subsequently divided his constituency. He said there were only about a dozen countries where corruption was "quite exceptional and regarded with grave legal and social disapproval". But in many others "corruption is a way of life". In some "you cannot do business without greasing someone's palm... You've got to make sure that those accepting money are punished".

This last observation suggests that host governments need to be involved. That is one of the practical difficulties.

A year later, in March 1977, Shawcross's ad hoc commission reported to the executive board of the ICC which circulated to all national affiliates the commission's draft report, which was then to be commented upon and returned. An amended report was finally approved by the ICC Executive Council in late November, and will be published in January 1978.

A comparison of the two is revealing both of the considerable differences between attitudes of businesses in various countries towards public disclosure and monitoring of business practice, and of the circumscribed role that at best the ICC can hope to play in what remains a highly competitive international business environment.

The amended report is a shadow of the draft –

In essence the amended report is but a pale shadow of the original draft. Detractors have gone so far as to suggest that it is nothing more than a face saving gesture agreed upon by other national members of the ICC at the behest of the British, American, and Canadian delegations who have consistently backed it, to avoid openly embarrassing the ICC. While the Anglo Saxons on the ICC concede that this may well appear to be the case, they point out that the proposed code, vague and inconclusive as it may seem, is but a first step, and therefore an important step towards the international business community being seen to be sensitive to and doing something about practices about which public opinion has become cynical. They maintain that ICC members have now accepted in principle that the ICC should have a code of conduct covering the payment of bribes, kickbacks and agents' fees, and a panel with powers to investigate and adjudicate cases which may arise.

What remains is to define the composition and functions of the panel. There is the question of who appoints members of the panel, its method of procedure, and the vital issue of whether its findings on cases referred to it should be publicised. An ad hoc committee is soon to be appointed by Professor Rolf Stoedter, the outgoing ICC president, to report its recommendations on this to the ICC executive council in June.

The original draft document was forthright and specific in its recommendations in a manner probably not compatible with the consensus and voluntary nature of the ICC.

Among its main points were:

'States should draw up and adopt as soon as possible, under the aegis of the UN, an international treaty providing for international cooperation and judicial assistance in dealing with corrupt practice.

These, it went on, should include clauses facilitating investigation and prosecution of officials suspected and subsequently found guilty of corrupt practice. These provisions should, further, be written into all future extradition treaties.

These proposals proved too sweeping for several national committees of the ICC to accept. Quite aside from the major initiatives in international law that they would entail, there was a marked reluctance to accept that commercial practice should be bound further by new provisions, the consequences of which would be extremely unpredictable, particularly in host countries.

As for the role of the ICC, the original draft proposed:

'The ICC supports the growing practice of making government procurement dependent on undertakings to refrain from improper payments. The ICC would recommend that governments should make the conclusion of government contracts dependent on adherence by the enterprises concerned to an appropriate public or private code of conduct such as the one drawn up by the ICC, and on the inclusion in such contracts of an appropriate clause safeguarding against illicit payment.'

The Shawcross commission provided a model code as an appendix to the original draft. Its first 'rule' reads – 'No enterprise, nor any employer or agent thereof, should offer, promise or give anything of value, directly or indirectly, to any official of a public body or to any employee or agent of another enterprise or to any person exercising any degree of control or influence over such enterprise or accede to a request for any such offer, promise or gift, with a view to influencing improperly his conduct in relation to such public body or enterprise.

The commission further proposed that parties to a contract could effectively sue for damages against other contractual parties who infringed the code. These would have included either termination of the contract in question, recovery of the full value of the illicit payment, or recovery of consequential damages caused by such illicit payment. The ICC would establish a Council on Ethical Practice to apply the code.

Other provisions called for full and open auditing of companies' facilitation payments, agents' fees and such like; public listing of all agents paid over $25,000 a year; and a ban on secret accounts.

– despite British and American attempts to strengthen it

It is hardly surprising that the Germans, French and Swiss argued strongly that it is not properly the role of the ICC to take such initiatives. They did not accept the British and American argument that the private sector has an important consultative role to play prior to the introduction of any potentially restrictive legislation, partly no doubt because continental countries, so far, have been relatively free from the sort of legislative controls recently introduced in North America.

The Japanese committee, for its part, declined even to comment on the circulated draft. The British committee, on the other hand, went to considerable lengths, making detailed emendations. Suggesting that the code be retitled 'Guidelines', to emphasise its voluntary nature, they pointed out particularly that:

– responsibility for firms' adherence to the code be best redefined as 'not knowingly violating the guidelines in connection with their conduct', and

– that a distinction be drawn between facilitation payments and bribes (defined as "an offer to have a man act contrary to his duty and reward him for it"),so that ordinary facilitation fees would not fall under the code; the distinction is, needless to say, not very clear.

These suggestions were incorporated in November into the version finally approved by the ICC executive council. The document only suggests that governments should enforce legislation against bribery and extortion, and that the ICC's 'Rules of Conduct' should be abided by, but not through force, with regard to the customs and conditions prevailing in particular countries. The 'rules' as now proposed state that companies should not accept or offer bribes or kickbacks, and that lists of agents receiving over $50,000 a year be available to auditors and, on specific request, to appropriate and acceptable government departments. There is no mention of damages or of making the awarding of contracts dependent on accepting the ICC code.   65

A straw poll among several of Britain's largest overseas contractors and MNCs the week the report was approved by the ICC council found senior executives somewhat sympathetic, but generally sceptical of the usefulness of the ICC's initiative. Respondents insisted that knowing the right people and seeing that their interests are well looked after is as essential to winning contracts throughout the world as it was two years ago when the Lockheed revelations were publicised. Several of the firms have taken the steps publicly, though, of publishing codes of conduct inveighing against just those sort of practices. Executives also stressed the ease with which they obtained Bank of England exchange control permission to make such payments overseas.

The commonest reaction to the report is that bribery continues to be one of the most sensitive and competitive aspects of international contract tendering and market penetration, and that the less said about it, publicly, the better. If the ICC report helps to end this, and can further improve the often acrimonious climate surrounding competition for large contracts, then the various national committees represented on the ICC executive council in Paris may have found some worthwhile common ground on which to agree.

IV. THE LABOUR ENVIRONMENT

The Changing Structure of Trade Union Response to the MNC

DR. G. K. BUSCH [•]   No. 4 1978

At the recent meeting of the IMF's[1] Ford World Council in London a delegate was heard to
mutter that "International solidarity is great - all these people coming here to discuss collective bargaining; but I still think it is going to cost us a lot of jobs when Ford pulls out of
Britain". This was not sheer cynicism on the part of the Ford representative; there is a
fairly widespread feeling among unionists that the great breakthroughs in international
collective bargaining are still a long way off and that rather than worry about developing
transnational negotiations with the multinational companies on harmonisation of wages and
working conditions, the international union organisations had better begin discussions with
the multinationals on employment maintenance and redundancy payments.

The international trade union bodies have not been very successful in bringing multinational
corporate management to a bargaining table with representatives of workers in the many
nations in which the multinational operates. This fact has not surprised nor upset the multinational managers or even most trade union leaders. The experiences which have been
absorbed in the process of trying to create transnational bargaining have indicated to the
leaders of the international union bodies the tremendous difficulties - both political and
financial - of such an undertaking. This is not to say that the international trade unions are
not interested in continuing to build up countervailing power to confront the multinational
corporations, but rather that the focus of these efforts is tending to be primarily directed
to problem areas which will not involve a major effort to negotiate an international collective
agreement.

The key to this phenomenon is that there have emerged a number of international trade union
bodies which are competing with the international trades secretariats for influence and power
within the context of the multinational corporation. Their efforts, while often parallel to
those of the secretariats, are more frequently in competition with them; a competition based
on political rather than economic interests. One could put this crudely, at the risk of over-
simplification, by saying that the heterogeneous welter of international trade union bodies
that has appeared on the scene during the past decade has become so embroiled in inter
union differences of a political nature as to impair their ability to mount concerted international bargaining strength to counter the bargaining advantages which most trade unionists
believe multinational companies enjoy through ability to shift production across frontiers.

International union efforts began with international use of corporate information

Historically, the first efforts to confront the multinational corporation involved an individual
trade union attempting to expand its power in a collective bargaining confrontation by using
information about the company's international operations in its negotiations. It was of value,
for example, to the UAW's General Motors negotiators to know that General Motors had
agreed to profit sharing in its Mexican subsidiary as early as 1947. It was decided that this
type of information was vitally necessary for all the companies with which collective

---

[•] Chairman of Multirees Ltd, consultants, London. He was formerly assistant to the
general secretary of the International Chemical Workers Federation, and previously research
director of the International Affairs Department of the United Automobile Workers (USA).

1   The International Metalworkers Federation is the largest of the so called international
trade secretariats - international confederations of trade unions organised on an industry
basis, very broadly defined. Their functions were described in Multinational Business No. 1,
1971 - our first issue. For other abbreviations see the glossary below.   67

negotiations were being conducted, both for the additional muscle it provided in bargaining and for the information it provided about the company's investment plans. Using the Automotive Department of the IMF as a vehicle, the major auto unions of the USA and Western Europe began to create world company councils in which all the unions with membership in the multinational company would participate. It was intended that these company councils would develop an information base for each company and would provide assistance to the weaker unions in developing their representational strengths through technical and financial assistance. This was not entirely altruistic, although the effects certainly were. If jobs were to be protected in the developed world, the wages and working conditions of auto workers in the less developed world could not (it was felt) be allowed to remain substantially lower than those in the USA or Western Europe.

From the beginning, trade union international solidarity was designed primarily as a defensive strategy by unions to prevent lower labour costs in low wage countries being used as a major factor in corporate investment and employment plans. Indeed, for the American unions this was virtually the sole objective. Among European unions there was perhaps greater concern over the possible scope for short term shifting of production between plants in different European countries during a dispute.

The weaknesses inherent in the endeavour to develop a common trade union strategy towards the multinational corporation could be swept under the rug or ignored as long as alternative trade union vehicles were not created. However, the formation of councils by the secretariats has generated a new set of organisations which are designed to perform essentially the same function as the company councils but at a level of trade union activity more in concert with the structure of Western European trade unionism than that of North America.

International company councils proved of limited effectiveness

The weaknesses of the company council approach manifested themselves in a number of important areas. First, it became obvious, particularly in the car industry, that trade unions outside of North America are only rarely organised on an industrial basis. Either the unions were part of a national metalworkers' federation or they were a smaller section of a general workers' union. In the case of Japan they were organised into company unions, or at least a separate union for each company. In Britain, in particular, the unions were highly craft oriented and bargained jointly with some employers and separately with others. Most bargaining outside of North America was conducted between employers' federations and national or regional trade union organisations. In countries like France or Italy union organisation rarely exceeded 35 per cent and this was   split between three separate union organisations often more hostile to each other than to any corporate management.

It is this political division among trade unions in Western Europe which has posed the greatest difficulties for the development of company councils. In some countries this division exists within a single central congress of unions (or "national centre"), while in others it is reflected in two or more competing centres. Within France there are at least three trade union centres; Italy boasts three; Holland has three (recently changing to two); Belgium has two; Spain has three or four; Portugal more, etc. In West Germany and Great Britain, as well as the Scandinavian countries, opposition to the dominant political attitudes of the national centres exists as internal counter currents - an opposition which is not very powerful on the national level but has strong followings in particular regions, industries or plants. Paralleling the decisions made by the International Confederation of Free Trades Unions (ICFTU) and the World Confederation of Labour (WCL), the secretariats have barred from membership those union centres which do not profess to believe in similar political ideologies, i e the French CGT and the Italian CGIL - both communist - were barred from membership in the activities of the ICFTU or the WCL because of their affiliations to the World Federation of Trade Unions (WFTU) and their sectoral unions in metals, chemicals, building, food etc were barred from membership in the respective secretariats because of their close ties to the Italian and French Communist Parties. This is so despite the fact that to a large degree, in both France and Italy, a modus vivendi has been established among the rival union federations on domestic issues (although this is not true in Spain or Portugal). This exclusion has had a profound effect on the development of world company councils, particularly for the European based multinationals. As long as the North American unions continued to play a major role in the ICFTU, the ILO and the trade secretariats, the process of trade union detente was likely to move at a very slow pace consonant with their harder line on East West contacts and Eurocommunism. The withdrawal of the AFL-CIO from the ICFTU and the absence of the USA from recent ILO deliberations has had a substantial effect on the secretariats as well, owing to the financial contribution of the North American unions to the funding of the secretariats' world company councils.

The secretariats are not wealthy organisations. For most of them the budgetary questions are a significant limiting factor in their ability to fulfil the tasks assigned to them. Their experience in trying to create and maintain world company councils in addition to their usual tasks has proved to the secretariats that such an activity places great drains on their financial and manpower reserves.

Effectiveness depends on unions' strength in the firm's home base

The strength of any secretariat's efforts is directly proportional to the interest and strength of the union organisation in the parent company's home base. This is why it is easier for the IMF to engage in serious discussions with Ford or General Motors than for the ICF to show much muscle against Kodak; the UAW has virtually 100 per cent of Ford or General Motors organised in the USA and Canada while Kodak is almost totally unorganised in North America. This is also why those trade unionists honoured by being appointed to head the company councils in virtually every council are the trade unionists who represent the union at the company in the home base of the multinational. Within the context of the secretariats this has meant that the research necessary to the functioning of the councils, the circulation of current plans of the corporation, and the funds which permitted meetings of the councils, have derived largely from contributions from the union with the greatest interest in the corporation. This subsidy was easiest when organised North American corporations were those for whom a council had been created, partly because of the greater discretionary resources of the North American unions, and partly because for a national metalworkers' federation or a general workers' trade union each separate company's employment, however large, is often only a small part of the total number of workers organised in that federation or union. However, for a sectoral union or a general workers' union to devote the sums of money necessary for the basic minimum level of sustenance for a world company council, a political decision within the union is required which must be weighed against opposing claims on its resources. If, in addition, this sectoral union or general workers' union is in direct competition with other rival unions on ideological or religious lines, the willingness to fund or fully support a world company council is markedly less. Consequently, world company councils organised by the secretariats have been less strong for European based MNCs than those for North American based multinationals.

Political schisms have impaired joint confrontation of companies

The initial efforts by the secretariats to confront the multinational companies have been widely reported (often in hyperbole) as have the successes and failures discussed in terms of the power of the international labour movement to build a bargaining relationship with the companies involved. What has not been reported has been the deep and important political schisms which have accompanied these efforts. For example, in the recent Chrysler/Peugeot-Citroën council meeting in London delegates were present from the IMF's affiliated unions in both France and Spain (as well as other countries). These French affiliates from the CFDT and the FO represent a small fraction of the workforce of the company in France; the Spanish UGT also represents a minority of the workforce. Their rival unions of the CGT in France and the Workers Commissions (CCOO) in Spain do not represent much more but play an important role in developing a trade union response nationally. The CGT union tried virtually every method to get a presence in the meeting; they invited the Spanish unions to meet separately with them; they invited British stewards to discuss employment with them; they cajoled and they threatened but to no avail. They were not affiliates of the IMF so they could not participate in the work of the IMF. Despite the urgings of the British unions, notably the TGWU, only IMF affiliates were allowed to participate. This decision to keep the unions under the influence of the communist parties out of the secretariats was not made because of blind anti-communism; rather it was made because those unions and the unions affiliated to the secretariats are competitive organisations whose rivalries mean a great deal in the domestic political arena. The growth of company councils and the practical programmes of international exchange which has grown with them have given a new dimension to the competition within the international labour movement.

If a union like the CGT in France is isolated from international trade union affairs in the West (with the exception of other communist unions) it cannot claim to be effective in meeting its responsibilities to its membership organised within the MNCs. If international councils exist and engage in solidarity activities without them they are diminished in the eyes of those who may join them or maintain their membership in their unions. They cannot command the same respect from their own local and regional officials, for whom international travel to union meetings is a time honoured reward for work well done.

Exclusion of communist unions has led to improvised "underground" bodies

This exclusion of the CGT, CGIL and the CCOO from the work of the secretariats has led to the creation of a new structure of international labour cooperation. The first efforts made by these unions to develop a parallel activity to the secretariats centred on developing what amounted to virtually an 'underground' world company council, organising meetings of shop stewards from the various countries. A good example is the case of the development of the Dunlop-Pirelli Shop Stewards' Committee in 1970. Following the merger of Dunlop (head-quartered in England) and Pirelli (headquartered in Italy) the two companies announced major layoffs and redundancies as well as short time working in their joint plants in Britain and Italy. The resultant problems these decisions created for the unions led to the affiliated unions of the ICF requesting that a world company council for Dunlop-Pirelli be created. The ICF called together a meeting of the Dunlop-Pirelli unions affiliated to it and established a company council under the leadership of Bob Edwards, a Labour MP and TGWU national officer. This council requested a meeting with Dunlop management to discuss the problems of disemployment in England and Italy as well as the investment plans of the company. The CGIL unions were excluded from the council, as were the CGT unions of France. In order to participate in this pressure on Dunlop-Pirelli to discuss the several problems with an international trade union body, the CGIL assisted one of its adherents (Chris Gilmour - a Briton married to the daughter of Pietro Ingrao, the head of the CGIL's International Affairs Department) to form a coalition of shop stewards representing workers in Dunlop and Pirelli plants. The CGIL made funds available for shop stewards to travel from Britain to Italy, and vice versa, to discuss the problems in Dunlop-Pirelli, and provided the necessary assistance for a "eurostrike" in 1972 in which some British Dunlop plants went on a token strike against Dunlop for a day, along with a two hour strike demonstration in Italy. This "eurostrike" was called by the stewards without official union sanction. It was followed by CGIL and CGT unions' efforts to create similar shop stewards' committees in other European multinationals such as Michelin, Solvay, and Unilever, and in the European operations of North American multinationals Ford, ITT and Continental Can. These shop stewards' com-mittees were designed to undermine or discredit the activities of the company councils of the secretariats. To the extent that the corporations' managements took these shop stewards' efforts seriously and as worthy of discussions with them, they appeared to be successful.

These efforts by the CGT and the CGIL to weaken the power of the secretariats using an MNC's activities as a platform were not restricted to the creation of company councils. While the IMF was meeting to draft a programme for common action against the multinationals in March 1977, another meeting was taking place in Rome; a meeting convened to discuss the role of the MNCs within the area of the Mediterranean basin. Attending this meeting of international metalworkers were unionists from the French and Italian organisations along with some from Algeria, Egypt, Yugoslavia, Cyprus, Syria and the leftist federations of Spain and Turkey. Their conclusions included a call for "...a struggle against the multinational corporations which must be deprived of their role as intermediaries between rich and poor countries". The IMF did not send any representatives, nor did any of its affiliates (outside of Italy). This type of sectoral conference has been arranged in other industries and financed by the WFTU or its affiliates; good examples include the World Automotive Conference held in Britain in which WFTU members participated, and the Geneva conference of European Labour Organisations on the subject of occupational health. The fact that these meetings were capable of being organised was largely the result of the breakup of the international trade union movement into regional groupings, a development which has resulted in a major shift of power in the alignment of forces opposed to the multinationals.

European regional collaboration has cut across wider structures

Regionalism within the international trade union movement is not a new phenomenon. The ICFTU had established a regional organisation for each of the major world   areas at its founding in 1949. The WCL, too, maintained its regional organisations. These regional organisations were geographical divisions which grouped national centres (organisations like the TUC, or DGB) into convenient bodies meeting to consider common problems. Following the signing of the Treaty of Rome,the ICFTU's affiliates met in Düsseldorf to form a European Trade Union Secretariat independent of the ICFTU's European Regional Organisation (ERO). This, it was argued, would keep together a European trade union unity in the face of the separation of EEC and Efta national blocs. The same year, the Christians set up a European Regional Organisation at their congress in Amsterdam. This creation of European regional union bodies was well suited to consult the EEC Commission and its committees. The CGIL and the CGT, while not members of either of these two groupings, maintained a joint permanent committee in Brussels.

The period until 1969, when the AFL-CIO left the ICFTU, did not involve the unions of the ICFTU or the WCL in much confrontation with the permanent committee, largely because the EEC Commission excluded the CGT-CGIL committee from participation in its debates because official representatives and the French and Italian governments did not nominate them as delegates to the Economic and Social Committee. By 1969, the European Commission lifted the ban on the CGT/CGIL and their respective governments nominated them to take their seats on the Economic and Social Committee.

The participation of all three strains of European trade unionism within the context of the EEC made it easier for these unions to join together in forming a European Trade Union Confederation (ETUC) in 1973 uniting the trade unions of the ECFTU and the Efta-TUC. The British TUC wanted to form the ETUC out of affiliates of the WCL and the WFTU, but this was resisted by many of the others. The TUC motion was not carried, but shortly after the creation of the ETUC, the new organisation invited WCL affiliates to join with it as well as the CGIL of Italy. The CGT was not invited, largely due to the opposition by the FO, but moves in that direction are currently under way. What is most important about this ETUC and the development of European regional trade unionism was that this ETUC decided that it, too, must have a direct role in confronting the multinational corporations.

The ETUC created six industrial committees (the European Metalworkers Federation, the European Federation of Agricultural Workers, the PTTI Trade Union Committee for the EEC, the FIET Regional Organisation for Europe, the Metal and Mineworkers Committee, and the European Committee of the Entertainment Secretariats). These European Committees are independent from the trade secretariats with whom they share some common membership. This development of eurosecretariats only loosely connected with the international trade secretariats marks a distinct change in the trade union approach towards the MNCs. It is the first time that industrial level organisations with memberships joining unions from the ICFTU, the WCL and the WFTU have been created and have actively attemted to play a role in corporation level interaction. The activities of the EMF in developing a bargaining relationship with the Philips company are well known, although apparently abortive. This Eurosecretariat structure is supported, and subsidised, by the EEC Commission. It poses a direct challenge to the international secretariats and to their world company councils. While the secretariats can argue that excluding the workers in CGT or CGIL unions represents no loss of power in that they often comprise less than 6 per cent of the worldwide employment of the multinational, the eurosecretariats cannot effectively exclude them because, within the confines of the EEC, French and Italian employment percentages are significantly higher. During the recent struggles in Spain and Portugal, in which union rivalry and reliance on external support was a major feature of the industrial scene, the ETUC and the secretariats often found themselves supporting different organisations and different goals in these two nations. In many cases, the creation of European regionalism has constituted a back door through which the CGT, the CGIL, the CCOO and the Portuguese Intersindical can gain a voice and a role in European social affairs.

ETUC has become important in the EEC context

This European regionalism has not been limited to the creation of rivals to the secretariats. The ETUC has played an important role within the EEC in the development of the body of rules and regulations designed to create a European company law. The Community's Green Paper envisages a body made up of European Works Councils which will engage in Europe-wide collective bargaining. The ETUC has made it clear that participation in the European Works Councils will be conducted by its affiliates; indeed, that the process of industrial democracy within the European company will involve the ETUC in nominating the representatives of the workers on the European company's board of directors. A European Trade Union Research Institute has been recently created to provide the necessary backup for research and training to build European trade union participation in corporate affairs. The continuing relationship which will exist between the euroorganisations on the one hand and the secretariats on the other is not yet clear, nor will it be uniform for all the secretariats. The euro-Fiet and the Agricultural Workers appear to be having few problems of cooperation. In general, however, such cooperation has been easiest among unions which are in industries in which enterprises are not mainly multinational ones. Those who have felt the competition most strongly are those secretariats which actually represent workers in MNCs and whose major affiliates include large contingents from North America and Japan. It is they who have had to face the challenges of regionalism.

The ILO may be weakened by regionalism too

This move towards creating regional substructures has had its parallel within the ILO itself. Following the walkout of the American delegation the organisation began exploring ways in which funds, now in short supply, might be best conserved. The various sections of the ILO began discussion on what is being called "structural changes" within the organisation. These structural changes will involve dividing the ILO into regional sub parts in which the tripartite nature will be preserved. What this means for Europe is that there will be a European Regional ILO which will bring together governmental, employer and trade union delegates from both East and West European nations in a common body. The move to create regional sub divisions within the ILO has been welcomed by the African and Latin American groups but has received less than full support from the Canadian and US governments.

The American unions are growing quite concerned with the increasing trend towards regional groupings, as they see some political dangers in such developments. The MNCs, perhaps because they view a division in the trade union camp as ultimately beneficial to their interests, have largely not taken any position on the issue. The various governments of Western Europe have welcomed eurounionism as the inevitable consequence of European integration.

The expected joining of the EEC by Spain and Portugal has raised some serious questions within the European labour movements about the roles to be played in their organisations by the CCOO and the Intersindical since, in both these countries, strong rivalries continue to divide the movements along political lines. There are also signs that there is a growing disenchantment among non-communist unions in France and Italy with the growth and development of eurocommunism. The Italian metalworkers, long the bellwethers of Italian labour unity, appear to be less than satisfied with the "Lama line" of wage moderation and labour union strikebreaking. The breakup of the French Union of the Left in the recent elections has raised a number of questions about the possibilities for trade union cooperation within France.

International secretariat representation on company boards may be the most effective union role

The trade union interaction with the multinationals which will prove the most effective and beneficial in the long run appears to be that which was pioneered by Herman Rebhan of the International Metalworkers; he now sits as worker representative on the Ford of Europe board. In that position he is best able to be informed about and to influence the decisions which will vitally affect his members throughout Ford. If the jobs of Ford workers are going to be maintained, the presence of Rebhan on the Ford board is likely to play a far greater role in that process than any euro-secretariat's resolutions.

GLOSSARY OF ABBREVIATIONS USED

AFL-CIO American Federation of Labour-Congress of Industrial Organisations. The single US national centre formed by the merger of the AFL and the CIO in 1955.

CCOO Comisiones Obreras (Workers' Commissions). The trade union centre in Spain closely allied to the Spanish Communist Party.

CFDT Confédération Française Démocratique du Travail. The French national centre formed from the deconfessionalisation of the former French Christian-Democratic national centre.

CGIL Confederazione Generale Italiana del Lavoro. The Italian national centre closely allied with the Italian Communist Party.

CGT Confédération Générale du Travail. The French national centre closely allied with the French Communist Party.

CGT-FO Confédération Générale du Travail - Force Ouvrière. The French national centre composed of Socialist and Social Democratic unions formed from the postwar split in the CGT.

DGB	<u>Deutsche Gewerkschaftsbund.</u> The major West German national centre comprising 16 industrial unions; closely tied to the SPD.
ETUC	<u>European Trade Union Congress.</u> The European regional trade union organisation joining together affiliates of the ICFTU, the WCL and the CGIL within Western Europe.
FGTB	<u>Fédération Générale du Travail de Belgique.</u> The Belgian national centre closely allied with the Belgian Socialist Party.
FIET	<u>International Federation of Commercial, Clerical and Technical Employees.</u> The Geneva based trade secretariat composed largely of bank, insurance, office and professional employees engaged in white collar employment.
ICF	<u>International Federation of Chemical and General Workers Unions.</u> The Geneva based trade secretariat composed of chemical, energy, glass, rubber and general workers unions.
ICFTU	<u>International Confederation of Free Trade Unions.</u> The Brussels based international trade union organisation formed in 1949 when the non-communist unions walked out of the WFTU; composed primarily of Socialist and Social Democratic national centres.
ILO	<u>International Labour Organisation.</u> A UN body formed by the League of Nations in 1919 and comprising a tripartite membership of government, employer and union representatives; sited in Geneva.
IMF	<u>International Metalworkers Federation.</u> The largest and most powerful of the trade secretariats comprising unions in the metal, shipbuilding, aerospace, auto, engineering and similar industries; Geneva based.
Intersindical	<u>Intersindical</u> is the Portuguese national centre closely allied with the Portuguese Communist Party and which was, until recently, recognised by the government as the only legitimate national centre.
ITS	<u>International Trade Secretariat.</u> A general term for the 16 international organisations uniting national unions with membership in similar sectoral employments such as metalworking, postal workers, miners, etc. Based mainly in Geneva, Brussels or London.
PTTI	<u>Post, Telephone and Telegraphic Workers International.</u> The Geneva based trade secretariat for unions representing workers in the post, telephone and telegraphic industries.
TUC	<u>Trades Union Congress.</u> The British national centre closely allied with the Labour Party.
UGT	<u>Unión General de Trabajo</u> (the General Workers Union). The Spanish national centre comprising both Social Democratic and Christian Democratic unions.
WCL	<u>World Confederation of Labour.</u> The international organisation of national centres predominantly Christian Democratic in orientation although some have deconfessionalised in recent years.
WFTU	<u>World Federation of Trade Unions.</u> The Prague based international trade union organisation composed primarily of Eastern European trade union national centres and some Communist national centres elsewhere, notably France; the CGIL claims associate membership.

Compensating International Executives

Against a changing global workforce –

The changing mix of the international workforce, according to a survey of 500 multinational companies carried out in late 1977 by Business International[1], is having a marked effect on corporate remuneration policies. Under pressure from host governments, more local employees are being hired at all levels; a new group of third country nationals (TCNs), a permanent international workforce, is of growing importance, and these,together with expatriates from the home base,constitute a more heterogeneous group because of the increased use of technical, scientific and skilled personnel. At the same time MNCs appear to be taking a more global view of their workforces. As a result, frequent short service moves between affiliates are more common, reinforced by the escalating costs of keeping expatriates abroad which encourages firms to reduce the length of foreign assignments.

– international salary structures are being rethought

Against this background far more attention is being paid to establishing and simplifying international salary programmes. Multinational companies are faced with the difficulty of establishing equity between conflicting demands – from the expatriate employee for his earnings to be competitive within the career structure of the parent company, from the national for earnings competitive both with the expatriate and within the context of the local salary environment, and from the TCN in relation to the international market. They have reacted initially by engaging in an elaborate process of definition.

Amid a wealth of case histories, one of the few major trends noted by the survey is that European based MNCs have apparently been more successful in adopting a truly multinational outlook. In their international salary schemes payment is most closely related to needs in the country of assignment. US based MNCs, on the other hand, still tend to conform to the principle of US base salaries plus add on schemes, leading to spiralling costs and leaving local relativities unresolved. European and US companies also diverge in their approach to tax, the former tending to pay all an employee's taxes in the country of assignment. The survey found taxation bracketed with repatriation as the companies' most recurrent problems, repatriation being increasingly seen as needing as much planning as expatriation has normally received.

Employee satisfaction has diminished

However, the problems of expatriation have evidently received too little attention. Reluctance or refusal of employees to take international assignments is a recent phenomenon reported by MNCs. According to the authors of the survey, this is less to be attributed to financial considerations or even social reasons than to companies' failure to engage in career planning; employees tend to see overseas assignments as 'at best neutral in terms of career development and at worst a step backward'. The major variations reported in company practice over selection, preparation, assessment of local performance and repatriation and reassimilation would seem to confirm some of these suspicions.

The companies' task has not of course become any easier in recent years under the impact of inflation, the decline of the dollar and floating exchange rates. The value of their employees' remuneration is,as one company put it,'in perpetual doubt'. The international salary

---

1   Compensating International Executives; New Perspectives and Practices. Business International Corporation, October 1978.

paid by the majority of firms surveyed consists of four main elements; the base salary, environmental equalisation allowances, incentives (profit sharing and bonuses) and employee benefit plans. The US companies, in tying the base salary to the US domestic salary structure, are evidently faced with much greater problems of adjustment for inflation than the European firms who have related it to needs in the country of assignment. Employee benefit plans, notably pension schemes, are bedevilled by differing inflation rates in either case. Inflation is less of a problem for the second category, which consists of overbase allowances for housing, education, tax etc and cost of living, all of which are designed to prevent the employee from suffering financially from the overseas posting. Non-cash benefits are of course increasingly subject to tax in all countries, and a lump sum to cover all or some of these is becoming more popular for the sake of simplicity - though the soaring cost of housing in many areas complicates any such calculation.

In view of the diminishing attraction of overseas posts, it is paradoxical that one element in international salary schemes - premiums for foreign service - appears to be on the way out. Just as candidates for international posting are growing scarce, firms have begun to feel foreign service premiums inappropriate. Only 43 per cent of the MNCs surveyed offered such a premium as distinct from the cost of living adjustment, and hardship allowances, once common, have almost disappeared. One reason given is that life styles in foreign capitals have become far more homogeneous; the other, interestingly enough, is that companies, unlike their employees, argue that international assignments are steps in career development, and the opportunity for promotion is its own reward. Failing further work on career structures, they may need to return to the principles of the market place.

V. THE ECONOMICS OF INTERNATIONAL INVESTMENT

Location of Affiliates; Fiscal Factors in the MNC's Choice

GEORGE YANNOPOULOS •

No.3 1973

For a number of years there has been controversy in business and academic circles over the importance of fiscal factors in the choice of location of operations in foreign countries. It may seem surprising, at first blush, that anyone could regard differences in tax rates, tax holidays, grants and subsidies, and the like, as unimportant; yet many businessmen and academic writers have contended, in effect, that they are. This contention has applied both to the question of whether such considerations ought to be regarded as of minor or major importance, and to that of whether multinational firms do in fact treat them as important (although frequently the writings in question blur this rather important distinction).

The various fiscal factors in question would make a fairly lengthy list. Rates of tax on corporate profits (including withholding tax on repatriated profits) are an obvious category and are considered neutral in terms of their influence on factor inputs. In addition, there are various input related incentives such as investment grants and investment allowances, accelerated depreciation, and tax holidays in respect of certain kinds of investment. Interest rate subsidies, although "current" in accountancy terms, are also clearly capital related.

There are also subsidies related to employment and to certain kinds of sales (e g exports). Often they vary regionally within countries. Among the less easily classifiable incentives and aids may be counted special tax treatment of capital gains, royalties, and loss carryover.

It is difficult enough to appraise how multinational companies ought to treat these matters in their decision techniques; it is even more difficult to generalise about how they in fact do so, not only because of the usual problem of corporate secrecy, but also because some of these variables may be objectively taken into account in the decision making process, while others may be only subjectively appraised or not even considered at all.

Why fiscal factors have been considered unimportant

Broadly speaking, the view that differences among countries in tax and related matters are unimportant as far as investment location decisions are concerned is held for two reasons.

First, it is argued that, owing to unpredictable changes in fiscal treatment, calculations of after tax and after grant profits in location decisions would give a false sense of precision.

Second, the overwhelming importance of other factors, in relation to fiscal ones, renders the latter unimportant, in any case.

Long term tax policies have not been unpredictable

Those who argue that government fiscal programmes over a period of years are too un-predictable to warrant decisions being based on fiscal factors conclude that multinationals should therefore locate their plants where pre tax profits are maximised. It may then be open to such firms to use their intra group financing (by varying the repatriation of profits in the manner which maximises profit for the group, and meeting capital requirement by intra group lending, where necessary) and transfer pricing policies (including the use of holding companies in low tax jurisdictions) in order to maximise after tax profits.

• Lecturer in the Department of Economics, University of Reading.

This school of thought tends to disregard the fiscal factor altogether in investment location decisions. A number of objections to this view can be raised, however. One is that some kinds of fiscal treatment are less sensitive to policy changes than others. Capital grants and interest rate subsidies (or other subsidies) can sometimes be obtained on a basis guaranteed for a number of years. Secondly, using the UK as an example, although tax rates have varied frequently, in fact, the effective overall rate of taxation of company profits, after non taxable grants (treating this as negative tax), has altered very little (at around 20 per cent) since the early 1960s, despite a number of tax reforms, changes of regional policy, and changes in rates of tax. (This is not to deny that the effective rate has altered sharply on occasion in specific cases, however.)

In some other highly important countries from the standpoint of multinational investment, such as West Germany and Switzerland, tax programmes have remained considerably more stable than in the UK. In West Germany, there have been counter cyclical changes; but the surcharges and/or reductions in capital allowances which have been devised to tax profits more heavily in boom conditions (when profits are likely to exceed expectations), cannot be said to frustrate the investing firms' investment objectives.

Scope exists to shift taxes

A fairly considerable technical literature is now available on the shifting of taxes through the appropriate fixing of product prices, both in terms of intertemporal changes (mainly in the USA, where most of these studies have been undertaken) and in terms of international comparisons (where the mechanism operates through transfer pricing). There is a tendency for pre tax profits to be relatively high where effective rates of tax are high, probably due to shifting. However, the shifting of taxes depends on the degree of tariff protection and may be severely limited where this is low. Opportunity for the use of transfer pricing, where it exists, is not an argument for ignoring tax factors. For the opportunity to indulge in transfer pricing to maximise after tax profits is to a large extent the result of lax administration on the part of national revenue authorities. This can also be the subject of change and uncertainty for the firm. The application of strict "value for duty" provisions by the host country can frustrate such practices. Transfer pricing, moreover, is not open to any substantial extent to all firms. Generally speaking, the scope is strictly limited for firms dealing in homogeneous products. Moreover, to take advantage of transfer pricing a firm must in any case have some substantial part of its operations in low tax countries.

Other considerations may be overwhelmingly important, however –

The second reason for disregarding international taxation is that other factors, principally differences in overall policy and political climate, and differences in production potential and unit costs (particularly labour cost), have an overwhelming importance in making site location choices. These considerations are most sharply highlighted in the context of underdeveloped countries. For example, tax concessions given by African countries, while often very liberal, have not attracted much foreign investment there in recent years. Instead, a very few countries have attracted most of the foreign investment going to underdeveloped countries mainly on grounds of their favourable political climate. But for groups of countries where the investment climate is similar, and exchange controls, nationalisation and other barriers do not present overriding objections, fiscal differences would seem logically to become more important.

– although difficulties persist in assessing true costs

In addressing the view that international differences in effective tax rates are so small (when compared with other cost considerations) as to be unimportant, it must be noted that wages in money terms are fairly meaningless as measures of labour cost, since differences in

78

productivity often tend to offset them. In the case of natural resource industries, it goes without saying that the availability of the resources in question may well be more important than either. But in manufacturing and services, the truly low wage countries that can offer productive labour are very few in number.

Also, it cannot be too heavily stressed that rates of tax on corporate profits do not give an adequate picture of the effective rates after allowing for all fiscal policies. In the case of the UK, already mentioned, the effective rate after allowing for grants (as well as investment allowances, etc) has been of the order of 20 per cent with some consistency; whereas nominal rates of corporation tax have varied from 40 to 56.25 per cent during the period in question (the higher rates in this range having been subject to various forms of relief in respect of dividend distributions). In the USA, the effective rate in these terms has not usually differed much from the nominal rate (currently 48 per cent) through grants or accelerated depreciation, and in addition there is frequently a state profits tax to be paid. Among underdeveloped countries, variations are even greater - although in some cases the true or effective rate will not be apparent until the withholding tax on dividends is taken into account (this tends to be high in several Latin American countries).

Moreover, a multinational must take into account the effect of national tax rates and systems on its global operations. Here, there is not only the question of withholding taxes to be considered; of even more importance may be the availability of tax credit in the parent country against foreign tax.

Tax credits sometimes offset inter country differences

In most cases, according to the tax laws of investing countries, taxes are levied on profits from all sources and tax credit is allowed for any taxes paid in the country where affiliates have generated and repatriated profits. This tax credit system tends to eliminate the tax advantages offered by host countries in respect of repatriated profits. To this extent, the argument that the consideration of fiscal advantages in a multinational's choice of affiliate location is unimportant is valid, because profits taxed at a low rate in a foreign country get taxed up to the rate prevailing in the parent country.

But several qualifications must be entered on this point. Where the effective rate of tax abroad is higher than in the parent country, the credit system does not level the foreign tax rate down to that in the parent country - the effective higher rate abroad is borne by the firm. Even if the profits tax rate is lower abroad, it is frequently higher after withholding tax on the dividend. Secondly, grants accelerated depreciation, and other non-tax incentives, are usually unaffected by the tax credit system. The "tax makes no difference" argument is probably most valid in regard to the rate of corporation tax, and less so with almost all other fiscal considerations. And thirdly, even low tax rates will normally be unaffected by levelling up through tax credit in the case of profits retained by the affiliate abroad.

In the USA, the tax credit system may confer a fiscal preference to foreign over domestic investment, even regarding distributed profits. But state taxes are not accorded similar treatment. State taxes levied in the US range from 0 to 10 per cent, broadly speaking. Thus if both a multinational and a national firm earn $100 in profits from the same operation, and the rate of foreign tax on the multinational's investment abroad is 10 per cent, the same as the national firm's state tax, the federal corporation tax (at 48 per cent before credit or deductions) to be paid will be $38 in the case of the multinational and $43.20 in the case of the national firm.

But profits can be retained abroad at low rates

But most of the argument in the USA to the effect that fiscal arrangements give foreign investment a preference over domestic investment concerns earnings retained in the subsidiary. The argument is of course valid only insofar as the tax rate abroad is lower than in the USA. There have been a number of representations in the USA that the law should be reformed so that the tax credit system would be applied to earnings retained abroad as well as earnings repatriated. However, it has been pointed out that the principal effect of such a reform could be to increase the tax receipts (from US multinationals) of foreign countries, rather than of the USA. For if the US multinational companies were induced, by losing the tax preference for profits retained in foreign countries with low rates of tax, to repatriate dividends more heavily, they would be paying greater amounts of withholding tax to foreign governments, and the additional US tax payable might not be very great.

It has been argued by some directors of multinationals that the privilege of keeping profits retained in a low tax country without paying tax in the parent country is a dubious one because the firm is unable to distribute such profits to its shareholders. This is of course true where the profits so retained cannot be profitably reinvested. Where they can, however, they may substitute for new direct investment. The tax preference is valuable, therefore, in that case, though the calculation of net benefit here must take account of the cost of the ultimate repatriation of profits. The benefit must therefore be seen as that of a deferral (as with accelerated depreciation) and not as a total gain equal to the difference between the tax rates in the parent and the foreign country.

Recently, the changes in UK taxation of profits earned abroad have resulted in a situation where dividends paid from such profits are not allowed the credit against UK corporation tax, which is now enjoyed in the case of profits earned in the UK. This will in some cases create a fiscal preference for certain multinationals for investment in the UK. Accelerated depreciation of fixed assets, also available in the UK, may also cause multinational enterprises to take profits in the UK (in order to make full use of the capital allowances) which they might otherwise take elsewhere.

It would be surprising, despite the levelling tendency which the tax credit system has in many situations, if the above facts did not cause, in the majority of cases, a different ranking of preferred alternative locations by using expected post tax profitability instead of pre tax profitability.

The survey evidence evaluated

The question as to how far tax factors and fiscal incentives do in fact influence the investment location decisions of multinational companies is essentially an empirical one. Models of investment behaviour explicitly incorporating tax variables have been used to determine either how far the global distribution of multinational investment is influenced by effective corporation tax rates or how far tax rates and taxation policies in general influence dividend remittance policies. Using data on British overseas investment made available through the Reddaway Report, J Mellors[1] of the University of Reading has found that the geographical distribution of the investment portfolios of British multinational companies is influenced more by post tax rates of return than by pre tax returns.

---

1   Mellors J L. International Tax Differentials and the Location of Overseas Direct Investment: a pilot study, University of Reading discussion papers in International Investment and Business Studies (1973).

Studies on dividend remittance policies of the multinationals (like that of G F Kopits[1] of the Graduate School of Georgetown University) indicate how inter country differences in tax policies can influence the global distribution of the internally generated funds of the multinationals. Where differences in corporation tax rates between parent countries and host countries affect the pay out ratios of these affiliates, then it was found such tax differentials affect the rate of reinvestment of the multinational's internally raised funds between the country of the parent and the rest of the world and, in consequence, exert an influence on its global distribution of investment.

The relative importance of political risks, supply considerations and fiscal incentives

Research along the lines pioneered by Mellors and Kopits has, as yet, been rather limited, and for this reason resort must be made to other forms of evidence based on survey work that purports to show the factors that were taken into account by multinationals when deciding on the location of plants by new or expanding affiliates. Survey work needs careful interpretation since apart from the problem that the design of the questionnaire may predispose particular types of answers, the replies of foreign investors may quite often reflect an ex post rationalisation of a decision based on other, quite different, considerations. A global questionnaire survey covering a total of 140 multinational companies based in the USA, UK, France and West Germany conducted by H Schollhammer[2] of the University of California, invited these firms to rank, in order of importance, some 78 possible influences on investment location decisions. Among the 78 different factors suggested five fiscal ones were included, which were ranked as follows:

Multinational Parent Company	US	UK	French	West German
Tax rate differentials	17	5	9	23
Tax incentives	32	12	30	19
Joint tax treaties	39	67	65	28
Tax loss carry backward & forward	41	24	53	30
Taxation of export income and income earned abroad	49	48	52	47

Given the nature of this survey and especially its coverage of the global spectrum of location possibilities, it is not surprising that perception of political risks and supply considerations topped the list as the two main factors influencing the choice of a particular country as a location for a new affiliate. When the 78 individual influences on locational decisions were grouped into nine distinct categories the fiscal factor was ranked third in the list by the firms from all five countries. Schollhammer's survey revealed, however, that European based multinationals tend to place a lower mean evaluation on the political factor and a slightly higher valuation on the tax factor. Indeed US based multinational companies ranked the political factor first in importance, followed by the supply factor, the labour factor and then the tax factor. Those that are European based ranked the supply factor first, the tax factor second, and the political factor third.

---

1 Kopits, G F, Dividend Remittance Behaviour within the International Firm, doctoral dissertation, Graduate School of Georgetown University (June 1971). 2 Schollhammer H, Locational Strategies of Multinational Corporations, mimeo (1972).

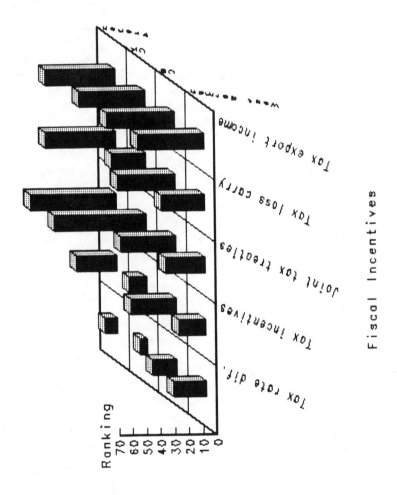

Fiscal Incentives

The difference in the importance attached to tax and fiscal factors by firms of different national origin may be due partly to different characteristics of the parent company and partly to different product and production characteristics. However, it is highly likely that political factors and tax factors were significantly intercorrelated. First, the availability of fiscal incentives for foreign direct investment has implications about the degree of risk involved in such investment. Relief from profit taxes helps the investor to recover his capital quicker, thereby reducing his concern over possible nationalisation or expropriation. Second, the availability of incentives and related fiscal advantages may be taken as a reflection of the political attitudes of the government of the host country towards foreign investment.

Need to assess attitudes in terms of homogeneous regions

To identify better the importance of the various tax and fiscal measures of host countries in site location choices, it is necessary to reduce the spatial unit of reference to a geographical division with distinct but more or less similar characteristics regarding market potential, production conditions and political stability. Under such circumstances it becomes easier to isolate any additional factors such as tax incentives that may influence the choice of a specific location within the broad geographic division studied. Thus in examining the locational importance of fiscal differentials it makes more sense to see how a multinational, once it has decided to locate its production units within particular market areas (e g the Western European market), chooses a specific location within these areas. This means the problem must be approached from the standpoint of the affiliate in the host country. Following this approach, the emphasis is shifted to evaluating the determinants of the choice of a specific location rather than on the general issue of whether to invest with a market area rather than serve it by exports.

In another study of US multinational investment abroad, market potential –

In this context, the findings of D J C Forsyth in a recent study of US direct investment in Scotland[1] are extremely illuminating. Forsyth's survey work covered the most recent period where fiscal measures were in full operation and furthermore distinguished between the two stages in the decision to locate a new subsidiary (viz the choice of the broad market area to serve and the choice of a particular region to locate within that market area). In the course of his Scottish study, Forsyth interviewed representatives of 105 US subsidiaries located in Scotland and enquired both about their reasons for investing abroad and their choice of Scotland as a specific location. Of the 99 firms which answered the first question, 80 indicated that the major determinant in their decision to invest abroad was the expected growth of the market either in UK only (31 subsidiaries), the continent only (8 subsidiaries) or simultaneously in the UK and the continent (41 subsidiaries). Most likely, many US multinationals locating their subsidiaries in Scotland had taken market growth on a continental level into consideration in expectation of UK entry to the EEC.

– and financial incentives determined site location choices

Of the 99 firms answering the first question, 96 specified in more explicit terms why they chose Scotland as a place to locate their capacity to serve expected market growth in Europe. In fact 41 per cent of the firms gave as the principal reason for choosing a location in Scotland the availability of government financial inducements and the additional advantages derived from the UK development area policy. Another 21 subsidiaries specified these fiscal incentives as an additional factor in influencing their locational decision.

---

1   Forsyth D J C, US Investment in Scotland, Praeger Special Studies in International Economics and Development, New York (1972).

Financial incentives were less important for UK investment

It is interesting now to compare the above percentage of the US affiliates which chose a location in Scotland on the basis of the financial incentives available there to the percentage of UK indigenous firms that either transferred existing establishments or set up new branches in the development areas of the UK during more or less the corresponding time period. Such data are available from the report of the then Board of Trade[1] on the movement of manufacturing industry in the UK. Between 1960 and 1965 38 per cent of firms established in developing areas because of fiscal inducements (only 23 per cent between 1951 and 1960). This comparison illustrates the order of magnitude in the degree of responsiveness of the two groups of firms (indigenous and multinational) to tax incentives and regional policies. Although the comparison is handicapped by the fact that we do not have the comparable information from US affiliates located in the other UK development areas, nevertheless additional information available from the latest report of the US Tariff Commission[2] on American multinationals seems to strengthen the view that multinationals are more responsive than local firms to fiscal incentives, operating in the context of regional policies by a number of European governments.

The US Tariff Commission report estimates that 50 per cent of US direct investment in Europe up to the end of 1967 was located in regions where tax incentives and other fiscal subsidies were available. Although direct comparison with indigenous, national, firms in Europe is handicapped by lack of comprehensive data on the regional distribution of investment, it is highly unlikely that such a large proportion of investment by indigenous firms would have concentrated in these areas. Indeed, as the Tariff Commission points out, "tax incentives for regional development have been successful in attracting US multinational company investment" because US companies "have been much more alert than European companies in discovering how to take advantage of such depressed area incentives".

Evidence from France

A French survey by Falise and Lepas in 1970[3] covered 40 affiliates of multinationals located in France. This showed that the French tax system and the availability of state aids were considered by the affiliates approached as the most influential factors in the choice of France rather than another country for the location of their plants. More specifically, the coefficient of importance for the tax system was 81.2 per cent and that for state aids 74.8 per cent.

The evidence suggests the increasing pull of fiscal inducements in plant location

The evidence suggests that tax and other fiscal incentives tend to affect the pattern of affiliate location within a broad market area where political and business environment, market potential and production possibilities are similar. It also shows that, compared to indigenous firms, multinationals may be more responsive to tax and fiscal factors in their plant location decisions. The distinct characteristic of the multinational is its possession of a package of income generating assets in the form of knowledge of how to manufacture and market a particular commodity or managerial expertise, superior to that of its indigenous competitors.

---

1 Board of Trade, The Movement of Manufacturing Industry in the United Kingdom, 1945-65, HMSO (1968). 2 US Tariff Commission. Implications of Multinational Firms for World Trade and Investment and for US Trade and Labour, Washington (1973). 3 Falise, M & Lepas, A, Les motivations de localisation des investissements internationaux dans l'Europe du Nord-Ouest, Revue Economique (No 1 - 1970).

Because of its higher mobility of capital, due to its flexibility in moving resources across national frontiers, and because of its extensive use of corporate planning techniques, which make it much easier to perceive correctly the advantages offered by tax and fiscal incentives, the multinational will tend to show, in comparison with indigenous firms, a higher degree of responsiveness to these incentives and, in general, to tax differentials between countries. A multinational can take advantage of labour cost subsidies by concentrating its labour intensive activities in areas where labour costs become lower on account of labour subsidies (e g the old regional employment premium) and its capital intensive activities in areas where the costs of capital are lowered on account of more advantageous fiscal incentives.

In general, as the multinational enterprise increases the size of its foreign operations, its locational strategy will tend to be based increasingly on factors which can be evaluated objectively. By extending the scope of its operations to more countries, the multinational reduces its locational dependence on transport costs and local suppliers of raw materials. The more the importance of such locational determinants diminishes, the more important factors such as international tax differentials and the existence of various forms of fiscal incentives for industrial or regional development will become.

Corporate Investment and Production Decisions

SHERRY STEPHENSON ●   No.3 1978

Environmental controls are of concern to multinational companies because they directly affect costs of production and the firm's competitive position in domestic and foreign markets.

Moreover, the controls or charges which governments impose to regulate pollution may affect the companies' choice of plant location. While use of the assimilative (waste absorptive) capacity of the natural environment had little influence in the past on corporate production and investment decisions, this may no longer be the case. Noxious waste accompanying extracting and manufacturing activities is now considered, beyond a certain critical level, as a "public bad" whose impact on producers and consumers escapes the market mechanism. Economists define such public bads as examples of negative externalities - economic events which inflict damage on persons not consenting in the occurrence of the event. In the case of pollution, these are those who suffer the effects without having had any voice in the polluting production or consumption activities. As long as this externality is not charged in some way to the firms responsible for creating it, they cannot be expected to reduce the levels of effluents associated with production processes. The "internalisation" of this externality - the imposition of a charge for impairment of the environment - can be accomplished only through government action.

Public pressure for a cleaner environment has brought the environmental issue to the forefront and led in the 1960s and 1970s to the passage or tightening of pollution control legislation in most advanced industrial countries. In the UK the Department of the Environment was created in 1970, as was the Environmental Protection Agency in the USA. Legislation in these two countries covers primarily air and water pollution although solid waste and noise pollution are also of concern. The EPA undertakes a wide variety of monitoring and research activities, and its operating outlay in 1978 was $989 mn, an increase of 30 per cent over its 1974 budget.

Desired environmental quality is an outcome of the interplay of physical use of the environment and social perception of the necessity for clean up. The social preference is thought to depend mainly upon the wealth of society or its per caput income, a cleaner environment being considered as a luxury for whose purchase society is willing to divert the necessary productive resources only after a certain level of economic development and consumption of conventional goods have been attained. For the MNC, then, environmental issues should be considered enduring since in the long run increasing incomes in the industrialised countries are likely to lead to greater demands for a cleaner environment.

How much pollution should be cleaned up?

It is generally accepted by economists that the goal of a completely pollution free environment is neither realistic nor desirable, its cost being practically prohibitive. To the extent that a better environment is judged both desirable and realistic (i e not too costly in terms of production forfeited), economists prefer that pollution abatement be undertaken along the lines of the "polluter pays" principle. This means that those economic agents most responsible for the output of residuals are attributed the burden of clean up. (This is not the same as saying that the polluter bears the ultimate cost of the policy.) Adoption of the polluter pays principle as the general guideline for effluent abatement has been endorsed by the OECD.[1]

● Sherry Stephenson is a research associate with the Centre d'Etudes Industrielles in Geneva.

1 OECD, The Polluter Pays Principle, Paris, 1974.

Pollution control carried out according to this principle might be accomplished, for example, through an effluent tax imposed per unit of polluting emissions associated with output.

Economists see this method of effluent taxation as being efficient for two main reasons: it works through the price system and thereby assures that desired environmental quality may be obtained at the lowest cost. Firms are presented with the choice between abating pollution above a permitted level or paying the tax, the decision depending upon the cheaper alternative. This ensures that those firms which can abate most efficiently will clean up the greatest amount of pollution.

Theoretically, the price mechanism for cleaning up pollution may alternatively be applied through the auctioning of licences which give right to a certain volume of effluent emissions, or the sale, at a predetermined price per unit of permitted pollution, of rights to emit effluents up to any maximum chosen by the polluter. Governments, however, when legislating clean up, generally prefer the use of direct quantitative restrictions, variously termed "norms" or "standards", which fall in the general line of the polluter pays principle. According to this method pollution may be forbidden beyond a certain level. The advantages for the government in the use of norms lie in the administrative ease with which they can be established and enforced, removal of the necessity of finding the "correct" level of taxation which depends upon the determination of an often ill defined social damage function, and elimination of the onus for rejuggling the tax structure which would have been called for by the collection and distribution of the pollution tax revenue.

Alternatively, a subsidy scheme may be applied. If subsidies are linked to the reduction in the amount of waste, the effects on firms' behaviour will differ little in the short run from those of the tax scheme. However, in the long run such subsidies offer encouragement for new entrants into polluting production. Such subsidies are not commonly in use. However, it is standard practice for governments to attenuate the severe effects of pollution control in some instances by extending direct subsidies for the purchase of abatement plant and equipment or indirect subsidies in the form of accelerated depreciation allowance, tax relief and concessionary loans, among others.

The welfare increasing attributes of any abatement method chosen depend on the assumption that the value to society of the increase in environmental cleanliness exceeds the social value of reduced output. This is because the enactment of an environmental programme is at the expense of a reduction in the output of traditional goods and services and a slowing of the rate of growth of GNP measured in conventional terms.

Alternative corporate responses to environmental controls

Environmental controls implemented through effluent taxation or standards/norms place a positive cost on the use of environmental services. A profit maximising firm will use the environment in accordance with its marginal cost and marginal product functions, including environmental services in its calculations just as any other productive resource. The obligation to pay for an additional factor of production at any given output will increase the firm's cost of production and decrease its competitive position in domestic and foreign markets vis-à-vis less polluting firms or firms subject to less strict standards.

What options does the firm have in this situation? In the short run it has no choice but to pay the cost of environmental clean up. It may alter its variable costs but can do nothing to change its fixed costs of production. Depending upon the competitive framework within which it produces and sells, it may be able to pass on part or all of the increased cost in the form of higher prices. If the output in question is a standard product competing with supplies from other firms with low or nil pollution costs, the firm will be able to pass on little of its cost increase to consumers and must instead absorb these increased costs through a reduction in its wage bill, its profits, or some combination of both.

In the long run several choices are open to the firm. Both fixed as well as variable costs may be altered. This permits a modification in production techniques, a change in product lines, or a shift in production location. At the extreme the firm may shut down entirely if its costs become excessive under the pressure of alternative competition. It may alternatively use a new technology which permits less polluting output, but, in order to restore the firm's competitive position, the new technique must also increase efficiency enough to lower substantially the cost of production at the original site.

Evidence collected from questionnaires undertaken by the US Department of Commerce, Bureau of Economic Analysis, indicates that most pollution abatement is undertaken not by the introduction of new techniques ("changes in production process") but rather by "end of line" techniques which involve the separation, treatment and reuse of emitted pollutants. In bringing existing plant into compliance with regulations, the preference has been overwhelming for the second alternative. Business in the USA is estimated to have allocated about 80 per cent of air and water abatement expenditures to end of line methods in each year beginning in 1973.[1] Since end of line techniques do not lower the firm's cost of production (though they do occasionally yield extra production through recovery of usable products from waste matter), it is plausible that new plant will have to incorporate new, less polluting, in-process techniques or have to relocate, sooner or later.

Shifting of production sites is likely to be from areas where environmental assimilative capacity is most limited and social preferences for environmental cleanliness strong, to areas where environmental assimilative capacity is greater and social preferences for environmental cleanliness less pronounced. Such shifts may be inter regional (between regions of the same country) or international. Since environmental preferences depend on the level of income per head, the difference between countries at different levels of economic development is likely to be much greater than that between different geographical areas of one country.

It would therefore be expected that the shifts in question would frequently be international. This especially applies to multinational corporations which, by definition, have operations in two or more countries and which are capable of shifting production centres with relative ease.

In the long run, then, we should expect to witness a transfer of a certain amount of polluting production from high income, high standard developed countries to low income developing countries with low environmental standards, with an accompanying outflow of private foreign direct investment in polluting sectors.

Encouraging these shifts in production and investment flows is the expected shift in consumer preferences in developed countries from high priced domestic products of polluting industries to low priced foreign produced equivalents of the same goods. Thus imports of polluting products by the most advanced countries are likely to increase relative to domestic production of such products.

The importance of environmental controls in certain industrial sectors

Environmental control (EC) expenditure looks modest when compared with that going to other major social welfare programmes. The OECD estimates that average total pollution control

---

1 Survey of Current Business, "Capital Expenditures by Business for Pollution Abatement," US Department of Commerce, June 1977.

88

expenditure in the USA over the period 1970-75 represented 1.6 per cent of total GNP as opposed to 7.0 and 7.5 per cent for health and education and 8.2 per cent for defence.[1] Another OECD study shows that EC programmes, including expenditure on new plant and equipment plus operating costs to meet air, water and solid waste standards over the period 1971-80 will represent only 1.4 per cent of total US GNP but 6.8 per cent of the growth in GNP during that period.[2]

Comparable estimates for the UK are difficult to obtain as figures collected on costs of pollution abatement usually include only capital expenditure estimates and not operating costs. Estimates made for the UK therefore tend to understate the cost of pollution control programmes. Expenditure on investment in capital equipment is cited by the OECD as representing 0.2 per cent of British GNP during the period 1971-80 and 1.1 per cent of the growth in British GNP over the same period.[3] It is interesting to note that the US effort is concentrated primarily on control of air pollution (56 per cent of total EC expenditure in the USA, 13 per cent in the UK) while major emphasis in the UK is placed on control of water pollution (87 per cent of total EC expenditure in the UK, 29 per cent in the USA).[4]

Although expenditure for environment clean up may have a relatively minor impact on aggregate national output, the burden for clean up is felt unequally among industries and even among firms within the same industry, depending upon size and age of existing plant, etc. This is illustrated by Tables 1 and 2. Table 1 shows the cost of air pollution control in the UK for several industrial sectors and divides total expenditure between capital equipment, operating costs and research and development. The estimates given for the period 1958-68 update those in the 1954 Beaver Report and appear in the Fifth Report of the Royal Commission on Environmental Pollution (1976). Surprisingly, no more recent nor more complete estimates on pollution abatement expenditure by industrial sectors appear to be available for the United Kingdom. This may be due to a preference for collection of scientific and technical data on pollution and/or to the British policy of secrecy as regards information on the nature and quantity of industrial wastes. For example, the Health and Safety at Work Act 1974 prevents the Alkali Inspectorate from making public details about emissions from registered works except with the works' consent.[5]

The first report by the Royal Commission (1971) and those reports following have lamented the lack of economic studies undertaken in this area, considering existing cost estimates as "seriously deficient" and recommending that the government takes steps to improve the study of the economic aspects of pollution.[6] Such being the situation at present, we can only point out that in Table 1 the sectors with the largest expenditure for air pollution abatement were iron and steel, chemicals, petroleum, non-ferrous metals and cement. Whether or not this order would be altered by the inclusion of water pollution abatement expenditure and by more recent figures is impossible to say.

---

1 OECD Environment Committee, Collection and Analysis of Pollution Control Cost Data, Paris, OECD Document AEU ENV/72.4, March 1972. 2 OECD, Economic Implications of Pollution Control, Paris 1974, page 34. 3 Ibid, page 34. 4 OECD Observer, No. 71, August 1974, page 35. The remainder of US expenditure is for solid waste reduction. 5 UK Royal Commission on Environmental Pollution, Fifth Report: Air Pollution Control, January 1976, page 65. 6 UK Royal Commission on Environmental Pollution, Fourth Report: Pollution Control, London, December 1974, page 79.

Table 1

Cost of Air Pollution Control in the UK for Scheduled Processes, 1958-68
(£ mn)

Process	Capital expenditure	Operating costs (10 year)	Research & development
Electricity	75.7	126.7	0.86
Iron & steel	26.4	93.4	1.24
Chemicals	20.5	55.5	0.95
Petroleum	6.8	11.7	0.54
Non-ferrous metals	5.8	16.5	0.66
Cement	6.2	6.4	0.30
Coke ovens	2.9	6.1	0.24
Gas	2.8	4.5	-
Ceramics	2.1	3.0	0.16
Lime	1.0	0.7	0.04

Source: UK Royal Commission on Environmental Pollution, Fifth Report.

For the USA Table 2 shows the amount of pollution abatement expenditure undertaken by
various manufacturing industries and the percentage this expenditure represents of the value
of total shipments and of total investment in new plant and equipment for the years 1973-76.
These figures are given on a value added basis, i e as a percentage of the value given to the
product by processing within the industry, excluding purchased inputs.[1] Expressed in such
a manner, the bite of pollution control programmes is seen to be substantial in certain
sectors, notably pulp and paper, non-ferrous metals (aluminium, copper), chemicals,
petroleum refining and iron and steel. In all but two categories (fabricated metal products
and motor vehicles and equipment) pollution abatement expenditure constitutes at least 1 per
cent of value added. Within large industry categories certain activities are more affected
than others: pulpmills more than paper and paperboard mills, fertilisers, organic and
inorganic chemicals more than plastic and synthetic materials, etc. Looking at the importance of pollution abatement expenditure out of total investment in new plant and equipment
gives a slightly different rank ordering, but in general the same sectors are still found near
the top.

At what point does the amount spent on pollution abatement become important enough to the
industry to affect firms' production and investment decisions? This is a very difficult question to answer without a great deal of information about each industry and all other factors
affecting investment. If any cost increase above 5 per cent of the value of industry output is
considered as potentially threatening to the firm's competitive position in existing markets,

---

1 The value added coefficient used for each industry grouping was calculated from the
Input Output Structure of the US Economy. 1967, Volume 1, issued 1974 by the US Department
of Commerce on the basis of 1967 data and applied to figures on the value of total shipments
obtained from the Annual Survey of Manufacturers, 1976: Value of Product Shipments, US
Department of Commerce, December 1977, for the years 1973 through 1976, the years for
which estimates on the total cost of pollution abatement expenditure (investment plus operating
costs) were available in publications by the US Bureau of the Census. Pollution Abatement
Costs and Expenditures. The most polluting industry groups were chosen on a 2 digit SIC
basis and then further broken down where possible to indicate the most polluting activities
within each industry. These 17 groupings accounted for 81.1 per cent of total pollution abatement expenditure in the US in 1976.

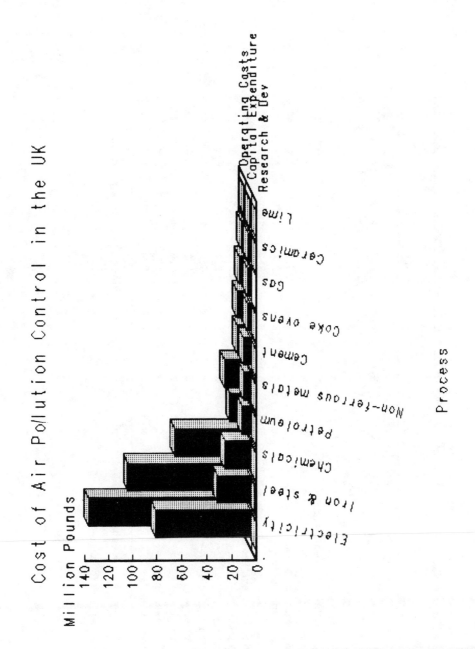

Cost of Air Pollution Control in the UK

Million Pounds

Process

Table 2

Ratio of Pollution Abatement Expenditures
to Total Shipments and Total Capital Expenditure for 17 Polluting US Industries
(%)

Industry	Total[a]				Total[b]			
	1973	1974	1975	1976	1973	1974	1975	1976
Pulpmills	28.3	25.7	28.2	28.9	59.9	81.6	40.0	35.0
Primary copper	17.0	16.1	26.9	23.4	129.6	136.8	115.6	377.6
Papermills	10.1	10.5	13.5	10.7	49.6	41.8	43.3	36.4
Primary aluminium	9.5	13.2	14.4	9.6	46.8	60.1	52.3	58.5
Agricultural – chemicals	8.7	8.1	10.0	12.0	39.2	27.3	26.0	27.5
Organic chemicals	7.9	6.4	8.3	9.6	34.8	26.5	27.6	30.3
Inorganic chemicals	5.8	8.0	9.8	9.2	35.5	38.1	42.4	42.6
Petroleum refining	7.8	6.3	6.8	6.3	58.4	47.7	46.8	46.0
Iron & steel	3.8	3.5	5.6	5.8	38.8	33.1	38.0	40.6
Plastics & synthetics	4.0	4.0	5.5	4.7	18.6	14.8	18.2	20.4
Cement	3.7	4.5	4.1	3.4	23.1	27.5	23.6	21.0
Rubber	1.5	1.9	2.0	2.2	5.1	6.6	8.4	8.9
Food products	1.1	1.1	1.1	1.2	16.6	15.6	14.0	14.5
Leather	0.5	0.5	0.7	1.1	13.0	14.8	21.0	31.8
Furniture	0.7	1.0	1.1	1.1	10.6	14.2	23.1	23.0
Fabricated metals	0.6	0.7	0.7	0.7	8.6	10.1	9.0	8.9
Motor vehicles	0.8	0.9	0.8	0.7	9.5	8.0	8.9	9.0

a Shipments on a value added basis and total.   b New expenditure on capital equipment.

Source: see footnote 1, page 85

we may find an increase in investment going abroad to areas with less strict environmental standards. The question examined in the next section is whether the data available on outflows of foreign direct investment reveal any significant increases in recent years, especially for those ten industrial polluting categories in Table 2.

Evidence on shifts in investment patterns

Examining investment flows within major polluting manufacturing industries is difficult because of the lack of data on foreign direct investment reported on the industry level. Such data as exist are not available on the same industry category breakdown as are the pollution abatement estimates.

For US private foreign direct investment, statistics are collected by the Department of Commerce in six broad categories, of which only two can be said to be polluting: chemicals and food products. Such aggregate figures show little, although in the case of the chemical industry net capital outflows to developing countries nearly tripled from 1971 to 1976, rising from $42 mn to $124 mn, at the same time that net capital outflows to developed country areas fell from $323 mn to $298 mn.[1] The increased investment in developing countries in the chemical industry was approximately equally divided between Latin America and Asia and Pacific. The concentration of investment in these two areas reflects the fact that a relatively small number of countries, most of them found in Latin America and Asia, account for the large majority of manufacturing production and manufactured exports from the developing world.[2]

A second data series published by the US Department of Commerce allows us to break down industries within manufacturing somewhat further. These figures relate not to investment flows directly but rather to sales by majority owned affiliates of US multinational companies abroad. Changes in the volume of sales by industries would presumably indicate changes in production capacity.

Five polluting categories can be identified in this series: food products, paper and allied products, chemicals, rubber, and primary and fabricated metals. Sales in these groups accounted for by developing countries increased between 1971 and 1976. The part of sales accounted for by developing countries increased in three categories, namely food products, chemicals and rubber. In these three groups the percentage increase in sales over the seven year period was greater than that for total manufacturing. However, in the other two categories the proportion of developing country sales out of total sales declined, by 0.3 per cent for primary and fabricated metals, where it is impossible to separate the heavily polluting activity (primary metals) from the relatively minor polluting activity (fabricated metals), and by 3 per cent for paper and allied products where substantial pollution control costs seem not to be reflected by production shifts to developing country areas.

---

1 Survey of Current Business, "US Direct Investment Abroad", issues October 1975, August 1976 and August 1977.   2 For example, in 1973 Hong Kong, South Korea, Singapore, Malaysia, Brazil, Mexico, Argentina, Colombia, India and Pakistan were responsible for 78 per cent of manufactured goods imported by the industrialised countries from the third world and accounted for over 70 per cent of industrial production in developing countries. Cited in Deepak Nayyar, "Transnational Corporations and Manufactured Exports from Poor Countries", The Economic Journal, 88, March 1978, page 61.

Judgment should be cautious in interpreting these results. Such changes may well be the result of random fluctuations in production or the net result of the influence of varied and numerous factors affecting output other than the environment. Corresponding data for the UK are not available.

This very incomplete picture is not enough to provide a conclusive answer as to whether locational shifts have been sensitive to environmental controls. Even the evidence available is contradictory. The impossibility of finding more disaggregated data on investment flows precludes searching further and places the burden of proof on other types of investigation.

Are we consuming more polluting
products from foreign production locations?

Another way of approaching the question at hand is through an examination of trade flows rather than investment flows, in an attempt to assess whether or not US and UK consumers have substituted in their consumption foreign produced versions of heavily polluting products over domestic versions. The higher cost of producing polluting goods at home, reflected in higher domestic price, should induce consumers to switch their source of consumption to low cost and low price foreign suppliers. While imports will grow in any event due to rising national incomes, we are interested in identifying the additional growth of imports of polluting products resulting from loss of price competitiveness by home producers. To do this, we examine the degree to which the growth rate of such imports has exceeded (if at all) the average growth rate of all imports excluding petroleum. In other words, have the import baskets of the USA and the UK come to contain a greater proportion of polluting goods?

Using trade statistics allows us to divide polluting products into much finer categories than did the available investment statistics. To compose Table 3 several groups of polluting product imports corresponding roughly to those polluting products listed in Table 2 were added for the USA and the UK and their total taken as a percentage of each country's total imports for the years 1971-76. Petroleum was excluded from both polluting product imports and total imports. Table 3 gives somewhat surprising results. For both the USA and the UK the consumption of polluting product imports grew less rapidly than did that of other import categories, as shown by the declining percentage share in 1976 compared with 1971. The share of polluting product imports coming from developing country regions, however, remained fairly constant in both cases.

Such comparisons are difficult to make while not knowing the importance of other factors which influence the propensity to import. For example, a change in supply conditions favourable to foreign exporters of polluting products may have affected the comparisons shown in Table 3 less than changes in demand conditions favouring imports of non-polluting goods. Again, aggregate data do not provide even indirect support for the argument that production of polluting goods has shifted from the USA and the UK to developing countries.

Table 3

Share of Polluting Product Imports[a] in Total Imports[b], 1971-76 (%)

| | USA | | UK | |
	From all countries	From developing[c]	From all countries	From developing[c]
1971	27.5	9.2	38.4	8.4
1972	26.0	8.5	37.0	7.6
1973	25.5	9.0	35.0	7.4
1974	27.1	9.8	37.3	6.9
1975	25.7	9.0	36.0	7.1
1976	24.5	9.3	34.4	6.7

a Polluting product imports are made up of the following SITC categories: Food and beverages (Section 0 plus Division 11); Pulp and paper (Division 25); Paper and paperboard (Division 641); Inorganic chemicals (Divisions 513, 514); Organic chemicals (Division 512); Fertilisers (Division 56); Plastic materials (Division 58); Leather (Division 61); Rubber (Division 62); Lime and cement (Division 661); Copper (Division 682); Aluminium, unwrought (Division 684.1); Iron and steel products (Division 67); Furniture (Division 82). b Both sides exclude Division 331, Petroleum. c Developing countries include Greece, Spain and Turkey.

Source: Calculated from OECD, Statistics of Foreign Trade, Series B: Trade by Commodities, various issues 1971-76.

What types of production shifts have taken place?

Despite the inconclusiveness of aggregate data, it would be wrong to surmise that environmental concerns have been totally absent from corporate investment decisions over the past few years. Available evidence at the firm level, usually involving the petroleum, chemicals and metals industries, confirms the contrary.

In the examples below the types of production shifts that have occurred appear to have depended upon the type and degree of environmental regulation involved. The mere presence of environmental controls alone was never cited as a determining factor in causing the rethinking of investment decisions. However, when environmental controls were imposed in the form of absolute prohibition, or accompanied by strong public pressure or long screening procedures for the granting of building permits, then firms often chose to modify their initial site location in favour of another.

Examples of absolute prohibition include the 1972 approval by the governor of Delaware (USA) of a bill outlawing the construction of any additional chemical plants, refineries or paper mills along the state's Atlantic coast. The City Council of Amsterdam's veto on a project of Progil's to build a carbon disulphide plant in the city vicinity resulted in the plant's construction in Belgium. A German court ruled against construction of (Bayer subsidiary) Erdoelchemic's planned ethylene plant expansion at Dormagen. The company decided to expand at Bayer's Antwerp site instead. And a $500 mn grass roots chemical complex planned by Dow Chemical in California was blocked by environmentalist pressure and the site relocated in the Gulf state area.

Sometimes what would have been a "no" decision was transformed into a go ahead but only after the imposition of specific conditions was agreed. For example, construction of a new paper mill at Sougy-sur-Loire was authorised by the French government only after due investigation and the assigning of certain norms. And permission to build a refinery at Brofjorden was not granted to the Swedish Oil Consumers Cooperative until it had pledged to use only oil with a maximum 1 per cent sulphur content.

Public pressure often seemed to play an important role in influencing corporate investment decisions, especially in areas already saturated with heavy basic industry. This was the case in Amsterdam in 1973 when residents protested against expansion plans by Mobil for further refineries. Dutch residents blocked the building of a mammoth steel plant by Hoogovens in the area around Rotterdam. Public pressure in Holland is manifested through several environmental groups, including the Rihnmond. The result of their action has been a decision by the Dutch parliament to place a tax on new investment in the congested western part of the country.

Such environmentalist pressure and consequent government regulation in the Amsterdam-Rotterdam areas have led to the diversion of new industry or the expansion of existing plants to Antwerp and lesser developed Belgian areas where firms are less under public attack and can take advantage of investment subsidies. The decisions to move "next door" rather than to jump continents were prompted by the substantial already existing chemical base in the area and the easy extension of water, rail and pipeline connections. In this way the Belgians have attracted new investments by Progil (France), Kanegafuchi Chemical (Japan), Union Carbide (USA) and BASF and Sandoz (Switzerland).

Screening procedures and delays in site construction permits because of environmental considerations have been cited by several German chemical companies, including Hoechst, Veba and BASF, as a major drawback in planning new plants. For example, Bayer's plans to build a glass fibre plant at Brunsbuettel were dropped in favour of a site in Western Europe outside Germany because of delay in granting licence for new construction. And Dow Chemical Europe waited more than a year for a site permit for a new chlorine plant at Stade. The technical manager for Dow Chemical Europe was quoted as stating that although environmental standards were pretty much the same throughout EEC Europe, the time required for getting a licence was less and the tax situation was better in other countries such as Spain and Belgium.

Perhaps the most dramatic example of environmental considerations which have induced shifts in plant location is provided by Japanese firms, especially in such industries as aluminium. The absolute shortage of industrial land in Japan available for aluminium smelting is said to limit capacity to 1.8 mn tons, forcing incremental capacity to be built overseas. Showa Denko is reportedly reducing its domestic aluminium output by 50 per cent and shifting the capacity to New Zealand, Indonesia and Venezuela. Nippon Light Metal has expanded its aluminium refining capacity in Canada and is participating in a joint venture in the Philippines for an alumina smelter. Such examples are typical of firms in other sectors as well where the limited availability of natural resources is placing constraints on industrial expansion and forcing Japanese firms to decentralise to other parts of the Pacific Basin and even to the USA.

Plant relocation thus appears to be a function not of the cost of environmental control but rather of the inconvenience imposed upon firms by public pressure and/or screening procedures related to environmental control, and in the case of Japan by the absolute lack of environmental resources. The level of already existing industrial congestion also seems to dissuade certain new investments (for example, the change in Grundig's plans to locate in the Saar rather than in the built up Moselle region and the desire of DSM to build in the relatively undeveloped northern area to escape the congestion of the industrial south) as well as negative tax incentives imposed to discourage investments in certain regions. However, in none of the above examples did the firm in question cite the desire to expand abroad as a reaction to environmental deterrents. The attraction of locating in a low environmental standard developing country was never mentioned. In fact, the shifts in question in the limited sample available were entirely intra national (within the same country) or inter regional, between neighbouring developed countries. This preference appeared to be attached to the presence of already existing regional infrastructure, well known markets and security of supply.

Research on an individual case by case basis, while ascertaining the importance of environmental considerations for certain investment decisions, fails to confirm the contention that such new investments go mainly to developing countries. Locational spillovers that have occurred seemed to stem from a blockage or exclusion of preferred sites in various developed nations and not from an active search for low cost environmental locations on the part of multinational firms in pollution intensive sectors.

Are environmental considerations of overall little importance to MNCs?

At the firm level evidence can also be cited of foreign direct investment which flows in the direction opposite to that which would be expected on environmental grounds. In the USA, the country with the most severe environmental controls, much of the inflow of foreign direct investment in recent years has been to polluting sectors. This has been especially true for German, Dutch and Japanese investors. For the chemicals and allied products sector the Conference Board has estimated that foreign based parent chemical companies are placing more than $600 mn a year into their US based affiliates. Most, but not all, of these new chemical production centres have been located in the south to take advantage of cheaper labour and unrestricted natural gas supplies.

How can this boom in inward foreign direct investment be explained? The reasons cited by company executives are varied and not related to environmental control. They include: the large size and profitability of the US domestic market; the rich endowment of resources such as oil and natural gas, and cheaper electricity; lower labour costs; a high rate of innovation; and the relatively minor intervention of the government in domestic price formation. To these reasons must of course be added the current decline in the US dollar exchange rate and a desire to invest behind US tariff and non-tariff barriers (the American selling price valuation system for certain chemicals, for example).

European and US multinational company executives do not claim to be greatly concerned about environmental controls. This was the opinion expressed in the survey carried out by Business International in the spring of 1978 attempting to assess the most important factors influencing the business climate and corporate operations in Europe in the 1980s. Environmental controls were given a little to moderate impact on future corporate operations, although concern was larger in the basic materials and chemicals sectors. As might be expected, the factors of greatest common concern were the instability of currency movements and high labour costs, along with inflation.

Two recent studies have also come to the conclusion that environmental controls have been overshadowed in foreign investment decision making by more orthodox investment criteria such as market proximity, transport and labour costs and political risk. One paper went so far as to suggest that, in general, environmental analyses are not even available to management when the investment decisions are made, although environmental studies are often undertaken after the commitment has been taken and frequently influence plant design.[1]

---

1 Thomas N Gladwin and Ingo Walter, "Multinational Corporations, Social Responsiveness, and Pollution Control", Journal of International Business Studies, Winter 1976; and Ingo Walter, "Environmentally-Induced Industrial Relocation to Developing Countries", unpublished paper, 1977/78.

Two words of caution might well be expressed, however, at accepting at face value the conclusions of such studies regarding the importance of environmental considerations in MNC investment decisions. First, while there is little detriment to a firm's public image in citing inflation, exchange rates, or union bargaining power as influencing investment decisions, such may well not be the case for environmental factors. Lending support to the argument that they export pollution to poorer countries or regions rather than clean up at home is far from being in the best   interests of MNCs already operating in a hostile world. Second, studies like that of Business International cited above are aggregate in nature and may understate the importance of environmental concerns for changing the competitive position of individual polluting industries. For instance, in a recent study done for the US Congress, environmentally related health and safety standards have been held responsible for a strong "pattern of flight" in the asbestos textile industry.[1] US consumption from domestic and traditional foreign suppliers (Canada, Europe and Japan) has declined in favour of imports from Mexico, Taiwan and Brazil. As a result of the Toxic Substances Control Act of January 1977 requiring the publication and testing (retroactively) of all chemical substances produced and sold in the USA, the arsenic, zinc, mercury, benzidine dye and pesticide industries have also become potentially flightbound.

Summary and conclusions

We are left with the overall conclusion that little concrete evidence is to be found for environmentally induced international shifts in production sites on any large scale. Firms seem to have preferred to expand in recent years at existing locations rather than go elsewhere, and when this has not proved possible they have undertaken intra national or inter regional rather than international shifts, moving to those areas (the south in the USA, the north in the Netherlands or nearby Belgium) where industrial congestion is not yet critical and the risk involved in new investments is substantially less than in overseas locations, particularly in developing countries.

Indeed, this study may still be a little before its time as the years under consideration, 1971-77, are complicated by the slack in industrial activity and the small increase in new industrial capacity, along with delays accorded in many countries for the implementation of environmental control legislation. Also, a critical level of government participation to aid firms in clean ups may have diluted the immediate impact of environmental standards. It is important to keep in mind as well the period of delay between the planning and realisation of new investment projects which take three years for pulp and paper plants and as long as five to eight years for petrochemical complexes and aluminium smelters. This would mean that the products of plants built during this period may not yet have come on to the market.

Most importantly, a study of the influence of environmental controls on corporate production locations cannot be carried out under "ceteris paribus" assumptions. The impact of pollution clean up on a firm's activities may be substantial when viewed in isolation but is only a factor at the margin in the locational calculus of international investment. The significance of this additional factor must be assessed within the complex structure of project costs, risks and returns - all the market and non-market considerations corporate managers must include in making their investment and production decisions on a worldwide level.

---

1 "Obey Releases Major Study of Export of Hazardous Industries", Press Release from the Office of Congressman David R Obey, Washington DC, June 29, 1978.

VI. FINANCE AND TAX FACTORS

Transfer Pricing in International Transactions

MALCOLM CRAWFORD   No.3 1974

Transfer pricing - the fixing of prices at which goods and services are transacted between different parts of a company - is an aspect of multinational business which the business journals, for all their diligence and occasional expertise, have found too recondite to explore. It is one of very few business related subjects on which there is almost no non-technical literature.[1] Not only is the subject matter technically difficult, it is also nearly impossible to mention firms by name. For except in the very few cases where tax disputes over transfer pricing have come before the courts, transfer pricing is discussed only behind closed doors. When called to say anything about it - as, for example, by the UN's Group of Eminent Persons in their two sets of hearings last year - managements of multinational firms say they do not practise it.

Strictly speaking, that contention can only be upheld where the firm has no intra firm trade. Given intra group trade, transfer prices must be struck at some level; and even if there is no intra group trade in merchandise, there is also transfer pricing in services (such as fees and royalties) and loan interest, where the very existence of foreign subsidiaries makes such transactions almost inevitable. The term is used in a pejorative sense when it relates to manipulation of such prices to affect the profits of constituent parts of a company.

Awareness dawned slowly

Serious concern about the subject was, it appears, limited almost wholly to the US Treasury and its Internal Revenue Service, until the late 1960s, when a small number of developing countries began to appreciate the size of the outward flows of funds which could be generated in this way. Business opinions continued, however, to express the view that it was a problem of small proportions. Outside manufacturing industry, this was probably true. With many primary products, transfer pricing is either organised by the exporting country through state trading or similar regulation (e g Chilean and Peruvian copper exports) or severely limited by specific taxes (e g tonnage levies on output or exports). With a homogeneous commodity it is also easier for revenue officials to check the transfer prices against market prices or some other version of an arm's length price. However, few revenue authorities do this systematically, for to do so involves considerable work, especially if the prices fluctuate widely, or if quality differences occur, due for example to dampness of cargoes or other such unsystematic causes.

In manufacturing, the flows generated or diverted by transfer pricing appear to be much larger than was generally believed a few years ago. It could well be that the practice has increased greatly, partly because intra firm trade in manufactures by multinational enterprises has become much greater, and partly because their managements have become more sophisticated. At the hearings of the UN Group of Eminent Persons, this issue emerged as one of the very few complaints against multinationals, by spokesmen for developing countries, which were neither contradicted by other complaints nor rebutted successfully by management representatives. It is therefore an issue which multinational management should consider carefully.

Systematic manipulation of profit taking

Transfer pricing alters or diverts financial flows to the advantage of a multinational firm through alteration of the prices at which goods or services are imported to or exported from

---

1 Author's note (1980): this statement is of course no longer true. Since this article was published there has been a great deal written on the subject.

a foreign affiliate, so that the allocation of profit between members of the group differs from what it would be if market or arm's length prices were used. It is obvious that, if transfer pricing is most rife where products are not homogeneous, there must be difficulty about determining what are arm's length prices. But, leaving that aside for the moment, the point remains that international allocation of profit can be manipulated in this way. Usually (but not always) the purpose is to maximise group net profit by shifting pre-tax profits out of jurisdictions where effective rates of tax are high, into ones where tax is lower. Usually the object is achieved by overpricing exports of goods (or services) to affiliates in high tax countries. Alternatively, exports from such countries may be underpriced.

Evidence that transfer pricing is now very big multinational business comes from a number of quarters. One is a number of surveys by developing countries of prices of imports compared with trade in the same products among other countries. The most famous of these was done in Colombia, which found that for a large sample of pharmaceutical imports, prices charged by multinationals to subsidiaries in Colombia were 155 per cent above the weighted average of comparable transactions discovered in other markets. The prices at which such goods were imported by Colombian owned firms were only 19 per cent above the "world" reference prices. The Colombian investigation also found that a selection of rubber imports by foreign controlled firms had been overpriced by 44 per cent, certain chemical imports by 25 per cent, and electrical components by 54 per cent.

In Spain, according to an Unctad report, overpricing of pharmaceuticals was revealed ranging from 100 per cent to 800 per cent; in Chile, 30 to 500 per cent; in Peru, 20 to 300 per cent; and in Mexico 40 to 1,669 per cent.[1]

Transfer pricing is distinct from monopoly pricing

These are of course big variations, but a qualification needs to be entered here. It is important to distinguish between transfer pricing (as defined above) and monopoly pricing, which simply means charging more in markets where competition is least. The fact that the most spectacular overpricing was found in pharmaceuticals is echoed in the findings of the UK Monopolies Commission regarding Librium and Valium sold in the UK by Roche Products Ltd (see Multinational Business, No. 2 – 1973) where similar wide divergences were discovered – although the prices in the UK were among the lowest. Transfer pricing – affecting the division of profit between the parent, Hoffmann LaRoche, and the UK subsidiary – was an issue, but was not really the main one, because the value added by the UK subsidiary was relatively small and the UK authorities were not chiefly concerned that it be enlarged. The main issue was the selling price of the end product, which was greatly in excess of the low prices at which similar pharmaceuticals were sold in Italy. This in turn was clearly due to the existence of patent protection in the UK that did not apply in Italy. Patent cover is an important source of monopoly profits in the pharmaceutical industry, a large part of whose sales are made in circumstances which make for minimal price sensitivity on the part of the final user. It would be dangerous therefore to generalise from pharmaceuticals to manufactured goods in general, as some writers – including the authors of the Unctad report – have recently done. Nevertheless, the manipulation of import prices to the disadvantage of the importing country appears to have been proven, even if the figures cited may not refer specifically to transfer pricing, or be capable of wider application.

US firms are the main exponents

A survey of American multinationals by the Conference Board, which (unlike Unctad) is sponsored by and favourable to US business enterprise, was published in 1972, showing

---

1 Constantine Vaitsos and Unctad, sources cited in Transfer Pricing by Multinational Firms, by Sanjaya Lall, in Oxford Bulletin of Economics and Statistics, August 1973.

indirect evidence of widespread transfer pricing by US firms. The survey[1] was aimed at ascertaining how the systems used by the IRS for correcting and reallocating international intra firm profits work in practice. In criticising the IRS concept of arm's length pricing, many of the respondents quoted made it clear that they arrive at transfer prices from a consideration of where it suits the organisation to show its profits, and how the prices of transactions would contribute to group profits, rather than from calculations based on market prices. The respondents argued, implicitly or explicitly, that arm's length pricing was impossible, or perhaps irrelevant; but the effect of such a contention is simply to establish that pricing methods do shift profits.

The greater centralisation of internal control of multinational companies has clearly reinforced such tendencies. It is well known that this tendency has gone much further among American multinationals than among European ones. Where overseas subsidiaries are largely autonomous, transfer pricing which would reduce the subsidiary's declared profit in favour of another part of the group is apt to be resisted by local management. Centralisation impairs such resistance. And where profit plans are drawn up on a divisional basis, transfer prices are less likely to allow for the susceptibilities and preferences of local management. It is fair to add, though, that the pricing policies quoted (anonymously) in the Conference Board report reflected a remarkable variety of approaches. Arm's length pricing rarely figured in them for international transactions, even though in some cases it was the established policy for intra group sales in the USA. Generally speaking there was little evidence of deliberate, large deviations from arm's length pricing; rather, that arm's length prices tended not to enter into the calculations.

Transfer pricing is rarely illegal

It is sometimes argued that transfer pricing is impossible (in the sense we are concerned with here) where foreign operations act as profit centres, because the transfer prices must then support the profit objectives for these centres. However, it is possible for profit targets to be set for overseas profit centres which take account of transfer prices, and which are lower than those which could be achieved if transfer prices were fixed to allocate profits to those centres. It is also possible to keep a second set of accounts for management control purposes, which differ from those shown to the tax authorities in that they are based on arm's length prices. This, however, would not be possible in cases where management genuinely does not believe that arm's length prices exist, even conceptually. Also, the tax authorities can ask if other records are kept; in which case their existence would constitute a prima facie case for profit reallocation by the authorities. And although in most countries transfer pricing is not a statutory offence (though firms have been fined in Latin American countries, including Colombia) fraudulent evasion is, so it would be dangerous to lie about the existence of other records. A case has occurred in Canada in which culpability was proven when the authorities established that the firm had given false information about its international profit split. Our impression is that not many large firms do keep two sets of accounts, in this sense.

Revenue authorities find assessment difficult

Criteria do exist for revenue authorities to use in arguing about transfer prices of goods. These are more difficult to apply to some kinds of services, however - especially technical knowhow. Fees for management services can be assessed in relation to management time

---

1 Tax Allocations and International Business, by M G Duerr, The Conference Board, New York, 1972.

allocated, but precision about this is bound to be spurious. There is some evidence that transfer pricing in fees and royalties is now more actively used to shift profits than pricing of goods. A European multinational company chairman interviewed by me expressed the opinion that in his industry (electrical and electronics) American multinational firms were now avoiding tax in Europe to a far greater extent by payments of fees and royalties than by manipulation of product prices. In most underdeveloped countries, where according to Unctad fees and royalties have been the fastest growing form of international transactions, not only is there a scarcity of officials capable of discussing such matters with multinational management on an adequately informed basis; some governments appear to prefer that foreign firms repatriate profits by these hidden routes, rather than as dividends, which may be politically sensitive.

According to the US Conference Board report:

> In Company 62, an executive explains that the objective is to get as much profit home as possible, so long as foreign subsidiaries' payments are deductible for local tax purposes. He prefers to repatriate funds as royalties rather than as dividends, because royalties are often deductible overseas and because they are classified by the United States as foreign source income - thereby raising the limitation on foreign tax credit. Actually, he feels, there is little basis for charging royalties overseas, because his company's intangibles have little value to the foreign subsidiaries until the subsidiaries them- selves develop them.

> "The best way to bring money back varies with the situation", he explains. "Some countries allow royalties to be deducted, but are tough on service fees. Others are the other way around. Some have a progressive withholding rate. We call the payments whatever seems best under the circumstances."

Repatriation of profits is the objective

Getting as much profit home as possible is not classically the main reason for transfer pricing. The practice first came to public attention when the US Treasury, finding that its powers to reallocate profits (Section 482) were inadequate to deal with the growing use of tax havens by US firms, gained, after years of effort, a provision in the Revenue Act of 1962 (subpart F) enabling it to tax the income of foreign sales subsidiaries derived from third countries, even if the income was retained abroad. The prime object of transfer pricing was, and still is to some extent, to store profits away in tax havens, such as Switzer- land or Panama. Subpart F has not put an end to the practice.

Profits required for dividend distribution to ultimate shareholders cannot of course be re- tained in tax havens, nor can profits required for reinvestment in the home country. But a portion can be retained in a jurisdiction with very low effective rates of tax, and recycled for other investment outside the USA, either through intra group lending or through the eurocurrency market. The controls on US direct investment abroad imposed in 1965 (and removed early in 1974) reinforced the incentives to indulge in such practices. Despite active investigation by the IRS, Panama is still the second largest recipient of profit dis- tributions from some South American countries, after the United States. Almost certainly the beneficial owners are American firms.

The IRS power to reallocate profits comes under Section 482 of the Internal Revenue Code. According to the Conference Board's report, half of the 271 surveyed companies which had suffered reallocations by the IRS involved a foreign affiliate in a low tax country. About a quarter more involved a Western Hemisphere Trading Corporation (a legal form of US subsidiary taxable at a reduced rate). A substantial minority involved affiliates taxed at US rates or higher.

The interest of the IRS is not to create an ideal world, but to collect more tax for the US Treasury. This means that it seeks to raise the prices charged to foreign affiliates, for both goods and services, and raise the tax base of US multinationals in the USA. Where royalties, or fees, or loan interests to foreign subsidiaries, are found not to be charged, it contends that they be charged. It has developed various guidelines for minimum rates of charge for all these non-merchandise categories. For merchandise trade, it first attempts to apply arm's length pricing; but where that fails, it resorts to a variety of other techniques, usually involving recalculation of the cost and profit structure of the products. Without doubt, it has developed the reallocation of transfer pricing to a science far ahead of any other revenue authority. In so far as the IRS succeeds in reallocating profits away from other countries to the USA, transfer pricing is thereby manipulated against the terms of trade of those other countries - whether US multinationals wish this to be so or not.

Little is known of the efforts of European tax authorities, apart from the fact that discussions have recently been initiated between revenue departments of certain EEC countries (including the UK, France, and West Germany) on problems of transfer pricing. Nothing has been publicly revealed about any collaborative measures on which they may have agreed. Whereas customs departments not infrequently check valuations with their opposite numbers in other countries, revenue authorities in Europe are more secretive. In Europe cases are never taken to court. And there is no survey evidence relating to European experience.

European revenue authorities have two problems in this area: policing US multinationals to ensure they do not transfer profits out excessively, and inhibiting their own firms' use of foreign tax havens. The UK Inland Revenue is said to be relatively easy going about tax havens, provided the UK firm does not load profits into them to such an extent that the glaring disproportion presents the inspector with an easy case. Exchange controls limit the scope for UK firms to retain profits abroad outside the sterling area.[1] There is no equivalent to Subpart F. There are powers to reallocate profits, however, under Section 485 of the Income Tax Act. It is up to the tax inspector assigned to the company to ask for an order under this section. The number of occasions on which this has happened are said to be few. According to tax accountants, a certain amount of regular bargaining takes place between inspectors and UK firms with substantial income from abroad, in which there is give and take on both sides. The oil companies are not overlooked, and the Inland Revenue does not accept oil transactions at posted price; yet even so, oil companies pay very little tax in the UK. New legislation is expected affecting transfer pricing of oil.

Foreign owned companies are always more difficult to police than domestic ones, because when arm's length prices cannot be found, alternative methods, such as apportioning global value added on a cost plus basis, cannot usually be applied. In the UK, the Inland Revenue does not have power to compel foreign firms to disclose unpublished data about costs and prices other than those of the UK subsidiary.

More important, perhaps, is the lack of qualified staff. There is no information about the number of inspectors assigned to multinational firms, but the total assigned to company accounts is under 3,000. A unit at Somerset House (at the chief inspector's branch) gives advice on transfer pricing and other international tax problems. Otherwise there is little

---

1 Author's note (1980): this ceased to be the case after October 1979.

specialisation, apart from a few very big companies requiring full time attention. It is hard to avoid the impression that the Inland Revenue regards transfer pricing as a problem of minor importance.[1]

Transfer prices affect international profit comparisons

Comparisons are sometimes made of rates of return on US direct investment in European countries in manufacturing – the USA being the only country that publishes information enabling such comparisons to be made. For the years 1964 to 1969, the returns are highest for Germany, after which in descending order come the Netherlands, Belgium, the UK, Italy and France. This is precisely the order in which US firms would choose to take profits, on the consideration of minimisation of tax (assuming a high rate of dividend repatriation from Germany, where retained profits are taxed at a high rate and distributed profits at a low one).

The effective rates of tax in the USA and the UK have been about the same, in the past, though this is now slightly altered with a UK tax rate of 52 per cent and no relief for imputation available for foreign owned firms. This may have created an incentive for US firms to transfer profits away from the UK. The most obvious area for this is eurocurrency banking, where profits can easily be taken in tax havens while margins in London only cover City office expenses.

Tax minimisation is the main consideration in Europe

For subsidiaries in European countries, tax (including withholding tax) is virtually the only relevant consideration affecting transfer pricing. Indeed, it is widely believed among those acquainted with the subject that tax minimisation is the only purpose of transfer pricing. With underdeveloped countries, however, the incentives to avoid showing profits can be numerous. And it seems fairly apparent that transfer pricing is the cause of very large concealed repatriations from such countries in addition to the stated profits. Apart from frequently high rates of tax on repatriated profits (many developing countries tax retained profits lightly) the inducements to allocate profits away from all but a few favoured LDCs include: exchange controls on conversion of currency; a tendency to apply price controls or to use licensing controls in a restrictive way when large increases in profits are shown by a foreign owned firm; multiple exchange rates whereby an adverse rate is allowed for profit remissions compared with that for merchandise imports; social pressures against the firm or its executives when large profits are declared; or merely an expectation that some of these conditions are likely to exist in future, even if they do not as yet. Exchange controls can sometimes be relevant not merely as applied specifically to remitted profits, but also to leads and lags (deliberate variations in timing of transactions) by which the firm would hope to gain advantage from exchange rate fluctuations on any payments of which the timing is alterable. Thus, where a currency is considered basically weak, transfer pricing can shift assets valued in that currency into assets valued in stronger currencies. The incentives affecting transfer pricing are discussed more fully by Sanjaya Lall in the August 1973 Oxford Bulletin of Economics and Statistics (see footnote page 112).

Local shareholdings may give room for manoeuvre

The existence of local shareholders in the subsidiary can be of crucial importance, though it can affect the issue in either direction. If the local shareholder is a state owned enterprise,

---

1 Author's note (1980): In 1977 the Inland Revenue expanded the central unit and assigned officials from it to work more closely with the inspectors engaged on accounts of a number of multinational companies.

or some other person or firm on whose loyalty the government can rely, and if the government is known to be opposed to transfer pricing, then the local shareholder is likely to be able to ascertain the methods by which pricing is determined. He (or it) has moreover an interest in avoiding over-invoicing of imports, since this would reduce the profit in which he (it) has a legal stake. This would tend to discipline transfer pricing.

Yet, as Lall argues, the existence of local shareholders enhances the incentive for the multinational to over-invoice imports because in this way it can increase the parent company's share of the "true" profits. If it has had the foresight to cost the equipment and other fixed assets in at high transfer prices, it will also thereby inflate the book value of the capital into which the local interests buy (and will also increase the base of net worth on which ceilings or surtax rates on dividend remissions are often calculated). And finally, Lall argues, the local shareholders could have a collusive interest with the group management, which may be providing assistance to the former in accumulation of funds abroad.

Tariffs are also a key factor

Tariffs also affect the issue. They too can affect it in different ways, given different circumstances; but in general, the effect of an ad valorem tariff is to offset the incentive provided by a high rate of tax on profits. For if imports are over priced, the additional value will cause more duty to be paid - thus tending to offset the saving of tax liability on profits.

True, the rate of import duty would have to be extremely high to offset (say) a 60 per cent rate of profit tax if, by overpricing the imports, the profits can be retained somewhere tax free. But usually transfer pricing has to be concerned with two rates of profit tax; typically one in the host country and one in the parent country, or else in the tax haven. Where the effective rate of tax on profits (including distributed profits) at the margin in the host country is 60 per cent, and that in the parent country (assuming no tax haven intervenes) is 50 per cent, an import duty rate of 25 per cent is sufficient to wipe out any gain from transfer pricing. Where high import duties are applied to the multinational's intra-firm trade, an incentive to transfer pricing other than high rates of tax on profits must normally exist, to justify rationally the use of it to shift profits to the USA, the UK, or France, where profits are taxed at approximately 50 per cent. The rate of import duty which makes for zero gain from transfer pricing merely to avoid tax, is $\frac{t-p}{1-t}$

where t is the tax rate on profit in the host country and p the rate in the parent country.[1]

---

1 This is derived as follows. Let Q_1 be the effect on group profits of one unit of pre-tax profit in the host country in the base case, and Q_2 the comparable effect after an increase of M in the transfer price of imports to the host country.

$$Q_1 = 1-t$$
$$Q_2 = (1-M)(1-t) + M(1-p)$$

If duty at a rate m is imposed,

$$Q_2 = [1-(M+mM)](1-t) + M(1-p)$$

If $Q_1 = Q_2$ (signifying no gain from changing the transfer price)

$$1-t = [1-(M+mM)](1-t) + M(1-p)$$

therefore

$$M(1-p) - M-mM+tM+tmM = 0$$
$$m(tM-M) + tM-pM = 0$$

therefore

$$m = \frac{p-t}{t-1} \quad \text{or} \quad \frac{t-p}{1-t}$$

Intra firm trade is very substantial for the USA and UK

Intra firm trade of course represents only a minority of total exports for any country. But for the USA, it is a rather large minority. Lall estimates that intra firm exports of US firms account for 35 per cent of total American exports of manufactures, and that foreign owned firms in the USA may account for a further 5 per cent. The value of intra-firm trade exceeded declared earnings on foreign manufacturing investment; and a 12 per cent change in transfer prices (in 1970) would have, theoretically, wiped out total remissions of dividends and interest.

In the UK, if a company with overseas investments needs distributable profits, the discrimination of the imputation system against distributable profits from abroad creates a further incentive for UK firms to overprice exports to subsidiaries, enabling it to show more profit as earned in the UK. This consideration does not apply to US firms, either in the USA or the UK, suggesting that British multinationals ought to be more avid manipulators of transfer prices than American. This does not appear to be the case, however. Moreover, UK multinationals tend to have much lower proportions of intra firm trade than American ones.

For the UK, the proportion of intra-firm trade in manufactures was 24 per cent of total manufactured exports. As a proportion of exports of multinational companies the percentages were naturally higher. American owned firms in the UK show 56 per cent of their exports as intra firm, according to Board of Trade data which Lall processed. The comparable figure for British owned firms was only 27 per cent.

It is arguable that transfer pricing is a necessary tool of self defence for foreign capital in an environment hostile to profits. This may be true where viable rates of return are not allowed to be earned or repatriated - as is the case in some South American countries, and even in some outwardly pro-capitalist countries, such as Greece. It may also be desirable where it appears to coincide with the preferences of the government. It is, on the other hand, difficult to justify where the rate of repatriable profits is high - say 15 per cent after withholding tax. Insuring heavily against fears that political conditions may get worse, by moving money out of a developing country, is a way of making them get worse. Data for both US and UK companies' overseas earnings and assets show that, until end 1971, earnings and rates of return on net worth (after local tax) have been about the same in less developed countries as in developed countries, or slightly higher. But circumstances differ greatly between countries. Given that transfer prices of transactions with less developed countries are known, in general, to be more affected by overpricing of imports than is the case (overall) with trade among developed countries, true rates of return for affiliates in less developed countries are likely to be understated.

Countermeasures by the LDCs -

How then are less developed countries to avoid exploitation by transfer pricing? A few (more) could turn themselves into tax havens; but this option is very like that of the small firm which can gain profits by undercutting the big ones, a course of action which can only cause losses if pursued by the industry as a whole. So it is with nations when designing tax policies for multinational enterprise; the third world would simply lose tax revenue. Without going to that extreme, they could, in principle, make their fiscal and other treatment of profits closely resemble that of the developed countries. Lall remarks that most poor countries would not subscribe to such an aim. As a matter of factual observation, this statement is probably correct. But it is entirely possible that this could be, for most of them, their welfare optimising course - subject to certain structural differences.

- mainly depend on possessing well educated revenue officials

The course of action which many of them are pursuing - many of those which have an adequate supply of well educated officials, that is - is to tighten up their control over pricing of intra firm transactions. The procedure of the US IRS has been studied by several countries. India and Argentina have been devising more elaborate forms of scrutiny, based largely on American techniques. The Andean Pact member countries (Chile, Bolivia, Peru, Ecuador, Colombia, and Venezuela) have set up an information sharing arrangement for the policing of transfer pricing. One fact which the academics have discovered seems to work in favour of such countries: intra firm exports of manufactures are highly concentrated among firms. Lall calculates that 7 per cent of American firms with overseas affiliates account for 65 per cent of the intra firm exports of US multinationals. For the UK, 2 per cent of the firms account for 52 per cent of intra firm exports. Thus, a high degree of success might be had by concentrating upon a small number of firms.

Even inter firm trade may involve transfer pricing

There is technique by which transfer pricing can be used in inter firm trade. There is no evidence as to how prevalent this is, but it is extremely difficult to detect. Assume that firms A and B are headquartered in the same country, and B supplies goods to overseas affiliates owned or controlled by A, in a country which is sub optimal for declaration of profits. B, by arrangement with A, overprices exports to A's foreign affiliates, which of course provides extra profit for B. B then makes a corresponding reduction in price on its sales to A in the home market; or else, if A is a supplier to B as well, A can recoup by overpricing to B in export markets. Not only is this form of transfer pricing difficult for officials to detect (they are overstretched just scrutinising intra firm trade). It also affects the supposedly arm's length prices to which such officials may refer.

The overall extent of transfer pricing is, it would appear, totally unknown - by anybody. It seems likely that transfer pricing as a device to shift profits is practised on a large scale by American firms, with the encouragement of the American tax authorities where this involves shifting the profits to US tax jurisdiction. It is apparently practised less systematically by European firms, though British firms make considerable use of sterling area tax havens as repositories for foreign earnings, to the extent that exchange controls allow.

Transfer pricing may make investment non-optimal

At any rate, much more is going to be heard about the problem. For transfer pricing constitutes a considerable qualification to the claim, made both by multinational firms and by many independent economists, that multinational enterprise tends towards a worldwide optimum use of real resources, and in so doing brings the maximum advantage to both host and parent countries.

Economists specialising in this subject increasingly believe that transfer pricing tends to make international investment non-optimal, where it is used to shift profits, and that this has occurred mainly at the expense of developing countries.

As will be apparent from the appraisal of the evidence presented here, our own view is that active use of transfer pricing to shift profits is not always in the interests of the firm; and although the constraints of which heads of multinational firms often speak tend to be less real than they would have us believe, the proportion of trade thus affected is probably quite small. Nevertheless it may well be large enough to exert a proportionately large effect on declared profits of foreign affiliates.

Offshore Corporate Tax Planning

THOMAS KELEN ●   **No.3 1977**

The use of "offshore" financial centres by the multinational corporations has over the years become a well accepted and established corporate financial technique. The advantages and disadvantages of using an offshore centre, or rather the real uses of these places, are now clear to corporate treasurers. The aim is to maximise the overall after tax profits of the enterprise, and, primarily, the use of offshore income, combined with tax deferral which enables the corporate treasurer to produce faster growth and accumulation of funds because of the tax free period.

Offshore centres may be used by the multinationals in three different ways: for profit creation, profit diversion, and profit extraction. To use these techniques the management of the multinational corporation must follow very closely the changing legal environment of both sides, i e the specific services offered by the offshore centres and the protective legislative framework imposed by the high tax countries to defend their revenue against erosion.

Profit creation means market considerations

These offshore places themselves may be simple <u>tax havens</u> or full <u>offshore financial centres</u>. A tax haven is a territory where assets can be held and profits can be earned and transferred without any local tax consequences, or at a cost of tax liability considerably less than in a major industrial country. An offshore financial centre aims to give a much wider scope of service than that. It is a place where international financial business can be carried on in a fiscally neutral way. The prerequisite is the complete separation of the domestic and international markets by means of a well thought out legal framework. The absence of direct taxation and the freedom from exchange control are desirable, but it is not the total absence of such barriers which is relevant but rather more the possibility of carrying out particular transactions free of tax and exchange control limitations. The choice of an offshore subsidiary of a multinational corporation is therefore mainly governed by the possibility of the flexible implementation of a series of appropriate transactions. It is not the case (contrary to popular belief) that the multinationals can solve most of their tax and exchange control problems by merely setting up a tax haven subsidiary. The object is to arrange that payments are deductible against taxable profits in the country of origin, thereby reducing the taxable income there. There may be withholding taxes in the country of origin, and taxes in the country of receipt.

It is in the nature of tax havens that not very much business is likely to be found there. It may be possible to build up a fairly substantial operation with substantial tax advantages, but one which by multinational standards is limited by a market of trivial size. In the case of manufacturing operations, it is often better to make $1 mn and be taxed as well as being allowed depreciation and other deductions, than to make $0.5 mn in a tax haven. Along these lines, however, there are possibilities of low tax profit creation in places like Ireland or Puerto Rico, which operate free zone facilities - preferably when such an operation is used as an operating centre for a wider market in the area. This kind of profit creation within a low tax territory offers the least problems but the fewest commercial opportunities.

● Thomas Kelen, now with County Bank, a merchant banking arm of the National Westminster group, was a member of J F Chown & Co Ltd (London) at the time of writing.

Profit diversion is a more common objective

Profit diversion, on the other hand, is an attempt to arrange matters in such a way that profits which would arise somewhere in the course of a company's trade occur in a low tax jurisdiction instead of a highly taxed one. The commonest technique for profit diversion is transfer pricing. Let us take an example of an American company manufacturing goods which are subsequently sold to another associated company, say in Belgium. If the final selling price of the units is $10 each and the American parent sells to the Belgian company at $9, $1 taxable profit will arise in Belgium. If, instead, these units are sold to the Belgian affiliate at $10, this taxable profit will arise in the USA. The simple tax haven possibility would seem to be to interpose a tax haven subsidiary to which the US parent sells the goods at $9 per unit, reinvoicing from the tax haven to Belgium at $10, leaving the $1 per unit profit accumulating free of tax in the tax haven. Similarly, it might be possible to pay a $1 tax deductible sales commission from one of the high tax companies to the tax haven company.

Unfortunately it is not as simple as that, because all high tax countries have legislation giving them the right to query inter company transfer prices and to substitute arm's length prices for the prices actually shown on the invoices. These provisions have been in existence for about 15 years in many countries, and by now detailed regulations have been published for establishing a wide spectrum of proper arm's length prices. Naturally, where these powers exist they are applicable to all cross frontier transactions, not only to transactions through obvious tax havens.

Under these circumstances if the US parent company in the above example was to sell directly to the Belgian company, the actual transfer price matters little to the group as a whole because the tax rates in the two countries are much the same. It does, however, matter to the two revenue authorities. In principle the same profit could be taxed in both countries, as both of the revenue authorities became more aggressive, making adjustments on the transfer prices at both ends. Under double tax agreements there are procedures for eventual readjustments and subsequent recovery of tax, but there is no compensation given by the governments for the extra legal and accountancy fees incurred, not to mention the loss of management time in negotiating these highly complex adjustments.

Another line of attack could be delivered on the basis of the place of 'management and control'. The place of incorporation is not necessarily the decisive test for the tax residence of a company. It may be registered, say, in the Bahamas, but if the real owners or managers live in a high tax country the revenue authorities of that country will try to establish that the company is really resident there. If this is held to be in the USA, or in the UK, the company will be liable to tax in exactly the same way as a locally incorporated company. To avoid this directors must meet and management decisions must be made in the country of registration or at least outside any particular high tax country. It is usual to have a majority of directors resident in the country of incorporation, and to ensure that they really run the company they must not be given instructions, only some 'advice', from head office. Strictly speaking this is not necessary. All the directors could be, for instance, UK residents provided the UK Inland Revenue is convinced that they only exercise their functions when they are physically outside the UK. Under UK law, however, even if all the directors are residents in the country of incorporation and it can be shown that the strings are really pulled by a UK resident with no formal connection with the company, it still may be deemed to be managed and controlled within the UK. Neither 'management and control' nor 'trading within' in this sense has anything to do with shareholding control. American and continental European law often gives less weight to the concept of management and control than UK law.

Profit extraction

The third technique in using offshore centres is profit extraction. In this case profits arise and are taxed in a high tax country, but the actual tax charge may be substantially reduced by having a low tax subsidiary charging management fees, royalties or interest against these profits. Apart from the revenue rules of transfer pricing which are applicable here too, in all these cases the country where the profits arise is likely to have legislation limiting the effectiveness of the technique. Many countries, especially Latin American ones, tend to regard management and similar fees as a fake distribution – and tax them as such – rather than as a charge against profits. Very often this technique can be made more effective when the advantages of existing double tax treaties are considered. As a result of these, payments of this kind are often routed through countries which are not really regarded as tax havens, such as the Netherlands.

Offshore borrowing and exchange rates

An offshore company may also be used as a 'financing vehicle', and indeed many companies use financing subsidiaries based on offshore centres. The use of an offshore financing subsidiary may not produce any particular tax advantage but it enables a company to borrow money without restriction from the most advantageous sources, paying interest to holders of eurobonds without deduction of withholding tax. This enhances its financial flexibility. It will, moreover, invariably ensure that the same income is not taxed twice in different countries where there are no appropriate double tax treaties. There are sometimes restrictive tax and exchange control rules in the country of residence of the parent company when the guarantee of that parent company is required for the undertaking of such borrowings.

Although the choice of currency to be borrowed by offshore financing vehicles is free, the decision itself is quite complex and far from easy. The combined effect of fluctuating exchange rates and possibly asymmetrical taxation of foreign exchange gains and losses have on many occasions caused the apparently less expensive currency to become one of the most expensive within a few years. Exchange control reasons have compelled British companies to finance overseas expansion by foreign borrowings, of which the real cost has risen sharply with the depreciation of sterling. These problems have occurred in other countries too, though to a lesser extent. Careful planning and the use of a financing vehicle could always have ensured that at least part of such losses occurred in a tax deduction form.

In managing the cash assets and liabilities of a multinational group in several countries in several currencies there are four very important factors to be watched. The first two are non-tax factors: currency risk and exchange control; the second two are the tax treatment of interest paid and received and the tax treatment of foreign exchange gains and losses.

Features of offshore locations

The choice between low and no tax jurisdictions again is not as straightforward as commonly supposed. A low tax or sometimes even a high tax country, with the relevant set of double tax agreements, is often the more advantageous place for a particular operation. In international banking business, for instance, a modest rate of withholding tax is a much more serious deterrent to intermediation than a 50 per cent tax on net profits. Central bank deposit and liquidity requirements also tend to increase the effective interest rates paid by banks for deposits, and apparently small penalties such as deposit insurance premia and stamp duties can also be sufficient to make international operations uncompetitive.

In choosing an offshore location one must bear in mind that it is very often only a place where a particular transaction is conveniently recorded. The centre of decision making, the location and movements of funds or goods may well be somewhere else at the convenience of the parties concerned. The infrastructure must be suitable to support the operations envisaged and it must also be efficient enough to be relied upon. This, of course, implies political stability, the availability of well qualified local lawyers, accountants, bankers and skilled staff, including relatively easy access by public transport and at least adequate communication services.

Developments in the scope for use of tax havens should be analysed by looking at the offshore centres themselves as well as the major industrial countries. Generally, changes in the offshore centres are rarely revolutionary since their livelihood depends on a stable and secure legal and political environment. Most dramatic changes have occurred on the offshore banking scene, because the Lebanese civil war has eliminated Beirut as a regional financial centre. The newly emerged centres like Bahrain and the UAE are, in fact, rather more natural developments which would have occurred anyway, even if there had not been a need for replacements for Beirut. The respective systems of Offshore Banking Units (OBUs) and the Restricted Licence Banks (RLBs) are quite similar, with the advantage of the RLBs being allowed to take deposits in local currency from residents and generally being able to engage in full scale banking operations both offshore and onshore in any currency including the local one. Offshore banks in Bahrain pay an annual licence fee to which they are not subject in the UAE. On the other hand, in principle the UAE would levy 20 per cent tax on offshore profits, though with the exception of Dubai the tax is unlikely to be imposed. Telecommunication facilities are good in both centres, though both places are overcrowded and expensive. Bahrain now commands a very sizeable market and, being better ruled and regulated, has not had a banking crisis like the UAE. Services in both places are expanding very rapidly, apart from insurance and money market operations. Modern company law facilitating offshore companies is now available in Bahrain and implementation is under discussion in the UAE. Sharjah, after a very ambitious start of physical construction of its "Wall Street" and some work on a new legislative framework, now seems to be almost abandoning the original ideas. Nevertheless, eagerness to acquire a slice of the petrodollar business has led to a general liberalisation in the area,with the notable exception of Saudi Arabia. Even in Kuwait, foreign banks, with Kuwaiti equity participation, are now permitted to open branches. Jordan has implemented new legislation enabling the country to provide full offshore services. Tunisia has also joined the club and now has an offshore banking law.

Cairo and Teheran have both aspired to become the leading financial centre of the region. Conferences were held in both where experts of the international financial community discussed the possibilities with government officials of Egypt and Iran of improving the environment for international business. Law No. 43 of 1974, which regulates foreign investment in Egypt, has been amended to end the confusion over multiple exchange rates and rules regarding repatriation of profits which have deterred foreign investors. The corporate tax holiday was increased from five to eight years and generally it is hoped that other new regulations will lessen the bureaucracy involving the administration of foreign investment. Iran, however, is no longer in direct competition because of the new political situation.

Singapore has further liberalised its exchange control regulations, and fees, interest or commissions received by Asian Currency Units (ACUs) on transactions involving offshore letters of credit are now taxed at a reduced rate of 10 per cent. Non-residents holding Asian dollar bonds, government bonds and deposits with ACUs are now exempted from estate duties. Tax rates in Hong Kong have been slightly increased in the last budget and further modernisation of company law was carried out. Countries like Cyprus and Greece have also removed a number of obstacles from the further development of international business.

The eagerness of governments to participate in the offshore bonanza is not restricted to the Arab world. Nauru, a remote island in the Pacific, which is one of the smallest and wealthiest countries of the world, now offers full tax haven facilities. Offshore banking along the lines of

Bahrain are now available in the Philippines. The Seychelles became an independent republic on June 29, 1976, and in August of the same year announced a proposed offshore banking legislation based on the Singapore and Bahrain models. Unfortunately further developments were again aborted by subsequent political changes. The government of Barbados also announced that, in principle, offshore operations will be permitted but the date of implementation is not yet known.[1] The British Virgin Islands is also considering modifications in its legislative framework for the revival of offshore business.

In some of the established offshore centres, costs are rising relatively fast. The Bahamas now requires non-Bahamian companies to pay higher stamp, property, emigration, and company registration fees. The Cayman Islands have increased bank licence fees.

There are also developments in the Channel Islands. Company law reform proposals have been published in Jersey and there are new regulations for non-resident trusts and bank deposits. Local bank deposit interest, held by non-residents in trust, will not in future have to be included in the tax return of the trust.

The Luxemburg government is empowered to set a minimum capital requirement, between LF1 and 10 mn, for holding companies registered there. Companies which do not comply with the required level within a specified period will lose their special holding company tax concessions. This regulation may well cause some small private holding companies to move elsewhere but it is expected that the majority will remain.

In Liechtenstein and Switzerland the respective national banks and bankers' associations have concluded an agreement on the practice of bank secrecy and on the precautions to be taken by banks in the acceptance of funds. It is not the end of banking secrecy, but a voluntary agreement to screen out improper business. There are higher cantonal taxes in Switzerland and negative rates of interest have been imposed on non-resident held Swiss franc deposits at various times. All these changes have made Switzerland a less desirable place to operate from. The Swiss franc is less attractive as an investment currency, but the many corporate financial advantages offered to non-residents remain unchanged.

Legislation against the use of offshore centres is on the increase

The major industrial countries are continuously closing ranks at two levels to close existing tax loopholes and to control the flow of capital and profits.

The first level includes rules and regulations by international organisations, such as the EEC, Gatt and Efta, including voluntary agreements such as the OECD draft model for negotiating double tax treaties. The European Commission is actively engaged in the implementation of tax harmonisation within the Community, although it seems realisation is still far away. The privileges enjoyed by certain European centres were highly disapproved by the Commission, but, as far as specific action goes, its report suggested that legislating against the existing European offshore facilities would simply cause the business to go elsewhere.

The other level is the weaponry of the major industrial countries, which consists of exchange control, tax, specific anti-avoidance legislation and transfer pricing policy. Most of these provisions have been incorporated into the existing legal framework since as far back as the early 1960s. The American concept of 'controlled foreign corporation' means that attributable profits of these companies (i e parent and subsidiaries) are subject to US tax regardless as to whether they are distributed or not. As an exception some of the export profits may be accumulated freely if specific permission is given; this concession was later consolidated through the concept of the domestic international sales corporation (DISC).

1. Early in 1979, Barbados implemented its offshore legislation.

112

Regulations governing the finest details of intercompany pricing have also long been established in the USA and in many cases other jurisdictions are coming to regard the US regulations as the model for this type of legislation. US revenue protection over the years has become so aggressive that several of the double tax treaty negotiations with other industrial countries had to include specific provisions for avoiding unacceptable levels of double taxation on the normal international commercial activities of US based groups.

The 1971 Canadian tax reform brought in a set of anti avoidance provisions which only came into force at the beginning of 1976. These rules are settling down into an established routine.

Since 1972 German resident companies or individuals controlling foreign companies can be taxed on the profits accruing to such companies. Since then the basic legislation has progressed and currently the rules do not apply provided that the foreign company itself pays tax of at least 30 per cent on the profits.

The Australian anti avoidance legislation goes as far as listing the tax havens for which the exchange control authorities will not consider applications without reference to the tax department. The Hong Kong government has protested against its inclusion. In the UK the transfer of trade of a UK company to a foreign company, and a number of other transactions, are prohibited without Treasury consent. This simple sounding rule in practice proves to be very efficient.

Measures like this are likely to spread, making more and more difficult the life of the corporate financial planner. On the other hand, as legislation becomes clearer and definitions more accurate, the scope for intelligent structuring of multinational operations will correspondingly increase.

Multinational companies continue to find ways to break down the barriers to capital movement between countries. Intercompany loans and infusions of equity into foreign subsidiaries
by parent companies are the classical devices for transferring capital within an international
group, but different arrangements have been developed which have certain advantages.
Among the earliest of these was the back to back loan. This means that a company deposits
money with a bank, and a branch of that bank will lend the money, in the same currency (the
bank takes no currency risk), to an affiliate or sister company of the group in another
country. There can be a number of advantages. The operation may legally avoid or
minimise the effect of exchange controls, may make repayment easier in some countries,
and may utilise funds that cannot be deployed as intercompany loans either because of
unrequited withholding taxes or the nature of the lending affiliate (in the case of certain
kinds of cash-storing subsidiaries in tax havens). Also, the borrowing affiliate will often
find the interest charge lower than if it borrowed in its own name, even with parent company
guarantee.

Parallel loans and (more recently) long term currency swaps have developed from the back
to back loan. A parallel loan involves a multinational company, say a British company,
making a loan in sterling to the UK subsidiary of an American company, while the parent
US company makes a dollar loan to the British company's affiliate in the USA. A bank will
normally be involved as an intermediary, but instead of taking the spread between the deposit
rate and its lending rate, as would normally be expected if separate deposits and loans were
involved (and this may often be 2 per cent or even more), it charges a flat front end fee of
perhaps $\frac{1}{2}$ per cent to each party. Borrowing costs can be 1 to 2 per cent cheaper than
through conventional borrowing.

For the UK company, the exchange control attractions are obvious. It is not a question of
avoiding the controls, since British firms may borrow foreign currency to finance investment abroad, but the parallel loan can be a cheaper and more flexible way of doing this than
an issue of loan stock or a medium term bank borrowing. For the American company,
there is no exchange control advantage in the UK, indeed there could be a drawback because
foreign firms in the UK have to match fixed assets with finance raised outside the UK.
Assuming that condition is fulfilled, though, the parallel loan meets another problem for
the US firm in Britain - the lack of recourse to capital markets. This is not due to exchange
control, but results mainly from the virtual drying up of the supply of long term fixed
interest capital for companies in the UK. Parallel loans offer a further advantage in this
connection: the two companies have a considerable range of choice in setting their reciprocal
interest charges. Since few American companies in the UK have a UK tax liability against
which to charge interest, their effective interest costs are very high. While neither the
Bank of England nor the US Internal Revenue Service would allow a widly uncommercial rate to be
struck, there is considerable latitude.

Currency swapping is a refinement of the parallel loan. The main difference is the way it
appears in the accounts. No loan is recorded in either company's balance sheet. Instead,
each enters into a spot forward swap with the other, or with a bank acting as intermediary.
The American company sells the British spot dollars, against a forward contract to pay
sterling for dollars in, say, ten years'time. The UK company sells the American spot
sterling against a contract to pay it dollars (in return for the original amount of sterling) in
ten years. The effect on the balance sheet of each company, once the money is invested, is
that cash is reduced and fixed assets are increased. Nothing is altered on the liabilities
side. There is no loan agreement as such, which saves some work and cost; there is merely
a pair of forward exchange contracts, enforceable under contract law in each country.

There is no currency risk, since each firm gets back the currency it advanced to the other, after ten years. There is, however, a credit risk. This does not arise so long as the exchange rates do not change, because if one party fails to fulfil its forward contract, the other will not either; in that case they are evens. Currency movements could, however, cause one party to have a potential gain by defaulting. This has been dealt with by a "top up" clause, whereby periodically the party which is enjoying the potential gain due to the devaluation of its currency must pay to restore the equality of risk. It must be stressed, however, that this is a credit risk, not a currency risk as it may seem on the face of it, because exchange loss can only materialise in the event of default. However, where a top class bank acts as principal in such a deal, taking each side of the swap itself so that the credit risk for each firm is with the bank, not the other industrial company, it is not clear that there is any need for such a top up clause. Continental Illinois Bank, which has pioneered in this field, acted as principal in this way in the recent swap involving Consolidated Goldfields and an unnamed American firm.

There is no interest charged on a swap; instead the firm whose currency is at a premium in the long term forward currency market pays an annual charge reflecting the expected interest differential. Recently this has been 2 to 2.5 per cent by US to British firms in dollar sterling swaps. The first long term currency swap was in 1975, between a Dutch company, Bos Kalis Westminster, and an unnamed British firm; but most of the transactions have been between US and UK companies.

As with back to back loans, the causes of mutual attraction to long term currency swapping can be numerous. But perhaps the main one at present is the ample liquidity of many US and UK firms, combined with financing problems among their overseas subsidiaries.

VII. CASE STUDIES IN CORPORATE DECISION MAKING

SKF Reintegrates Internationally

JAMES POOLE•

No.4 1976

For the past four years SKF, the largest maker of ball bearings in the world, has been implementing a programme to integrate the production operations of its big five European operating companies. This reorganisation, which is now largely complete, represents an extraordinary departure for the company which exemplified, perhaps more than any other multinational firm, the philosophy of complete independence for affiliated operations.

SKF has been run like a federation of sovereign corporations since before the last war. We last commented on this unique structure in Multinational Business No. 2 - 1972, when the group opened a central research laboratory at Jutphaas in the Netherlands. The location was highly significant. Each of the big five SKF companies in Europe - operating respectively in the UK, Sweden, France, Germany and Italy - contribute proportionately to the costs of the centre. So that none of them would exercise undue influence, the laboratory was located on "neutral" ground, in a country where SKF presence is small. The headquarters in Göteborg, Sweden, reluctantly shifted its research work to the Netherlands along with the other four - a remarkable example of deliberate avoidance of centralisation in one of the key strategic areas of a highly technical business.

The new integration of purchasing, production and sales within SKF's European subsidiaries will have a far reaching effect on the way the group is controlled. At the start of the 1970s the group as a whole produced a range of about 50,000 different types and sizes of bearing. The simple explanation of this variety lay in the fact that each subsidiary, particularly the larger subsidiaries which SKF calls Division A, had complete autonomy to make virtually anything that it could sell. The change away from this system was virtually forced on the company to garner the benefits of scale. The immediate cause of the change was an onslaught of competition from bearings made on large mass production lines in the Far East.

GFSS - the basis of reorganisation

The development of what SKF calls its Global Forecasting and Supply System, or GFSS, is the competitive answer to this challenge. In the SKF context it has meant first and foremost deepening the relationships among the main subsidiaries. Intra group trade has expanded significantly, to more than a third of global turnover. GFSS involves the elimination of duplicated bearings made by separate subsidiaries and the concentration of the high volume lines in one centre of production only. This then supplies the rest of the group. International specialisation within the group, already common among more centrally directed multi-nationals, has involved a number of subtle changes to the SKF method of operation. The GFSS experience, which is planned as a five year programme to be completed by 1978, is more than an interesting study in multinational operation. It can be argued that SKF is the best example of the kind of supranationality that many commentators have predicted as the future of the MNC.

Firstly, there is little doubt about SKF's multinational credentials. The company produces in 33 countries and has its own selling operations in 69. Sales generated by the home companies in Sweden are £190 mn (including exports) of the £746 mn group total, but sales in the Swedish home market are only 9 per cent of turnover. And that figure is inflated by the inclusion of sales of surplus quantities of SKF's own special steels production. For bearings alone, the core of the business, still accounting for three quarters of turnover, only about 5 per cent of the group's output is sold in Sweden.

• At the time of writing a business journalist on the Sunday Times.

SKF is worldwide, but thinks Swedish

This type of overseas dependence is quite typical of multinationals based in the smaller European nations. Of itself it does not dictate any particular kind of management philosophy, but it does tend to lead such companies to adopt a decentralised management approach, while remaining firmly rooted in the country of origin. SKF is no different from many other similar companies in this respect. It is firmly a Swedish company, with a predominantly Swedish board of directors, local auditors and bankers, and the group is evidently susceptible to political pressures from the Swedish government and Folketing. Managerially too, SKF thinks Swedish. In the example of the research laboratories in Jutphaas there was a strong, but minority, voice from the Swedish management, who argued strongly that a tighter central grip should be kept on vital knowledge, by locating the lab in Göteborg, where there was an existing technical facility.

What distinguishes SKF policy over that episode was the fact that the initiative for the transfer of research to the Netherlands came from the subsidiary companies. The autonomy of the subsidiaries was - and still is - based on financial independence and profit responsibility. They originated differing standards and product types demanded by predominantly national engineering customers. But there are degrees of independence within the group. Division A includes the big five European subsidiaries already listed and SKF Industries in the United States. Division S is a group of non-bearing subsidiaries, of which the most important are in special steels and tool sales.

A mini reorganisation in 1975: tidying the outer fringes of the empire

The smaller bearing companies were split into two divisions, B and C, in 1975. This rationalisation separated the more self sufficient operations in Argentina, Brazil, Mexico, Canada, South Africa, Yugoslavia, and Iran, into Division B. The remaining group is a more highly coordinated one, including Austria, Chile, and Belgium, whose worldwide sales are handled by a divisional sales company. Individual operating units often reinforce their independence by the existence of minority shareholdings, usually in the hands of customers who have been historically linked to particular production centres now in the group. RIV-SKF in Italy for example is only 66.7 per cent owned, with Fiat interests holding the balance. The US operation is 96 per cent owned, Germany 99.9 per cent and SKF-CAM in France only 81.3 per cent controlled.

Added to the diverse history of many of SKF's overseas companies is a differing pattern of specialisation as each followed its own line of market development. The automotive sector is a key area throughout the group accounting for a fifth of total sales. Heavy bearings are another important speciality. The Swedish company has developed types for mining machinery, for example. Railway rolling stock is another strong point, but particularly of the German company. RIV was acquired in Italy in 1965 and more recently Sarna in France (1975) to bolster the position in aerospace engine bearings. These specialisations have been a fundamental aspect of SKF's development which are being retained in the recent product rationalisation programme.

SKF was faced with a lack of a mechanism for rationalisation -

As explained previously, the company wide range was about 50,000 bearings at the start of the 1970s. The problem was that within the company there was no mechanism for rationalisation or elimination of overlapped products. Coordination of budgets and financial results worked well, however. Technical matters receive a highly organised airing through a hierarchy of committees, both national and international, coordinated centrally. The so called Machinery Committee plays a crucial role in determining the means and methods of production.

Management is kept on its toes on everything from raw materials to quality testing. Centralised planning keeps an over view on all investment.

But decisions are still taken locally. Finance is raised locally. Investment in line with the development of export markets and the local GNP goes ahead automatically. A cardinal SKF principle seems to be never to take from Peter to invest in Paul. Another is to respect local sensitivity to allowable exports, labour relations, etc. All multinationals claim something of the sort, but few go to the lengths of SKF. The new GFSS idea is to reduce the whole company bearing range to less than 20,000, with a "core" of 7,000 main ones. Manufacture is being concentrated into the single most economic location in each case. And SKF will cease to produce small quantities in several subsidiaries and import instead. Such proposals, for this organisation, are revolutionary indeed.

GFSS grew out of an analysis of the actual sales of each bearing across the company in 1972. This document, called the ABC analysis, became the basis for assessing the profitability of each of the existing products, a decision base for plans to meet the growing competition from Japan. Each of the five European Division A subsidiaries agreed to coordinate a rationalisation programme in 1972. They agreed to set up a committee, to meet once a quarter, made up of the managing directors of each of the five companies and production executives from HQ. Again after a discordant discussion a neutral site was selected, in Belgium. This time the choice of location was useful. A potential hazard of the programme was that it involved sharing out markets and production by subsidiaries. The Swedes were concerned about EEC antitrust and competition laws. Normally these rules leave the internal operations of multinationals strictly out of consideration. The closest they have come to the opposite course are certain cases involving independent distributorships and the restricted selling area agreements which some multinationals used to impose on such agents. But SKF wanted positive clearance from any future hassle. So on their own initiative SKF cleared the plans with the EEC Commission and Efta secretariat (Sweden is part of Efta and has a free trade agreement with the EEC). The company's interest was made even more acute by an antitrust attack in the USA on SKF's European acquisitions. This action in 1974 reinforced the decision to eliminate SKF US from GFSS.

- but equal group relationships had to be preserved

The plan as it evolved demonstrates a typical care to preserve equality among the participants. For a start it was agreed that companies would be free to continue making their own specialities specifically for their own markets, independently of the GFSS plans. This required defining a "speciality", but,beyond and above that, two guiding principles were enshrined. Each GFSS company would retain its relative share of total production; and optimum use would be made of each partner's knowledge and technical resources. In the Göteborg headquarters, where the planners responsible for drawing up the detailed programme and for monitoring its implementation are to be found, they put their objective more simply. No jobs, and where possible no profits, are to be transferred across frontiers under the GFSS process. Each of the five major operations retains a global sales responsibility for the bearings it produces.

By the middle of 1978 a complete overhaul of the manufacturing programme of the five companies responsible for producing 88 per cent of the group sales will have taken place. The switch is already 80 per cent completed, as of autumn 1976. All production of deep groove ball bearings is now concentrated in Göteborg, for example. In future no bearing will be made in more than one place. On the really high volume lines, on products like electric motors, which are in the biggest slump at the moment, the same type of bearing will be produced in different factories but each size will be made in one spot only. Work in progress has already been halved by the process but the effect has been masked because so many of the subsidiaries are manufacturing for stock in the present recession. The decision to push the programme ahead during a recession was deliberate, with a view to minimising any disruption of deliveries due to changeover problems.

It is clear that a major overhaul has been in progress throughout the European operations of the company. GFSS is not just a means of integration. It has only been made possible by a switch in bearing manufacturing economics. SKF used to make bearings by batch methods. A major five year investment programme has reequipped the major factories for continuous production. Two complementary new techniques were developed which the company calls Permaline and Flexline, the first making only individual standard bearings, the second being capable of turning several differing sizes. Since the company image concentrates on offering a quality product, the key to the switch has been an improvement in at least some of the technical performance aspects of the new mass produced bearings, at perhaps a small sacrifice in overall running accuracy. It certainly has been the case that the customers used to a highly customised product have not welcomed the attempt at standardisation. Some, particularly in the UK and Sweden, have made full implementation of the GFSS plans rather awkward.

It is the nature of such a project that the implementation becomes progressively harder. The first 10,000 low profitability product candidates for scrapping were identified easily. A technical review of 45,000 products produced a list of 20,000 more or less redundant bearings. Several low sales items can be found in the remaining 25,000, but are retained for what is euphemistically described as "commercial reasons". Getting down to a "basic" product range of about 7,000 will be very difficult. By the end of 1975 the original plan was 58 per cent implemented, and it is now more than three quarters done. One of the immediate problems is that, increasingly, it is significant sales items that have to be brought into the system. 1975 was also the first year when meaningful commercial operation was conducted with the new system alongside the more traditional activities of the individual companies. No positive cash flows have emerged yet, and, perhaps not surprisingly for SKF with its lack of past experience in international manufacture and coordination, the system has not worked smoothly and flexibly, but jerkily, and with some considerable complaints by the sales forces. Savings consequently have not matched expectations, though in a sense they were not expected to in the early days.

The system is coordinated on a day to day basis by an executive counterpart to the five managing director committee, the Forecasting and Supplies Office located in Brussels. All materials flow through to stock keeping and finished products at the five companies are now controlled centrally by the FSO. This computer coordinated agency now links data from the manufacturing and sales companies. In addition there is a link with a key Export Agency in Sweden which controls all sales to SKF outlets outside the five countries. The agency, at the Göteborg headquarters, is, the company admits, of equal status in GFSS to the five operating companies. Planning is based on estimates of demand from these six members, plus data on available manufacturing capacity located at Göteborg headquarters. The centre has in its hands the means to take factory loading decisions affecting all the federation of companies. The FSO computer plans regular manufacturing and stock shipment schedules for the 85 per cent of the range that represents standard bearings, obviously to increase SKF's ability to deliver ex stock. This is very important in the current recession, as a high percentage of sales are going into replacement markets rather than original engineering manufactures. The whole optimisation programme is in fact located in a new 1975 group subsidiary, SKF Data, based in Göteborg, which holds all the data on company operations. The process works on monthly and quarterly cycles.

Jacques Dubost, the industrial director of SKF-Clamart in France, admits frankly that the continuous computer updating leads to far too many changes in manufacturing rhythm, and has therefore proved expensive. The experience is particularly relevant because at the

Fontenay le Comte factory a new automated production line has taken over from the old batch plant. The Swedish sales director is most happy with the fact that it is now possible to go to a store with an order and purchase ex stock, leaving the FSO computer to adjust manufacturing. Increased availability and improved operating economies have been made on the high volume lines now in production. Experience is much lighter on the interface between the old and new systems for bearings produced in intermediate quantities. In many ways the subsidiary which has progressed furthest with the system is at Schweinfurt in Germany. Perhaps because the market pressures were greater, earlier, this company, the largest entity in the group (25 per cent of sales), has reduced its basic range to about 8,000 bearing types already. But perhaps it is the Swedish company which has had the most favourable experience. Traditionally the HQ has benefited from a larger share of export business than the rest of the group. Göteborg has about double the export proportion of the rest at 66 per cent of sales. In 1975, thanks to the GFSS programme, exports accounted for 80 per cent of sales, and the parent company was the only one in the group to maintain its level of production, from a completely new automated production line facility opened in 1974.

A byproduct of the new integrated manufacturing plan is that it has increased group sales in Europe, largely through the effect of increased intra group trade as described earlier. The expansion of the EEC in 1973 and Sweden's association with it by free trade treaty were undoubtedly contributory factors in the GFSS decision. Britain as a member of both Efta and the EEC was a key market for the new strategy and in fact has been closely involved with the GFSS, although it is less than half the size in sales terms of any other of the big five. Rebuffed in its attempt in the early 1970s to rationalise the UK bearing industry in order to meet the Japanese challenge, SKF decided on an investment expansion at Irving, Scotland, and Sundon, near Luton. The old plant at Luton was closed down and production switched to new GFSS production lines. The commercial results in Britain have been disappointing. Though GFSS sales trebled in 1975, the programme is a heavy loss maker. The performance would have been worse had it not been for the international exports and intra group deliveries of the GFSS range. But a long term commitment to the UK was demonstrated at the end of July 1975 when SKF successfully bid for the Sheffield Twist Drill company.

It is clear from the foregoing review that a radical change has overcome the federated multinational SKF. Decision making still has a federal form, with a whole hierarchy of committees of international executives and key HQ personnel together managing both day to day and long term operations. The internationalisation of the process was enshrined in a famous 1967 decision by the company chairman, Folke Linskog, to make English the operating language for all executive activity in SKF.

The federal decision process of the future

The process of integration has been going on quietly for four years and is still not complete. Changes have been far reaching. As a direct result of GFSS a new organisational and personnel policy had to be designed. That was completed in 1975 and from now on all decisions in this area will be taken in conjunction with central staff. Financial integration is progressing with a special subsidiary, SKF International in Göteborg, responsible as a cash clearing centre for four fifths of all internal SKF transactions for 30 group subsidiaries. If SKF has eschewed transfer pricing policies that discriminate between subsidiaries, as it claims, then it has not given up managing its foreign exchange transactions to maximum advantage. SKF is learning to cope with increasing confidence with running a more centralised international operation. And though SKF remains unique, even in Scandinavia, its new operating philosophy develops the idea that multinational companies could all one day become supranational federations. SKF's centrally coordinated, federal decision taking is an object lesson in how such a system works in practice.

The Multinational That Wanted to be Nationalised

MALCOLM CRAWFORD and ROGER EGLIN●

No.1 1976

To all outward appearances, the arrangement between the Chrysler Corporation and the UK government which enabled the former to continue manufacturing in Britain, instead of shutting down and liquidating Chrysler UK as John Riccardo, chairman of the parent corporation, threatened to do, was a remarkable achievement on Riccardo's part. The Detroit News called it "a triumph of negotiation", which it said "established Riccardo's leadership". The New York Times commented that the deal protected Chrysler Corporation from future losses. Chrysler management, in announcing the agreement on December 19, declared that "the agreement is a good one, not just for Chrysler and the people of the United Kingdom, but especially for the employees, dealers, suppliers, and customers of Chrysler UK".

In the end, instead of a liquidation which would have more or less forfeited total assets of £170 mn at book value, plus redundancy payments and other liquidation costs, Chrysler Corporation retains full ownership of the UK subsidiary, subject only to 50-50 sharing of any profits that may be earned in years up to and including 1979. To assist Chrysler UK to return to profitability, it will receive £90 mn in government (or government guaranteed) loans and up to £72.5 mn in grants in aid of losses.

Chrysler's financial weakness gave it bargaining strength

It is commonly written that multinational companies threaten the sovereignty of national governments through their financial power, their ability to shift production among countries, and their ability to influence decision makers in the host country. What strikes one immediately in the case of Chrysler's crisis in Britain is that an American multinational company which, while middling large, was financially weak - indeed, in severe straits - succeeded in achieving what it did mainly because of its financial weakness. Had it been in a stronger financial condition, it would not have been able to mount a convincing case for UK government support. It was Chrysler's inability to earn profits either in Britain or in the US that placed the government in the awkward position in which it found itself, and which led it with great reluctance to rescue the firm's UK subsidiary.

Domestic British companies in shaky financial circumstances have also been rescued from disaster. One would not have expected that being part of a foreign owned multinational group enhances a firm's chance of this sort of treatment. Chrysler's multinational character did however affect both the company's objectives in the affair, and the final outcome.

Chrysler UK has made more losses than profits –

Since Chrysler took over the deeply troubled Rootes Motors in 1964, consolidating its ownership in 1967, its financial performance has been erratic, culminating in a sharp deterioration during the recent industry wide crisis. In the ten years to mid 1975, Chrysler UK incurred losses aggregating to £58 mn, while in good years profits totalled only £10 mn. Even in 1973, the British car market's last boom year, Chrysler could manage a pre tax profit of no more than £3.7 mn. The report on the motor car industry in the UK published in December by the Central Policy Review Staff (CPRS) (the so called Think Tank) shows that on the measures of return on shareholders' funds, on capital invested and on trading assets, the performance of Chrysler UK was significantly worse than that of any of its major European or Japanese competitors, and much worse than that of Simca, Chrysler's affiliate in France. In terms of market share, between 1971 and December 1975, Chrysler UK's share halved from just over 10 per cent to 5.1 per cent.

● Industrial editor of the Sunday Times.

Chrysler's output in the UK has never risen to a level sufficiently high to keep the two major car assembly plants, Ryton and Linwood, fully employed. Between them these two plants produced 220,079 cars in 1964. It was not until 1970 that production again approached this 1964 total. In an industry growing on a Europe wide basis by as much as 10 per cent or more a year until the recent crisis, Chrysler UK car output was still only 265,000 in 1973 and fell to 227,000 in 1975.

Exports to Iran of cars in CKD form (completely knocked down) have been very important to the company, since 1974. CKD sales in 1974 were some 90,000 units. In 1975, Chrysler exported 102,000 units CKD to Iran alone - underlining Chrysler UK's dependence on this business, which accounted for 10.8 per cent of the total value of British car exports. Chrysler had planned to increase sales to Iran to 220,000 units by 1977. The CPRS has questioned the long term future of this business, however, suggesting that there will be a big increase in local manufactured content and that the Iranian company, INIM, may procure supplies from elsewhere in Europe.

Simca's financial position has been rather better. In recent years, the company has been able to finance its own operations, but both companies have been suffering from an ageing model range and a failure to establish models on an integrated basis, as Ford of Europe has done. The last attempt to achieve this was with the Chrysler 180. Chrysler originally planned to make this in France and Britain. For a variety of reasons, including the poor productivity record in Britain, the idea of UK manufacture was dropped. Again, original plans laid down that the Simca Alpine would be made in the UK and France, and these were shelved, to be resuscitated in the rescue operation, in the form of manufacture in France and assembly in Britain for the UK market.

- and the US parent has been in financial trouble

Nor in recent years has the US parent been in a position to underwrite unlimited losses incurred overseas. Last year the US corporation lost $259 mn, following a profit of $52 mn in 1974. Its survival has been openly debated, especially as this is the third financial crisis the US company has undergone since the start of the 1960s - thus promoting speculation that Chrysler is the "marginal" company, capable of making profits only during market upswings. At the end of the third quarter of 1975, Chrysler Corporation's short term debt amounted to $446 mn - better than the $619 mn at the end of 1974, but still worse than the $326 mn debt at the mid point of 1974. The recent labour troubles at Barreiros in Spain and the uncertain future for this plant have aggravated the parent company's present difficulties. Fears about the political stability of Spain appear to have been a significant factor in the Ford decision to produce the Fiesta at other European plants as well as at Valencia, and these considerations may have weighed substantially with Chryslers too in the outcome of its confrontation with the British government.

Chrysler took the initiative in bringing the issue to a head

The first signs of UK government interest in Chrysler's immediate problems came in mid summer 1974. At that time, the company's name was added to the Whitehall list which is intended to give early warning of potential "lame duck" situations. But there is no evidence of any high level contact between the company and the UK government in the period immediately after this. Nor is there any sign that efforts were made to mount contingency plans, either to aid Chrysler in the event of a shut down or to mount an emergency programme of job creation in the Linwood area.

Table 1

Chrysler UK Financial Performance

	Pre tax profit or loss (£ mn)	Pre tax return on net worth (%)
1964[a]	1.6	3.9
1965	-2.5	-4.7
1966	-3.4	-5.8
1967	-10.8	-18.4
1968	3.7	6.2
1969	0.7	1.1
1970	-10.7	-15.3
1971	0.4	0.6
1972	1.6	2.5
1973	3.7	6.3
1974	-17.7	-34.2
1975[b]	-15.9	

a Strictly speaking. 1963-64. Only 1974 figures correspond
with the calendar year. b Six months.

Table 2

Chrysler UK and Subsidiaries Consolidated Statement of Net Earnings

	13 Months ended Dec 31, 1973 (£'000)	12 Months ended Dec 31, 1974 (£'000)
Sales	322,192	313,275
Other income and (deductions). net	223	(1,229)
	322,415	312,046
Cost of products sold, other than items below	294,699	302,730
Selling and administrative expenses	15,191	16,063
Depreciation of property, plant and equipment	5,187	4,176
Amortisation of special tools	1,960	1,719
Exceptional item	(1,103)	–
	315,934	324,688
Operating Loss (1973 profit) before interest and taxation	6,481	(12,642)
Interest paid, less interest received	(2,998)	(6,168)
Non-operating profit	241	1,076
Loss (1973 profit) including minority interest before taxation	3,724	(17,734)
Taxation	(26)	(60)
Minority interest in net earnings of a subsidiary		60
Net Loss 1973 profit	3,750	(17,734)

After receiving this amber light signal from Chrysler in the summer 1974. government attention was distracted by the more immediate needs of British Leyland. But in January 1975. concern about Chrysler was mounting. Wedgwood Benn. then secretary for industry. wrote to Riccardo asking about his intentions. The next day. Wilson himself dined with Riccardo in London and then flew to Washington where he discussed the position of Chrysler with a surprised President Ford.   At this point. Wilson must have felt reasonably optimistic.

because he gave a reassuring statement in the Commons on the Friday. But the question
of UK government money had already, apparently, been mooted. During the May 1975 strike,
Wilson exploded in the Commons: "I am not prepared and the government is not prepared for
one moment to contemplate the use of one penny of taxpayers' money, or money borrowed
by the government, to gratify that kind of politico industrial ambition."

Again there was a lull until government's expression of surprise at Riccardo's Detroit press
conference at the end of October, 1975. On November 3, Riccardo and five other Chrysler
directors dined with Wilson, Eric Varley and Edmund Dell at Chequers, a meeting switched
from Downing Street because of fears of trade union demonstrations. At this meeting,
Chrysler's line was apparently bleak: the company would have to pull out of Britain. It
offered the government its UK operations. Riccardo also offered an alternative, whereby
Chrysler would retain its UK affiliate, if provided with a substantial sum from the government. Press reports of the figure here ranged from £100 mn, initially, to £450 mn during
the subsequent fortnight. Varley asked the Industrial Development Advisory Board (IDAB)
to comment. During the next few days, a Cabinet sub committee of ministers and officials
was formed by the prime minister to explore the various options.

Initially, the issue was withdrawal and how to cope with it

The discussion, however, still centred mainly on how to cushion the impact of Chrysler's
withdrawal. During this period, the possibility of submerging Chrysler UK into British
Leyland was explored, and dropped after meeting opposition from BL's senior executives.
What hopes remained were at that stage centred on the Iranian contract and the commercial
vehicle business, the general presumption (outside Scotland) being that the rest would be
allowed to close.

The warning from the IDAB on November 17 that Chrysler UK's prospects looked gloomy
did not surprise those involved in the negotiations. Varley was later to tell the select
committee, in what was certainly an understatement, that the IDAB "had doubts and reser-
vations and recognised the risks". After another meeting with Riccardo, the government
was steeling itself to take a tough line with Chrysler. Wilson warned the Commons on
November 25 that "we have a long way to go before we can hope to save any bit of Chrysler".

Scheme B - Chrysler to manage a state owned company

At that time, what came to be known as Scheme B was evolved by the Department of Industry,
with some prodding from the Scottish Office. This was a variation on Chrysler's offer to
"give" the government Chrysler UK. Under this plan, Chrysler would manage the remnants
of a slimmed down operation under a management contract. Chrysler offered to put in
£35 mn - against which Varley estimated total liabilities of £170 mn (without deducting
realisable assets). This figure implied, incidentally, that Chrysler UK was verging on
technical insolvency - or would have been had not Chrysler Corporation just put in £20 mn
in fresh capital.

Under Scheme B, the UK company, with car production centred at Linwood, engines being
made at Stoke and commercial vehicles in Dunstable, would be nationalised by the government. The attraction of the plan was that it would save the Linwood plant, and most of the
profitable commercial vehicle output, and would also save the Iranian contract. And, of
course, the act of nationalisation would appeal to Labour's left wing.

Table 3

Chrysler UK and Subsidiaries Consolidated Balance Sheet

	Dec 31, 1973 £ '000	Dec 31, 1973 £ '000	Dec 31, 1974 £ '000	Dec 31, 1974 £ '000
Property, plant and equipment		37,348		33,141
Unamortised special tools		7,084		6,777
Investments		534		1,296
Current assets				
Balances at bank and cash	3,532		2,509	
Debtors and repayments	22,962		21,015	
Amounts owing by subsidiaries	–		–	
Amounts owing by fellow subsidiaries of Chrysler Corporation	11,879		9,502	
Inventories	77,682		93,635	
	116,055		126,661	
Less				
Current liabilities				
Bank loans and overdrafts	19,285		33,527	
Short term notes payable	1,000		9,000	
Trade creditors and accruing charges	56,263		60,073	
Amounts owing to subsidiaries	–		–	
Amounts owing to Chrysler Corporation and fellow subsidiaries	13,662		6,300	
Current portion of long term debt and deferred liabilities	10,453		6,631	
Accrued interest on long term debt and deferred liabilities	349		325	
Taxation payable	363		121	
Provision for foreign exchange adjustments	132		132	
	101,507	14,548	116,109	10,552
Net capital employed		59,514		51,766
Financed by				
Share capital		33,742		33,742
Share premium account		13,330		13,330
Reserves		201		560
Accumulated loss		(4,574)		(22,308)
Shareholders' interests		42,699		25,324
Long term debt and deferred liabilities		16,815		26,128
Minor adjustment in net assets of a subsidiary		–		314
		59,514		51,766

Several variations upon Scheme B were considered. One was that Chrysler would retain a 20 per cent interest in Chrysler UK. In terms of capacity to be retained, a shrunken version was considered, which would include only the Iranian contract (presumably concentrated at Stoke, Coventry) and commercial vehicle production. This would have retained a work force of only 6,000 out of 25,000.

Clearly, large sums were required from the government, whether nationalisation or rescue of the operation under existing ownership was the chosen solution. The variants that included saving Linwood as well as Stoke would have involved substantially larger financial commitments from the government than the £100 mn which was the bottom figure leaked early in the negotiations. It is possible that the £100 mn represented the grant or grant equivalent element in a larger package of soft loans and loss funding, however – in which case it closely resembled the deal ultimately agreed.

The nationalisation proposal: doubts about Chrysler Corporation's likely methods

The notion of paying Chrysler such sums to induce it to continue in Britain was rejected by the Cabinet in November, mainly out of concern that the money would be applied directly or indirectly to Chrysler's international solvency problems without assuring a continued presence in the UK on any substantial scale. Negotiations therefore focused on nationalisation, which was in any case politically less repugnant to ministers than supporting an ailing foreign multinational.

Nationalisation within a British Leyland framework was obviously the most attractive formula, and, had BL been capable of the job, the precedent of the absorption of Associated Electrical Industries into General Electric in 1967 was encouraging. There were however two fundamental obstacles to BL "doing a Weinstock" on Chrysler UK. One was that BL management was already fully stretched with its own internal problems. Another was that whereas Arnold Weinstock had been free to close AEI's worst plants and reorganise its best ones, Chrysler UK did not readily present such possibilities. The Stoke plant – the least modernised of all the major Chrysler factories – was essential to the Iranian contract, while the top political priority was Linwood which, while fairly modern, had the worst track record in labour relations and (so far as one can tell) of low productivity. Ryton, the most modern car assembly plant in the UK at the time, might have been attractive to BL, but the latter's management refused to consider acquiring even that, for fear of possible repercussions on labour relations in their own plants whose future might consequently be jeopardised.

Nationalisation, with Chrysler continuing to manage whatever remained of its UK affiliate, presented different difficulties – quite apart from the cost to the government in capital outlays. Even with a 20 per cent stake (and even more so with none) Chrysler Corporation would have had little incentive to earn profits in the UK. To maximise group profits, it would have to load the UK end with the least profitable elements of an integrated European business. It would have been provided with powerful incentives to shift profits elsewhere by transfer pricing, and to use its dealership system to sell cars from plants abroad. Its relations with its government partner would have been uneasy at best. The government could had had an unlimited commitment to underwrite losses. That it would have possessed two competing state owned car companies, an objection cited by Varley in testimony to the select committee, was not in itself a serious argument against a state takeover; but the government would thereby have become politically committed to providing continued support to the operation even if the worst happened and losses continued to escalate; and this must have been a critical deterrent.

Civil service opposition to a major rescue

The Treasury and the Department of Industry were both opposed to any major rescue programme - the Treasury for reasons of expenditure control, and industry officials because
they had with some difficulty succeeded (they thought)in shifting the main thrust of industrial
policy away from the support of what Peter Carey, the second secretary responsible for the
policy, called "permanent pensioners",   towards one of selective assistance
to firms deemed viable on a criterion of long term profitability. Indeed, it is likely that the
government ignored the symptoms of impending collapse (before November) because both
the industry department and the National Enterprise Board regarded the demise of Chrysler
not only as a necessary reduction in the industry's alleged excess capacity, but also as
offering scope for British Leyland to increase its share of the market. The NEB chairman,
Lord Ryder, expressed resentment (November 28) when he found that the government was
beginning to change its mind.

The government's change of mind

Three principal factors influenced this change. One was the increasing pressure from
Scottish MPs, culminating early in December in threats by the secretary of state for Scotland, William Ross, and his parliamentary secretary, Bruce Millan, to resign unless
Linwood was rescued. In addition, the Department of Employment prepared estimates of the
consequential unemployment of about 50,000 for one year after closure, rather than the
25,000 which ministers had at first assumed to be involved. This higher figure led to an
estimate of extra benefit payments of £100 mn to £150 mn falling on the Exchequer. The
latter figure, which was the one given publicly, has been disputed (there are, logically, some
indirect offsetting effects to consider) but nevertheless they impressed the chancellor,
whose conversion to the ranks of ministers in favour of rescue was crucial. Finally, ministers became rather suddenly convinced that closure of Chrysler would cause a wave of imports. The idea that British Leyland would benefit from shutdown of Chrysler UK could no
longer be sustained, for the situation in BL was becoming worse; the NEB and BL management
were, by the end of November, preparing decisions in response to this, which emerged early
in December in the form of a moratorium on new investment. The 850 Chrysler dealers
would, it was now felt, go over substantially or wholly to foreign suppliers (including Simca).

On the scenario of Chrysler closing, the industry department put to the Cabinet a plan for
import controls for 18 months, along with a recommended running down of Chrysler UK over
twelve months. The controls were to be based in such a way as to affect most severely those
foreign suppliers which had increased their shipments the most in recent years, notably
Japan and to a lesser extent France. Nissan Motors, the manufacturer of Datsun cars, was
approached with the suggestion that it take over the Linwood plant, in which context the
import controls would be an incentive. Nissan declined the offer.

The chancellor, who had come under considerable pressure from abroad over the import
control question, and had given certain commitments, opposed this plan. Harold Lever
took a similar view, and also regarded the idea of a twelve month rundown as impracticable,
on the ground that Chrysler UK sales would slump even further and therefore the cost of
underwriting losses would be impossible to justify, either by Chrysler Corporation or the
government. In any case, Riccardo was adamant that if Chrysler UK had to liquidate,
December 31, 1975,was the deadline.

The Lever rescue package

On December 4, Lever offered an alternative proposal which, after a week of further negotiation (mainly over the loan guarantees and the sharing of losses beyond the first £40 mn)
was finally accepted. The contents of the package are now well known, and were published

by the government as a Declaration of Intent. The government agreed to meet by outright grant the whole of any loss in 1976 up to £40 mn, and half of losses above that to a maximum of £20 mn (i e. total exposure of £50 mn). Half of any loss is to be similarly met in 1977 up to a loss of £20 mn, in 1978 up to £15 mn, and in 1979 up to £10 mn, making the maximum exposure to loss cover £72.5 mn. The government will share half of any profit in any year up to 1979. It also guarantees a medium term clearing bank loan of £35 mn (for seven years at interest 2 per cent above sterling interbank rate) to fund short term loans already drawn to cover the cash flow deficiency in 1975 - towards which the parent company had already injected the £20 mn already mentioned. The government also extended Chrysler UK a loan of £55 mn, of which £28 mn is to be drawn by the end of 1977, and the balance of £27 mn after January 1, 1978. Repayments are in ten equal semi annual instalments after the end of 1985; interest is 12.5 per cent up to 1980, rising thereafter. This £55 mn loan is to finance the introduction of "new models", which we discuss later. Chrysler Corporation guarantees the first £28 mn, but the second tranche will be a charge only on the assets of Chrysler UK. Chrysler does not guarantee to remain in the UK (indeed, Varley said later in testimony to a Commons select committee that it could not possibly have given any such guarantee) but the whole of the £55 mn becomes immediately repayable if Chrysler Corporation reduces its equity interest in its UK subsidiary below 80 per cent.

Chrysler also promises to introduce, for assembly at Ryton, a British version of the successful Simca C6 Alpine, imported (as to about 50 per cent of its value) from France. This development is to be financed by the parent company. A mark 2 version of the Avenger is to be produced at Linwood. The government strongly emphasised the fact that this new pattern of production would integrate Chrysler UK much more closely with other Chrysler affiliates (Simca, in point of fact) implying that this, which does certainly mark a change from past production strategy, augurs well for Chrysler's continued presence in Britain.

Reductions in the labour force were agreed, totalling about 8,250. Of these, 3,000 were to occur at Linwood, 2,500 at Ryton, 2,100 at Stoke, and 500 through closure of a small factory at Maidstone. Shortly afterwards Chrysler agreed with the unions at Linwood to reduce the redundancies there to 1,500, making the total layoff about 6,750.

Was Chrysler serious in its threat to liquidate?

From the beginning of its current troubles, Chrysler management in the US claimed that the currently depressed economic conditions in Britain were the main source of the UK subsidiary's difficulties. This was the main thrust of Riccardo's letter of February 18, 1975, to the then secretary for industry in which he stressed that "the current times are very difficult ... substantial excess average annual capacity ... dramatically reduced markets ... sales of all motor products in the UK are depressed ..." and so forth. He urged the government to pursue "monetary and taxation policies which will stimulate the purchase of motor vehicles". He also made a thinly veiled reference to price control as a disincentive to investment. Despite a passing reference to productivity, there is little to suggest that Riccardo felt greatly concerned about any serious structural defects in Chrysler UK, either in management or plant. A similar outlook is reflected in press conferences given by Riccardo and the Chrysler president, Eugene Cafiero, on October 29 and on December 19 (after the rescue had been announced). In the latter, Cafiero explained the need for redundancies as follows: "These, really, have to do with the current state of the industry in the UK, which is down to about one million units a year from 1.7 mn in 1973, and the penetration of foreign cars". In another answer, Riccardo emphasised that the main problem was to survive the loss in 1975 and that expected in 1976, while Cafiero pointed to expectations of market recovery thereafter "hopefully to at least the 1973 levels, with some improvement in productivity".

All this must raise doubts, not only about the ability of Chrysler senior management to deal with its non-cyclical problems in Britain - problems of which it is surely aware - but also about the extent to which it seriously intended to liquidate the UK subsidiary. The prime minister was sceptical, on the latter point - as he implicitly revealed in his complaint that his government had been "presented with a pistol to its head".

It was bound to make sweeping changes,
but liquidation presented vital problems of its own

A cursory glance at the profit record of Chrysler UK might suggest that its US management would have been not merely serious, but determined, to liquidate its UK subsidiary. It is as certain as anything could be that Chrysler could not have envisaged carrying on Chrysler UK as it was. Model development work had been cut back drastically, so that there were no specifically British models emerging. Any future which Chrysler might have seen for its UK affiliate can only have been as a greatly slimmed down element integrated with Simca, functionally if not in terms of organisation. The Stoke (Coventry) factory, in which little had been invested, was clearly surviving only for the duration of the Iran contract. Doubtless Chrysler wanted to remain in possession of one assembly plant, and to continue making commercial vehicles, which were profitable. But it was undeniably true that it needed financial help to do any of this. And above all, the Iranian contract presented it with a grave problem, for its international reputation would have been irreparably damaged had it repudiated that contract in the course of shutting down in Britain.

Switching this contract to another source was a third possible course. However, the only place in Europe to which the Iranian contract could be re-sourced would be France; and given any recovery in Simca's sales (and these are off to a good start this year) the French affiliate would not have had the capacity, particularly to supply some 70,000 to 80,000 engines to Iran in 1976. Theoretically, the contract could have been re-sourced to the US, but the capital cost would have been very high, as Chrysler does not make car engines in the 1,700 cc range in the US.

Chrysler Corporation would also have faced liquidation costs in the UK. The Economist has reported these at about £120 mn. We cannot substantiate this figure, except to estimate as follows. Chrysler's share of redundancy payments would have been rather less than £10 mn. If Varley's estimate of total liabilities (other than to Chrysler Corporation) of £170 mn is correct, one should set against that realisable current assets of about £100 mn (mostly stocks of cars). What the fixed assets would have fetched in liquidation is anybody's guess. Although it has been reported that liquidation losses would have been offsettable against US tax, Chrysler Corporation did not have a federal income tax liability in 1975, and only a small portion could have been recovered against US capital gains tax, if any. The £120 mn appears high, but clearly there would have been a very substantial net cost of liquidation.

Chrysler management could not have been eager to abandon its UK operations, as some press comment declared. In his press conference on December 19, Riccardo indicated that nationalisation by HM government was what he was aiming at. He said: "We hoped that we could make some meaningful arrangement with the government for them to continue the company. We didn't threaten or want to liquidate ... That was an inescapable conclusion if no other arrangement could be made. But it was our hope that somehow the government could find its way to take over this operation. We pledged our full support, our managerial talent, the technical help, the use of our worldwide distribution network. That's the way the negotiation started, and it took a 180° degree turn to the form that finally evolved."

Nationalisation would have provided a good solution for Chrysler

There is every reason to believe that Riccardo was speaking the truth. He would not have offered the government £35 mn from the parent company, in the latter's strained financial condition, to encourage the government to nationalise Chrysler UK, had he not earnestly desired that outcome. The reasons why the government found nationalisation commercially and industrially unattractive made it best from Chrysler's standpoint. Apart from the instant release of £170 mn of debts, one must consider the ongoing possibility of adding to group profits while in partnership with the government, in the ways described above, which would have exceeded the scope offered by the present arrangement. Moreover, Chrysler would have earned a risk free management fee income from an enterprise assured of long term losses.

While Wedgwood Benn was still secretary for industry, Chrysler would have felt reasonably confident that nationalisation would be the government's preferred course. And although the change of policy after his departure became known before October, Chrysler UK management was fully aware too of the force of a threat of almost immediate shutdown, given the UK unemployment situation and the Iranian contract.

From start to finish, these were the two factors which preoccupied ministers the most - though. unforeseeably and almost accidentally, the problem of import controls turned the balance in the end. The prime minister was especially worried about Linwood, right from the beginning. Only a few days after the talks opened, he said in the Commons on November 11:

> "We are paying special attention to the problems of Linwood. I think that the whole House knows - and knew before there was an SNP (Scottish National Party) member in the House - the importance of Linwood .... We are certainly bearing that in mind as one of the high priorities in anything that we hope - I use the word 'hope' - may come out of our discussions with the Chrysler Corporation."

And on November 25, when the prospects for a solution appeared at their bleakest:

> "We are striving might and main to save the whole operation, if that is possible, and certainly to save Linwood, because of the high level of unemployment there."

Varley worried about the Iranian contract

Varley, although opposed to a rescue on industrial grounds, both as regards the rest of the motor industry and his industrial policy in general, was deeply concerned over the Iranian contract. Both its size as a proportion of total UK car exports, and the possible implications of cancellation upon exports to Iran in general, caused him to seek ways of salvaging this element, in all the various rescue plans he considered. He is even reported to have asked British Leyland to take it over, after BL had refused to take over Chrysler UK. Much of the time spent by his officials on the Chrysler rescue was devoted to the Iranian contract, and the costs and possibilities of re-sourcing it.

The Treasury was rather less convinced of its importance. It does not appear to have believed that the contract was being used to shift profits out of Britain to a co-subsidiary in Switzerland (a charge that has been levelled by Labour left wingers). On the face of it, this view would appear to be correct, because Chrysler UK has no corporation tax liability in the UK to avoid; nor would exchange controls have provided an incentive, assuming that Chrysler Corporation stood ready to meet the debts of its UK affiliate if the worst happened (and the injection of £20 mn of capital by the parent in mid 1975 suggest that it was). However, it is clear that the average price of the CKD units shipped to Iran last year was remarkably low; and the Treasury was aware of this.

On a customs basis, the number of built up cars shipped to Iran last year was 20,000, which agrees with Chrysler's figure for Avengers under the contract. The customs figure for cars shipped CKD was 102,000, compared with Chrysler's figure of 120,000 (scaled down from a target of 150,000). The difference is due to the fact that the customs closes its entries about three weeks before the end of the year. Chrysler is the only UK exporter of cars CKD to Iran. All but an insignificant number (192) of these were in the range of engine capacity 1,600 cc to 2,200 cc, and the average value last year was only £531, compared with £660 for all other exports of cars CKD by the industry in the same range of engine size (mainly Cortinas). Substantially the whole of these were at the lower end of the range, i e. the same or less than the 1,725 cc Hunter engine, so in this respect the figures are comparable. As the Iran contract was not routed through a foreign intermediary, however, it appears that the low prices realised were the result of the contractual terms agreed with (and highly favourable to) INIM, and that they do not reflect transfer pricing.

The remarkable telegram from Teheran

The strange incident of the telegram from Iran, relaying a message from the latter's minister of finance, proves that either Chrysler or the Iranian government (or both) considered Britain to be vulnerable over this contract. The telegram expressed the Iranian government's deep concern over the impact of a possible cancellation of the contract upon financial and industrial relations between the two countries. It is possible that it reflected genuine anxiety on the part of Teheran over disruption of its car import programme - though in that case, it is surprising that it was not sent sooner. It was transmitted on December 10 or 11, just as the Lever solution was being finally accepted in Cabinet. It is also possible that it followed representations in Teheran by Chrysler. In that rather more likely case, it illustrates great concern on the part of Chrysler management over the possibility of having to liquidate its UK affiliate - and perhaps, too, a sense of panic over the government's rejection of scheme B (nationalisation) which it had evidently thought the government would accept.

The telegram came too late to have been decisive in the outcome. The deciding factors were (1) the government's fears that a sudden collapse of Chrysler UK would not only turn 25,000 (or 50,000) workers into the streets (British Leyland had however shed 30,000 workers in a little over a year), (2) even more important, liquidation would increase car imports by perhaps 200,000 a year, and (3) the appearance of a plan which would provide the appearances of reviving Chrysler UK as a going concern, more integrated with the rest of the group, at a cost to the government which compared favourably with the likely cost to the Exchequer of unemployment and other benefit payments. Clearly, in these terms, a solution achieved in December 1975 was more important to the government than one that would be of any lasting benefit.

But can Chrysler UK survive?

The Iranian contract is also an important element in the future of Chrysler UK. Owing to delays in Iran in absorbing kits for assembly (partly due to slippage in commissioning plant for making body trim and other parts) and the existence of some 50,000 kits in stock or transit, shipments in 1976 are expected to fall to about 70,000. This is likely to be greatly exceeded in 1977, subject to any further problems at the receiving end. In 1978, however, the outlook becomes complicated by the introduction of a Mark 2 version of the Peykan which will not only have a much larger Iranian component element, but also a new or revamped engine. According to reports in the trade, Chrysler is planning to supply a Simca engine for the Peykan Mark 2. This would leave very little scope for continued operations at Stoke.

Doubts about the figures –

Varley's shadow on the Conservative side, Michael Heseltine, has publicly claimed that the sums required to launch the promised new models in Britain must be at least twice those outlined in the government's Declaration of Intent. He has documented his estimates with obvious signs of expert advice. Timing appears to be the essence of this matter. The bulk of the first £28 mn of the government loan is to be spent at Linwood, on a face lift for the Avenger (which Heseltine puts at £5 mn) and on a replacement for the Imp, to be produced largely from parts supplied from France. The retooling at Ryton for assembly of Alpines will be financed by Chrysler Corporation, which will inject £10-12 mn for this purpose. As the loss estimate for 1976 of £40 mn to £50 mn is described as including the cost of transferring the Avenger work to Linwood, it may be that all expenditure on that model in 1976 is being treated as current. In that case, the £28 mn of new capital is mainly to finance tooling up for the Imp replacement (designated the 424),which appears credible.

The main strain upon the credibility of the government's figures comes after 1977, when the remaining £27 mn is to cover a new car model and a new truck – not to mention more fundamental capital investment, of which there has been very little for more than two years. Chrysler has also to decide this year whether to increase the UK component element in the Alpines (to be made at Ryton) in 1978, at a further cost to Chrysler Corporation estimated at £23 mn.

One rational element in the new production pattern is the elimination of the curious practice hitherto of producing engines and major sub assemblies for the Hunter in Coventry and shipping them to Linwood for assembly, while producing similar sub assemblies for the Avenger in Linwood for assembly in Coventry. On the other hand, the reduction in the labour force at Linwood of only about 20 per cent, while only the Avenger will be fully manufactured there this year, suggests that the labour cutback there reflects plant under utilisation rather than increased labour productivity. Overall capacity of Chrysler UK will be reduced by 25 per cent (Varley has said) whereas the work force is to be cut by about 27 per cent.

– and about labour relations

Nor can Chrysler's recent labour relations be seen as an augury of permanence. The firm proposed a participation agreement last spring, which was rejected by the employees. Although a crisis such as that which broke in the autumn might have been expected to place the unions in a weak, almost supine position, there was no evidence that this was so, or that Chrysler was minded to react to it if it was so. One might have thought that a reform of the disputes procedure, ideally one involving compulsory arbitration of disputes (as when the shipbuilders were rescued) would have been sought; but no move was made in that direction. At Linwood, the unions successfully reduced the redundancies from 3,000 to 1,500 (fair enough perhaps since Chrysler expected the other 1,500 to be needed by mid summer) and later staged a plant wide strike over a pay anomaly involving a small number of workers. Don Lander, managing director of Chrysler UK, rebuked the Linwood workers rather lamely, with a warning that they were endangering "the jobs of their colleagues in the Midlands", and the management conceded the claim. Offers of voluntary redundancy at Linwood were heavily oversubscribed, and were fully taken up at Stoke.

The Bristol University motor industry research project, headed by Krish Bhaskar, which last year did an intensive study of the industry, has recently run the Chrysler rescue figures through its computer model a second time, and has concluded that on Chrysler's assumptions about market share (a 10 per cent market share to be achieved in 1977 and maintained thereafter) no profit would appear until 1978. Thereafter, profits would amount to only £16-17 mn a year in the two best years. Assuming a 7.5 per cent market share (Chrysler's

132

market share in February 1976 was in fact 4.7 per cent, including imports from Simca) losses would persist through 1978, with barely visible profits in the next two years. Both runs are founded on the optimistic assumption that there will be no further recession in the motor industry before 1981.

Incentive to Chrysler to earn profits in UK will be impaired

While the incentive provided to Chrysler Corporation to take profits in the UK would be greater under the present arrangement than if it were operating the concern on a fee basis, it will be in its interest to transfer profits elsewhere insofar as the resultant losses in the UK remain within the limits of the 50-50 sharing agreement. If by any chance Chrysler return to profit (and does so in the US also) it will have a tax incentive to shift profits out of Britain. The reason is that the 50 per cent government share in the profit would be more onerous to Chrysler than (say) a 50 per cent tax rate in France on profits of Simca, because the former would not be eligible for credit against US tax, whereas the latter will. While Varley said to the select committee that the two government members on the board of Chrysler UK would watch for any signs that profits were being shifted, this was later contradicted by the Treasury official responsible for industrial policy, Alan Lord, who said that it is not the role of such appointees to channel information to the government. The Treasury board member on Chrysler UK would not be a "government nark" he said.

A reassessment by 1978?

Besides the fact that loss cover by the government reduces in 1978 to £7.5 mn, that year is of signal importance in other ways. There is, as already mentioned, the Mark 2 Peykan in Iran, which could bring a quick end to supplies from Britain. There is the problem of raising the UK content in Chrysler UK manufacture of the Alpine, the cost of which is to fall on Chrysler Corporation. Replacement of obsolescent equipment, which has been deferred for the past year or more, will either place a strain upon cash flow, or else be further deferred, to the detriment of production. Since the £27 mn second tranche will not be explicitly guaranteed by the parent company, the government will not be eager to urge it to take it up if prospects look poor. Moreover, since all the credit extended by the government becomes immediately repayable if Chrysler reduces its equity in Chrysler UK below 80 per cent, Chrysler is unlikely to draw and spend the £27 mn second tranche without being very confident that the operation will prove a long term success. For, if in 1978 or 1979 Chrysler decided to liquidate (or bring in a joint venture partner), it would at that point be liable to repay a fruitlessly invested £27 mn (plus, in the event of liquidation, up to about £200 mn in existing liabilities). The end of 1977 would be an excellent point at which to reconsider fundamentals.

The significance of Chrysler's multinational dimension

The extent to which Chrysler's position as a multinational company affected the outcome can only be assessed by comparing the position of a British uninational in the same situation. The firm, when under the name of Rootes Motors, had already been rescued twice. Had it remained Rootes Motors in 1975, the political pressures in Scotland, and the awkward industrial logic of fulfilling the Iranian contract from the most antiquated plant, would have been every bit as difficult for the government. The "pistol to its head" aspect of the affair would therefore not have been the least bit different. And since the Iran contract would have been incontestably a UK-Iran matter, the case for a rescue on this account would have been far stronger than it was with the contract between INIM and Chrysler International.

Table 4

Bristol University Motor Industry Study: Computer Projections, March 3, 1976

	1976	1977	1978	1979	1980	1981	1982	1983
Government plans & Chrysler assumptions								
Total UK demand ('000 cars)	1.250	1.400	1.600	1.800	1.900	1.800	1.600	1.800
Total market share (per cent)	8.6	10.0	10.0	10.0	10.0	10.0	10.0	10.0
Total of built up units ('000)	154	198	224	255	265	260	240	260
Profit & loss account:								
Total revenue	298	380	433	436	433	400	376	402
Total trading profits	10	48	66	76	79	73	62	72
Net profit before tax	-44	-6	6	16	17	11	0	6
Government plans and "pessimistic" assumptions								
Total UK demand ('000 cars)	1.250	1.400	1.600	1.800	1.900	1.800	1.600	1.800
Total market share (per cent)	6.2	7.5	7.5	7.5	7.5	7.5	7.5	7.5
Total of built up units ('000)	125	163	184	210	217	215	200	215
Profit & loss account:								
Total revenue	255	334	378	374	367	347	320	339
Total trading profits	1	31	44	52	54	49	40	48
Net profit before tax	-51	-20	-9	3	3	-2	-11	-7

Study project leader: Krish Bhaskar.

It would not, however, have been possible to save the UK operations by adapting them to assembly of Simca vehicles. This comparatively easy solution would not have been available. Some sort of rescue might have been effected, but the much needed rationalisation could not have been deferred, as it has been. Solutions of problems such as that of Chrysler UK cannot ignore the industry's need for a much greater scale of fully replicative operations. Optimal scale of production is far in excess of the output of any model range in Britain. Bhaskar has concluded that the minimum efficient scale of production in machining operations is a million car equivalents a year (in components machined) and 2 mn in stamping operations. Minimum assembly production is put at 200,000 to 400,000 a year. Assembly operations require less scale than component manufacture, obviously; but, as the CPRS report showed, the British industry compares less favourably with foreign ones in assembly than in component and sub assembly manufacture, probably owing to organisational inefficiency. This does not bode well for a Chrysler solution which reduces component and sub assembly production in the UK while concentrating upon assembly.

Both parties have bought time

Chrysler Corporation did not get what it wanted. It has secured a stop gap arrangement which will probably cover its losses in 1976 and half of any in 1977 (when it might make a small boom time profit), and has been provided a small interest rate subsidy - not as great, however, as that on loans on concessional terms in developing areas, and not great enough to amount to a serious competitive advantage over other producers (though whatever market share it retains will affect them adversely). The loans must be repaid, and unless the use to which they are put can generate positive cash flow and profits, the loan repayments will in themselves comprise for Chrysler Corporation an unattractive aspect of the deal. Both Chrysler and the government have bought a little time; but it is hard to see that the company, in doing so, has gained any advantage.

Editor's note (1980): Chrysler Corporation, again in financial difficulty, sold its UK operations to Peugeot Citroën SA in 1979.

Brown Boveri: Six Years After McKinsey Came

JAMES McARDLE●

No.2 1976

Since the Swiss market is so small, Swiss companies of any substantial size are usually
multinational. Brown Boveri, the Swiss maker of power generating and other heavy electrical
equipment, has long been a classic example. Its German offshoot has for most of its life
been larger than its parent, and because of the nationalistic nature of the power generating
business, Brown Boveri & Company (BBC) has had to let its foreign affiliates have almost
complete autonomy in their national markets. BBC has shown over the years that it is
possible for a multinational supplier of power generating equipment to succeed without a
large domestic market. Nevertheless, in 1970 a thorough reorganisation was started, and
those apostles of centralised management control, the McKinsey management consultants,
were called in to recommend structural reforms for the Brown Boveri organisation.

The reasons for the reorganisation do not leap immediately to the eye from a cursory examination of Brown Boveri's accounts over the years, though it must be said that the interpretation of Swiss company reports raises difficulties at the best of times. BBC management
felt that operating results could be better; that the long standing and probably inevitable
policy of geographical diversification, which involved production of similar products in
affiliates in more than one country, was leading to an unnecessary amount of duplication of
investment; that research and development in particular needed to be centralised a good deal
more than it was; and that there was in general a complex problem in deciding exactly how
to gain what could be gained from the fashionable trend among multinational companies
towards centralised control and structure, in a company whose business and peculiar circumstances defied centralisation.

Whatever was contained in McKinsey's confidential report, it is clear that BBC management
imposed characteristics of its own upon the reorganisation. The company was and remains
deliberate and slow moving; it took considerable time to implement the McKinsey changes,
and is still in the course of evolution. The reasons for this are the very ones that caused
BBC to call in McKinsey in the first place: BBC's international marketing problems and
strategies.

BBC is a "national" company in its various markets

Fundamentally, Brown Boveri must still be identified as a "national" company in each of
the markets in which it operates. Competitors claim that BBC is 'foreign' and is therefore
a higher risk supplier and a strategic threat to the domestic industry. This can be a powerful disincentive to potential customers, most of whom are government owned or else closely
regulated. It is a major reason why BBC's hard won toehold in the US market is under
constant threat, and why its share of US business is disproportionately low, given its international standing.

The BBC companies in Germany and France do have strong local identification built up after
years of genuine independence of management. In Mannheim the company has been operative
since the turn of the century. The French division, Cie Electro-Mécanique (CEM) is even
older. Both of these companies form autonomous profit centre divisions known confusingly
in BBC as Groups, within the new five Group management structure. A third is formed by
the Swiss manufacturing base at Baden together with the former Oerlikon artillery engineering
company and the Secheron factory. The remaining two are the so called Medium Sized Group,

---

● At the time of writing a consultant with the EIU.

with seven manufacturing bases in Europe and South America, and Brown Boveri International, which encompasses the rest. In terms of products, there are five product subdivisions: power generation, power distribution, electronics, traction and industrial equipment. Thus each of the five Groups contains up to five product divisions, depending on its product range.

BBI controls export marketing

Brown Boveri International also performs the function of controlling all export marketing operations. Orders for export are allocated by BBI in Baden to member subsidiaries according to their capacity, and with a view to maximising overall "Konzern" profitability in the light of tariff barriers, costs, exchange rates, taxation, government incentives, and export finance. Exports are allocated to the Swiss manufacturing division on the same basis as to any other, at least in theory. But, presumably because of the presence of the highly successful international sales and marketing organisation in Baden, BBC Baden is geared to a level of demand quite unrelated to the size and type of its domestic market, and its production is remarkably stable. Exports for the whole BBC Konzern are somewhat under 30 per cent of sales, but for the last three years the export performance of the Swiss division has been 70, 70 and 80 per cent of sales.

This cross border selling is the key to BBC profitability, being generally more lucrative than domestic orders. Sales within the EEC area account for 60 per cent of the total, with another 20 per cent in other European countries. This indicates a large potential for expansion in the Americas, Africa and Asia. The heart of the business is power distribution and conversion (with 19.5 per cent of the Swfr7.7 bn - £1.75 bn - turnover last year) and power generation (21 per cent of the total). Another 20 odd per cent is accounted for by industrial and transport goods. Household and professional products are a meagre 4.5 per cent.

BBC damps the cycle through geographical diversification

Brown Boveri is thus heavily weighted towards the capital investment side of electrical engineering, and therefore must expect to be affected by investment cycles. Geographical diversification rather than product diversification is the key to company stability. Last year the German subsidiary, which accounts for 45.5 per cent of sales and 41 per cent of group employees, increased its sales by 15 per cent and its order book by a huge 55 per cent. None of this improvement was apparent in either the French group or the Spanish subsidiary, both of which lost money in 1975. A good deal of manufacturing overlapping still occurs because of the geographical organisation. This is judged to be inevitable given the political nature of power generation. In the major European markets, substantial domestic capacity is the prerequisite for major contracts. Hence it is possible for different parts of the company to experience quite different trading results. The barometer for the whole organisation, however, is the Swiss division or Group. This had sales in 1975 of Swfr1.76 bn, of which Swfr1.4 bn were exports. This represented a rise of a fifth, but it always has to be borne in mind that the strength of the Swiss franc means that BBC's results are understated. In 1974, sales in Swiss francs registered a rise of only 3 per cent. They would have been 18 per cent higher under a constant exchange rate - that is, if exchange rates in all countries had remained at their 1973 cross rates.

BBC is prevented from expanding employment in Switzerland

This financial peculiarity of Swiss multinationals affects BBC. In 1973 the company was asked by the Swiss government not to expand employment in Switzerland. Major investments in future had to be outside the country. Over the years this will necessarily increase the weight of the German and French divisions - although under the McKinsey structure they only have one seat each on the six man Konzern Managing Committee (one for each Group, plus a man

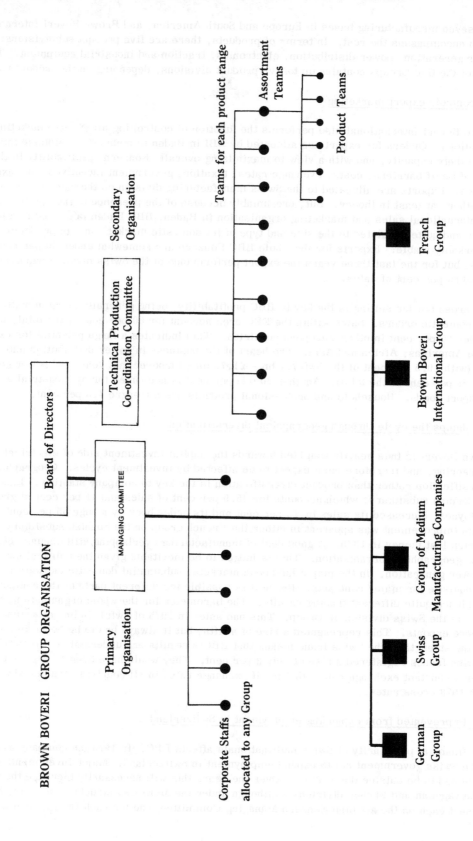

BROWN BOVERI GROUP ORGANISATION

Board of Directors

Technical Production Co-ordination Committee

MANAGING COMMITTEE

Primary Organisation

Secondary Organisation

Teams for each product range

Assortment Teams

Product Teams

Corporate Staffs allocated to any Group

German Group

Swiss Group

Group of Medium Manufacturing Companies

Brown Boveri International Group

French Group

for corporate strategy) which is now attempting to centralise all power and decision taking in
BBC. The other four seats are Swiss, i e occupied by Swiss citizens.

The power of BBI in Switzerland lies in its control over exports, although the Swiss manufacturing division is dwarfed by the German subsidiary which is a larger, more integrated
and diversified company. In particular the Germany company incorporates BBC's entry
into the nuclear power business. The influence that may bring to bear is of course tempered
by the fact that this strategic area has not been a conspicuous success. It has 55 per cent
of Hochtemperatur Reaktobau in Cologne, but the other 45 per cent is held by Gulf Energy
Systems, which is rapidly winding down its business after making massive losses on high
temperature reactors. BBC also has 26 per cent of a consortium company with Babcock and
Wilcox of the USA specialising in design and construction of nuclear power stations. This
cooperation with a US partner is important to BBC, which is under great competitive pressure
in the US from Westinghouse and General Electric. BBC has sold generating equipment in
the US to some of the largest utilities such as Tennessee Valley, and American Electric.
But recently competitiveness has been eroded by the upward revaluations of the key European
currencies - not least the Swiss franc - and a US manufacturing base is now an urgent
necessity if BBC is to hold on to a share of the market.

How to tackle the American market: a major problem for BBC

This constitutes a major strategic challenge for BBC. The company does not believe that it
can serve a major market without a major local manufacturing base. It has strong ideas about
quality control and the need for after sales service to maintain a long term market share.
The company has considered opening such a plant in the USA, but the investment is apparently
considered prohibitive, and moreover the market has remained relatively depressed, hardly
encouraging new entrants. New entry is also made much more difficult by the still unresolved pace of technical change, particularly that associated with nuclear power. Brown
Boveri has faced up to this problem many times in the past decade, without finding any
obvious solution. In fact the question has been shelved several times, particularly as US
competition was pushed back in other world markets. The large new business which has
been successfully opened up in the Middle East has provided further grounds for postpone-
ment.

In 1968 the stage seemed set for an arrangement with Rockwell for them to manufacture for
BBC under licence. Rockwell, heavily committed to space and military programmes, badly
needed to diversify. There seemed to be clear benefits on both sides. However, BBC
eventually backed away, not liking the financial terms. Rockwell approached BBC again as
late as 1973, on hearing that the latter was still studying the possibility of manufacture in the
USA, but was rejected. To date there are turbo generator service facilities, but no solution
to this key strategic problem of the US market is in sight.

George Kent provided an entry ticket to the UK -

A happier marriage - from BBC's point of view - was the acquisition in 1974 of 49 per cent
of the equity of George Kent, a major UK manufacturer of instrumentation and control equipment. The firm's capability in industrial control equipment complements the existing range
of BBC products and adds to BBC's all round competitiveness in international markets. It
is less obvious, however, whether this will help BBC gain a toehold in the UK heavy electri-
cals market - which is in any case not one of the most attractive world prospects.

The initial agreed bid was announced in August of 1974. This bid involved the transfer of all
George Kent assets, but excluding scientific instruments companies in which BBC was not
interested. A new company was planned, to be called Brown Boveri Kent. BBC would own
a majority, 53 per cent, of the equity of this company, at a cost of £6.1 mn. While this bid

was approved by the board of George Kent, it ran into immediate political difficulties, occasioned because the Department of Industry had ownership of almost 25 per cent of the company's equity.

Anthony Wedgwood Benn was secretary of state for industry at that time, and strongly opposed the idea of his department becoming a minority holder in a domestic company possessed of valuable technology but controlled by a foreign multinational. We have previously reported (Multinational Business No. 4 - 1974) how the department attempted to encourage a counter bid by the UK owned General Electric Company (GEC). GEC would own 50 per cent of George Kent's equity, the government 41 per cent and the remaining major shareholder, the Rank Organisation, 9 per cent. But BBC, and for that matter the board of George Kent, determined to fight and decided that the labour force should express its views. BBC was able to assure George Kent employees that within the context of a multinational organisation there would be massive export orders and possibly even 1,500 more jobs. At the same time BBC increased its offer on a per share basis and opted for a politically more acceptable 49 per cent of the equity. GEC weakly responded to the BBC thrust by promising George Kent employees that there would be no redundancies in the event of the GEC bid being successful, but with a reputation for ruthlessness arising from its takeover of AEI in the 1960s GEC was not believed. Predictably, in retrospect, the vote went overwhelmingly in favour of BBC. Benn observed that the workers had been properly consulted and voted for the BBC offer. GEC withdrew, and shortly afterwards Rank also capitulated.

- and an international network of subsidiaries

Prior to the acquisition of a controlling interest in George Kent Limited, the United Kingdom was virtually the only major European economy in which BBC did not have a strong manufacturing base, and consequently BBC was hardly represented in the British market. In addition to acquiring a British presence, BBC has assumed the international network of George Kent subsidiaries. These companies are located throughout Europe, the Americas, Australia, the Far East and Africa. Thus, it should be possible to integrate the international George Kent organisation with that of BBC on a European scale at least. The man much concerned with this problem, and with increasing the profitability of the group, is Erwin Bielinski, former executive chairman of George Kent, former head of corporate planning for BBC, and now head of Brown Boveri International, sitting on the Konzern Managing Committee. Bielinski has been reporting directly to the Konzern Managing Committee. However, as he has now become head of Brown Boveri International, George Kent Limited will be incorporated into the Brown Boveri International division and will report to Bielinski in Baden.

Will Brown Boveri Kent attain "Group" status?

The inclusion of George Kent within the BBI division reflects the special role that the company and its various subsidiaries will play in complementing BBC's international capability. Apart from the German, French and Swiss companies which form divisions in their own right, nearly all of the European BBC companies belong to the division of medium manufacturing companies. However, George Kent and its international network require coordination from the centre. Whether Brown Boveri Kent ever develops into a large enough organisation to achieve the status of a BBC division depends upon the policies of expansion and acquisition to be adopted. It is likely that profitability rather than growth is the immediate objective. The post merger strategy of improving productivity and delivery dates is still continuing.

More acquisitions in foreign markets are likely

The severe limits imposed on expansion in Switzerland since 1973, the current high exchange value of the Swiss franc, and the trend that customers demand manufacture, in so far as is possible, within their own national territory, points to a continued policy of acquisition in foreign markets. It is only in recent years that BBC has made a serious effort to coordinate its operations between countries. Prior to 1970 there was very little cross border coordination of product or marketing strategies. Member divisions and companies operated within their national territories independent of any central unifying strategy. Thus, BBC amounted to a loose federation of units with an historically built in duplication of resources to a greater extent than might be justified by market or political necessity. Possibly the protected nature of heavy electrical engineering markets resulted in the assumption at BBC that there was no choice but to allow member companies to function autonomously. However, this fragmentation and duplication of resources necessarily limited the scale of operations of the whole organisation at a time when it was realised that massive amounts of new capital would be needed. The new structure is built around the idea of central control of essentials, such as product coordination, while at the same time preserving the identities, and goodwill, of the major European components.

The new structure

Central to the new structure, following the 1970 McKinsey report, is the concentration of a great deal of power in one executive and policy making body at the summit of the organisation. This body is called the Konzern Managing Committee (KMC). As already mentioned, it is composed of the heads of the five divisions with the addition of one member with special responsibility for strategy. Such a structure may be a McKinsey trade mark but in the case of Brown Boveri it fulfils the additional aim of integrating the jealously independent national subsidiaries into some semblance of a single minded multinational corporation.

Corporate staff departments for research, technical coordination, management development, planning, finance and control, and marketing, supplement the KMC at headquarters. In addition,four Konzern Committees set policy for research, technical strategy, nuclear energy and marketing, but the fact that these committees are each presided over by a member of the KMC probably inhibits their originality and independence.

The KMC is represented at lower levels

The representative of each Group on the KMC is responsible for communicating KMC decisions to the Group concerned. The KMC is represented on the board of each manufacturing company by members or delegates additional to the KMC Group representative. The impression of decisions being handed down in the form of orders is carefully avoided; nevertheless KMC recommendations are usually carried out. It is felt that this is the case not because of the undoubted ability of the KMC to apply pressure, but because it is willing to take a pragmatic view of efficiency within the Konzern and is attuned to the political needs of the subsidiaries.

The management is Swiss dominated. The chairman of the Swiss home subsidiary also heads the six man KMC, which also includes the heads of BBI, the Medium Sized Group, and Brown Boveri technical strategy. These three are also managing directors of the Swiss Group.

A secondary organisation runs through the company

A secondary organisation runs horizontally through the company coordinating product specifications. This secondary organisation is three tiered and is made up of individual product teams, teams for each product range, and a technical product coordination body. These teams are horizontal counterbalances to vertical divisions. The principal function of the members of these teams is to obtain clearance for proposals made by their respective companies so that these can be incorporated directly into annual plans and budgets. Given this motivation it seems unlikely that teams would, on their own initiative, produce proposals for the rationalisation of any product throughout the Konzern. This is why the third layer was set up, in 1974, for "technical product coordination". This body is composed of three corporate staff senior executives and its main objective is to promote R & D and production rationalisation efforts in the product and product range teams. While the product coordination and rationalisation process might appear fragmented it does allow very full discussion. However, outside of the very limited scope of accepted local autonomy, all executive action in the field of product coordination and rationalisation is confined to the KMC.

The divisions negotiate for their share of exports

All Konzern international marketing activities are centred in Brown Boveri International in Baden. The head of BBI is a member of the Swiss dominated Managing Committee; he also chairs the marketing committee, and all corporate marketing staff come under his jurisdiction. BBI has profit responsibility for all activities outside Germany, France, Switzerland, and the Medium Sized Division. It has split this responsibility into four regions: i. Africa and Asia, ii. Canada and Latin America, iii. Europe (including Eastern Europe), and iv. United States of America.

The prime central activity of BBI is the allocation of export orders to member divisions. Corporate marketing staff within BBI decide to which affiliate an export order should be allocated. Allocation is made on the basis described above (see page 131). Each division begins the financial year with an export allocation budget based on their own forecasts. The forecasts are discussed at a meeting of the Konzern marketing committee - each marketing manager negotiating for his share of anticipated exports. This avoids dictation from the centre and enhances the autonomy of the affiliates. Over the years export based growth has, however, resulted in Swiss capacity being out of all proportion to the requirements of its diminutive home market. The allocation process permits the Swiss management to ensure that the Swiss operation benefits from available world demand. Exports by BBC Baden rose from 70 to 80 per cent of its total sales last year - a measure of Swiss "control of essentials". The average figure for the whole Konzern was 29 per cent in 1974.

Once an export order or enquiry is allocated it is the responsibility of the chosen affiliate to tender independently for the contract. Orders received by a division from within its own territory are not allocated at BBI's discretion but remain with the receiving group. It is free to subcontract elements of an order to other Konzern companies though there is no obligation to subcontract exclusively within Brown Boveri. It is interesting to note that since Brown Boveri Kent is part of BBI, contracts obtained in the UK for products outside Kent's capability automatically enter the BBI export pool for allocation, without having to be negotiated.

BBC enjoys a reputation for quality and workmanship of the highest order. The company has established a name with major utility companies in the United States, despite the enormous disadvantage of being foreign. When it rejected Rockwell a BBC company spokesman claimed that "US production standards and trade union practices being what they are, neither Rockwell International nor, probably, any other US firm would have been able to fabricate our equipment up to our traditionally high specifications". This attitude has not endeared BBC to North American manufacturers and no punches have been pulled in attempting to keep BBC out of the USA and Canada. Recently, BBC successfully defended a charge of "dumping" circuit breakers on the Canadian market. BBC went on to acquire the Tamper Electrical Division of Canadian Canron Ltd, making electric motors and generators and drive equipment for industrial plant and rail transport.

Research is centrally coordinated

Research is carried on at two broad levels: pure research and applied product research. In Group terminology, pure research is not divorced from profitability; however, it is in general concerned with fundamentals rather than with specific products. As might be expected, the main Konzern centre for pure research is in Switzerland. Limited research programmes are carried out by BBC Mannheim in Heidelberg and by CEM in Le Bourget, but the Segelhof centre at Dattwil keeps a firm Swiss hand on BBC's technology. The centre opened at the end of 1972. Its conception coincided with the streamlining of the Group's activities and epitomises central Swiss control of essentials.

Product research is carried out in Switzerland, Germany and France independently of pure research, but it too is subject to central coordination. Product research is normally financed by the specific manufacturing unit. Where the product is single sourced this generalisation is easily applied. Where more than one subsidiary is in a position to benefit, allocation of costs and the location and coordination of research is negotiated through a high level research committee. Pure research is financed according to much the same principle; costs are shared according to agreed central estimates of divisions likely to benefit from a particular programme. Predictably, allocation of costs not geared to immediate profit is seldom a cut and dried issue. However, management philosophy, here as elsewhere, incorporates the principal of negotiation. Conflicts in this as in any other area are settled by discussion of national and Konzern interests. Major decisions involving different national interests are, eventually, unanimous.

The centralisation that took place after 1972 increased the scope and scale of research, and the fund for such spending dropped by over a half in two years. It is replenished by royalties income, which more than doubled over the same period to 4.9 per cent of BBC Baden turnover in 1974.

Areas of research at Dattwil include one dimensional metals, permanent magnets, thyristors for high voltages, silicon in the context of high power electronic devices, high temperature materials, ceramics, lasers, liquid crystals in information displays, plasma physics, automatic control theory and super ionic conductors.

The reorganised BBC intends to remain a world leader

BBC is determined to remain one of the major manufacturers of heavy electrical engineering equipment in the world. About 6,000 people are engaged in research and development, on which the company spends some Swfr 450 mn a year. As a result of heavy research investment the company is technologically advanced and in some areas it is a world leader. One such example is circuit breakers for electrical substations. BBC specifications are probably ahead of any other manufacturer in this field - including the North American giants.

Following reorganisation BBC is more able to view the world market as one large oyster rather than as a collection of separate more or less succulent ones. Cross border production and marketing strategies have been established. Duplication of sales and manufacturing capability in different European markets is inevitable given the importance of being able to compete as a domestic supplier. However, multisourcing imparts great flexibility to the overall marketing function. Export orders can be allocated between subsidiaries to maximise advantage to the Group.

The company has a policy of careful acquisition and purchases are made with integration on an international scale in mind. The acquisition of a controlling holding in George Kent Limited is a good example of systematic expansion, since that company's capability in instrumentation and control equipment complemented the resources of BBC's major European divisions. The company is also able to consider selling out of loss making situations. It went a long way down the road to selling its loss making Italian subsidiary before negotiations stalled. The great question surrounding the future of BBC is whether or not the company will eventually set up manufacturing facilities in the United States, come to a licensing arrangement with a US company, or hope to improve on its modest but significant success with the American utilities from its European base alone. In 1974 sales in North America accounted for only 3.5 per cent of the worldwide total and no advance was made in 1975. Latin America and Africa are each more important, while Europe accounted for about 80 per cent of turnover. BBC recognises the importance of the US market; the board held a press conference to say so in 1973. But following a disappointing year in 1975, continuing overcapacity, and a successful shift to selling a quarter of the export order book to the Opec countries, it seems likely that the long term US strategy will continue to get fairly low priority.

Multinational Expertise
is Not Enough; The Sobering Story of Corfam

ANDREW ROBERTSON●

No.2 1975

There is more than a touch of irony in the fact that in 1974 a communist country, Poland, opened a new factory to manufacture a material invented and developed,but unsuccessfully marketed,by one of the largest chemical companies in the capitalist West, E I Du Pont de Nemours of Wilmington, Delaware.

It took Du Pont 18 years and cost an estimated $250 mn to realise that the world did not really need its ingenious synthetic leather, Corfam. Probably the company was a victim of "technology push", the hazardous situation in which science and technology based firms find themselves when they make a discovery in their laboratories which is attractive enough to be worth pursuing through all the phases of the innovation sequence from the initiation of a research and development project to the eventual launch on to the market. Various recent pieces of "research on research" have shown, however, that the majority of <u>successful</u> innovations do not begin with the technology but with the perception of a need. About 70 to 75 per cent of successful innovations in a number of samples began with "need pull".

Research, develop – and watch market

This is not to say that firms should discontinue basic research nor that they should not try to develop and market scientific discoveries. It does suggest that they should, however, pay much more attention to the market implications of the scientific and technical advances which they make.

In the case of Corfam, the R & D appears to have come first, with the development of a number of methods of making microporous polymer films in Du Pont's Central Research Department back in the 1930s. This work appears to have been directed at the packaging market, the textile industry and various forms of coating, but not at that stage the footwear manufacturing industry. Also, according to an article published in <u>Research Management</u> in 1965 (Vol. VIII, No. 1), written by three executives responsible for the innovation, the early work was done in the Newburgh Research Laboratory where there was a factory making vinyl coated fabrics on the same site. In view of the fact that it was shoes made with uppers of vinyl coated fabric which stopped Corfam from becoming economic in the cheaper, mass end of the footwear market, this is a fact worth remembering.

Corfam was expected to follow nylon's "invasion innovation" success route

The work done in the 1930s was not proceeded with as part of the Corfam plan until 1953. By that time Du Pont had experienced the overwhelming success of nylon, the big breakthrough in man made fibres, which also reflected part of the R & D in the 1930s. Nylon was a spectacular example of an "invasion innovation", a new material with superior characteristics to a number of natural and semi artifical fibres in current use. It was far stronger than any of its rivals,including rayon,and was much cheaper than silk, and eventually cotton fabrics too. Its adoption by the textile industry across the world (Du Pont extended a licence to ICI) brought immense benefits to Du Pont and its licensees. There seems little doubt that top management in the company believed that the same would happen with Corfam as happened with nylon: an invasion of the footwear industry that would replace leather.

● Reader at the School of Management Studies, Polytechnic of Central London.

In the Research Management article, which was evidently an authorised version of the story of Corfam up to that date, the then sales manager of the Poromeric Products Division ("poromeric" was a Du Pont coining from "porous" and "polymer"), Charles A Lynch, cites the company philosophy, "that a product must first be new, then serve a purpose, be of value to the user, and fill a need". In other words, the new product was expected to fill a need, rather than there being a need that had been perceived and a new product subsequently developed to meet it.

Leather was identified as the rival, but it was not the main one

In the case of Corfam, Du Pont's economists worked out that there would be a need for a leather substitute for shoe uppers, arising from a predicted shortage of natural leather relative to the growth in world population and the increase in the proportion of people wearing shoes. In these global terms, this projection was neither illogical nor necessarily wrong. At the time of the preparation of the chosen Corfam process for commercial scale application about 1960/61, the US market for all kinds of footwear was of the order of 600 mn pairs a year. This grew to about 800 mn pairs over the next ten years. But every one of the additional 200 mn pairs a year was imported, mainly from Japan and Italy, and the majority of them were with synthetic upper materials, designed for the cheap end of the women's fashion shoe market. This unexpected eventuality did not form part of Du Pont's economic forecast. Indeed, they appeared to be quite unaware, until they were fully committed to the Corfam programme, that non-porous synthetic sheet was the main rival.

Technology push

The sequence of events, in brief, was that in 1953 Du Pont had three industrial departments working on the development of a poromeric based on the research done before the war. These were the Fabrics and Finishes and the Film Departments, backed up by the Textile Fibers Department which was working on the fibre for the substrate. The material structure of Corfam was designed as an analogue to natural leather, with a smooth surface on a porous or permeable base, the substrate. Early versions of the material were three layer: the felted web or batt, made of compacted and needle punched polyester fibres of as fine a count as could be drawn (one to two denier), an interlayer to prevent foot perspiration attacking the surface, and a coating of polyurethane which was coloured and embossed with rollers to give it the appearance of natural leather.

At Du Pont research projects are overseen and evaluated by an executive committee and, in 1955, the appropriate committee ruled that the development work on what was to become Corfam should be concentrated in the Fabrics and Finishes Department. At this point the product was being made on two pilot plants, one in Fabrics and Finishes and the other in Film. The former had a product lacking in acceptable leather like characteristics, while the latter was able to make a similar material but more easily. The official account does not reveal why the Fabrics and Finishes Department won the competition. But there is a telling comment in that account which helps the understanding of Du Pont's predicament. Quoting from the Research Management article we find that "In 1956 and 1957 these materials were field tested, and more thorough consideration was given to where these products might find utility in the American economy". Clearly this innovation was technology push.

Hush Puppies denied one market –

By mid 1959 the company's commitment was almost complete. For one thing the price of leather had reached a new peak. For another, suede had become extremely popular. This was important technically, and appeared to be a brilliant piece of good luck, because a suede or napped finish meant that Corfam could be made more quickly and cheaply by cutting out the coating and embossing stages of the process. Unfortunately, it was at that time that the

146

Wolverine Shoe and Tanning Corporation, makers of horsehide work shoes but facing a shrinking market, decided to plunge on their pigskinning machine. They did a deal with the Chicago meat packers (their home was not far away, Rockford, Michigan) who paid in pig skins for the rent of the machine, capable of skinning a pig carcase without leaving the tallow on the hide. The brand name of these shoes was Hush Puppy. No one at Du Pont will admit that this was the reason for switching the production programme away from napped finishes to coated, but they do concede that "suede is a cyclical market" and they wanted a steady off-take. Anyway, no suede type Corfam was put on the market.

– while the tanning industry responded to synthetic leather's threat –

In terms of production complexity this change meant the addition of two processes, coating and embossing, and contributed to the unit cost of a square foot of the new material, which had been estimated at about $1 to be competitive with leather. There can be no doubt now that the whole research and marketing effort was aimed at replacing natural leather, a threat to which the American tanning industry responded energetically. The latter phenomenon was recognised in principle by S Gilfillan as early as 1935. In his Sociology of Invention he refers to what he calls the "sailing ship effect", the fact that the best and fastest sailing ships came into service after the arrival of the steamship. In this case the leather tanners began to make their leathers have Corfam characteristics – scuff resistance, toughness and durability.

– and a simpler, cheaper product was in the mass market

Yet here was another marketing enigma for Du Pont. Their plan for Corfam was logical. The footwear market would be invaded with this synthetic substitute for upper leather, which had the advantage of being uniform, unlike cowhide which is of an irregular shape and bears the scars of active life. At first it would compete only at the top end of the market but as the market grew and production increased and unit costs fell, it would descend into the lower ranges and eventually replace leather right across the board (except that cheap leather had already been ousted by vinyl coated fabrics at the really low priced end of the market). So as far as the cheap end of the domestic market was concerned, the Corfam plan was nipped both by cheap imports and by synthetic sheet of the kind produced by Du Pont themselves.

An encouraging start, then little growth

Corfam was launched in the United States in 1963, just ten years after the restart of the research programme into microporous sheet. It appeared to have had instant success in the market, selling the equivalent of 1 mn pairs of shoes in 1964, 5 mn in 1965, 12 mn in 1966, 20 mn in 1967 and 40 mn in 1968. After that sales seemed to have reached a plateau, and the domestic market share never reached even 10 per cent.

The international rivals

Nevertheless, competitors for Corfam were already on the market. In 1967 Chemical Week (Sept 23) noted that Goodrich had become a danger to Corfam with its follow up product Aztran. Indeed, there were by that time four American rival materials, four Japanese, one German and one British. The British contender was Ortix from the Fibres Division of Imperial Chemical Industries, hopefully building upon the development work done at Du Pont. The intention seems to have been to try to pip Corfam at the post in Europe.

Du Pont had signalled its punches by making an attempt to launch Corfam in Europe as early as 1967, two years before they realised that the invasion of the domestic market was not succeeding. Conforming with the general plan, the material had been offered to the top fashion shoe makers, such as Edward Rayne in London, but although some of the British manufacturers were willing to experiment, resistance was much tougher in France and Italy.

It is worth noting that while the Germans, the Dutch and the British, as well as the Japanese, made attempts to get into the temporarily attractive market for poromeric materials, neither the French nor the Italians bothered. It does look, with hindsight, as if the shoemakers of those fashion conscious countries were alert to the twin facts that their premium market wanted leather, while the ephemeral fashion conscious low priced segment had no preference for materials but rather for price and style. Asked about this shortly before Du Pont pulled out of the whole business in 1971, one of the chemists in Poromeric Products Division said, a shade wistfully, "we should have asked our daughters".

The mass market did not need Corfam's qualities, nor could it afford them

The hard truth of the market resistance to Corfam at the cheap end seems to have been that the majority of buyers in this price bracket are young women, with little money but a lot of fashion sense. As the shoes which they buy tend to be designed in various "open" styles (better ventilated than men's shoes, said a Du Pont marketing man bitterly) permeability or porosity does not matter, indeed is lacking in any marketing significance. Not only that, but the toughness and durability of Corfam are equally irrelevant. Who wants fashionable foot-wear to last? Most of the pluses built into Corfam became minuses in this unfamiliar market. Perhaps it was the fixation with nylon that blinded Du Pont senior executives to the shortcomings of their amazing Corfam. As we have seen, they were not alone in being misguided. As many as 20 other companies in half a dozen countries followed their lead.

One of the economic difficulties with all the poromerics was their high cost of production. Unlike the vinyl sheet plastic materials, they could not just be extruded, they had to be laid up. The felt or web substrate had to be provided with a protective layer and that layer covered with a coating. Advanced versions of the poromerics were two layer rather than three, but still the unit cost remained higher per square foot than the cost of cheap "side" leathers. It is possible that really high volume production would have changed this cost basis and made the poromerics competitive, but the vinyl coated fabrics prevented that happening.

Shoemakers, retailers and customers found fault with the product

In addition there were mundane marketing problems. Du Pont went to great lengths to convince footwear manufacturers that their new material was going to succeed. They encouraged 200 shoemakers to produce 16,000 test pairs of shoes. These were given to a wide cross section of users in the United States, from hard wearers like postmen and policemen to children and housewives. The researchers and marketing men were satisfied with the results from these user tests. The makers had technical problems, because their machinery was designed to make shoes from soft leather rather than tough, unyielding Corfam. And even when these production problems were overcome, there remained three more obstacles.

One was the retailer, interested mainly in the volume of his sales rather than the material from which shoes are made. The same applies to his sales assistants whose commission depends not on what kind of shoes they sell but how many and at what price. Finally the customer, not particularly keen on substitutes for the familiar leather, especially at high prices, but anxious to have the sort of shoes with which she or he is familiar, to like their looks and to have them fit and feel comfortable.

The cost of not having natural "stress decay"

A characteristic of Corfam which did not come to light until after full commitment (not indeed until 1964) is that it could not be regarded in any real sense as a synthetic substitute for leather, because of its relative coarseness. In 1964, for the first time, the scanning electron microscope, developed in Britain, became available to Du Pont. This device enables the user to scrutinise the structure of a material in complete detail. As soon as microphotographs of Corfam were examined and compared with those of natural leather it was obvious what was wrong. The fibre in natural leather is at least ten times as fine and therefore ten times as soft and pliable as that in Corfam as it then was. To spin manmade fibres down to the fineness of animal hair was not technically possible. The result was that the poromerics lacked an important quality as far as shoe uppers were concerned – they would not "break in". In the words of the Du Pont scientists they had no "stress decay", or in other words would not deform to fit the foot.

Making a virtue out of necessity

In 1964, with sales rising fast, this technical setback was taken in the company's stride. The marketing angle was subtly changed. Instead of Corfam being heralded as a manmade substitute for natural leather in shoe uppers, the line became that Corfam was in many ways superior to leather, not a mere replacement but something even better. This was making a virtue out of necessity. It was a good tactical move but it made little difference to the long term outcome.

There were other, comparatively minor, difficulties. Whereas in the United States it has become unusual to repair shoes, in Europe, at the time when Du Pont made the first attempt to introduce Corfam, 1967 and again in 1969, it was still customary. Apparently no one in Wilmington had paid any attention to this small international difference, but when Corfam shoes went to the cobblers trouble began. When heels or soles have been replaced it is usual to polish the shoe using a high speed rotary brush. The friction of the brush raises the surface temperature to several hundred degrees centigrade, enough to melt the polyurethane coating on Corfam. Shoes came back from the repairer with grooves in the uppers where the brush had destroyed the surface. Feedback on this defect was very slow.

There were other unforeseen problems. Manufacturers, used to leather uppers, forgot that Corfam relied on permeability for one of its unique selling points and lined their shoes with impermeable vinyl. They would line leather with leather or canvas, but this was a plastic, wasn't it? At the same time shoemaking technology was changing, from nailing and stitching uppers to the soles, to bonding them, and from using leather soles to using manmade materials. Again, the result was that quite a number of Corfam shoes went on to the middle range of the market, with bonded and manmade soles, allowing little or no permeability. There had been no serious problems with nylon in the textile industry (except a few, such as photo-disintegration of net curtains, static and discoloration of white nylon with age). Here the invasion innovation was not quite up to it.

The cost of the venture

The competition from native and foreign firms was comparatively negligible. The only leather like material to be marketed internationally against Corfam was Clarino, the brand name adopted by Kurashiki Rayon, Japan. Du Pont, having tried out numerous chemical routes to its poromeric, had also protected many of the more promising ones by patent in the industrialised countries of the world. Their Japanese imitators were caught by one of these and eventually had to pay royalties on the sales of Clarino to Du Pont. But this was a hollow victory. No one but the top management of Du Pont knows what the venture cost the company. When in 1971 they announced to a surprised world that they were withdrawing Corfam, shutting down the plant in Old Hickory, Tennessee, and selling the machines to the Poles, they said that the 18 years had left them at least $100 mn out of pocket. It was known that the launch in 1963 and 1964 had cost $25 mn on top of the R & D investments. Later estimates (unofficial) pushed the probable loss to $250 mn at least and a possible billion dollars. When it is remembered that they invested in a marketing department in Geneva, in a finishing plant at Malines in Belgium and in launches in the major countries of Europe, not to mention their legal costs and the continuous programme of education and service in the United States and Canadian footwear manufacturing industries, a ten figure shortfall sounds at least possible.

The bigger they come, the harder they fall.

VIII. IS MULTINATIONAL ENTERPRISE IN RETREAT?

Foreign Divestment in the Multinational Investment Cycle

The US Experience

PROFESSOR B. D. WILSON●

No. 2 1978

The expansion of foreign operations by the largest US corporations has been charted over the years by numerous studies. The proportion of overseas sales to total turnover of these companies continues to increase. To support this rising stream of foreign sales US corporations have expanded the number of their foreign subsidiaries. But, in more recent years, they have divested substantial numbers of foreign affiliates, and the ratio of divestments to numbers of new affiliates established has increased.

Such a pattern has been charted in previous articles in Multinational Business, particularly by J C Sachdev, using British data (Multinational Business No. 4 - 1975 and No. 3 - 1974). The divestment data from the USA and from European sources appears to follow a predictable pattern. From it a model can be constructed from which interesting implications for the future can be drawn.

In the studies made by Sachdev, not surprisingly, inadequate profitability was found to be the predominant influence behind disinvestment. Among other factors generally but not necessarily specifically associated were: organisational problems within the group (not necessarily involving poor profitability of the affiliate to be divested) and host government relations problems (though in very few cases was an actual expropriation involved).

In this article, Professor Brent Wilson, of the University of Virginia, describes his results from a study based on data arising from the Harvard Multinational Enterprise Study. Professor Wilson finds an inevitable economic logic in the processes which have led to rising disinvestment rates, and relates these to product cycle theory. Disinvestment, he contends, is the logical final stage of the international product cycle, and its increasing incidence is to be expected following the explosion of international investment opportunities in the first two decades after the war.

Endeavouring to document the growth of foreign subsidiaries of US corporations, the Harvard Multinational Enterprise Study[1] has traced the development of the 187 largest US based multinationals through 1975. These 187 firms were selected on the basis of their inclusion in the Fortune lists of the 500 largest US industrial firms in 1963 and 1964, controlling manufacturing subsidiaries in six or more foreign countries in 1965 or before.

The Harvard study documents some 13,795 foreign subsidiaries. From this population it is possible to examine the pattern of exits or disinvestments by US MNCs. Starting at a low level in the 1950s the annual number of exits increased during the early 1960s to a high of 329 in 1967. Since that peak the number of disinvestments has remained relatively constant at about 260 annually. During the whole period from 1951 to 1975, 3,152 subsidiaries were disinvested. These figures do not include exits by means of mergers and company reorganisations. Only those subsidiaries which exited from the parent system by other methods - i e sales, liquidations, or expropriations - were included.

Trends in the data for formation of new subsidiaries and for disinvestment of existing subsidiaries show that US companies may be gradually moving towards a net disinvestment

---

● Assistant professor of business studies, University of Virginia.

1 Data from this study are reported in Curhan, Joan P, et al, "Tracing the Multinationals"; Ballinger Publishing Co, Cambridge, Mass. 1977.

position abroad. The growth of US foreign investment has been very great, as is well known indeed phenomenal. Table 1 shows foreign sales and profits of 16 of the largest US firms in 1977. A study which estimated the sales of 282 majority owned US affiliates is summarised in Table 2, showing continual growth in dollar sales. The chart shows how this sales growth was achieved by the formation and termination of subsidiaries. The peak in net annual growth occurred in 1968 when the stock of subsidiaries was increased by 774. This rate of overseas net subsidiary formation has steadily diminished to 109 in 1975. The ratio of new subsidiaries to exits has fallen from over 10 to 1 in the period prior to 1965 to 1.4 to 1 in 1975. An examination of the data for manufacturing enterprises alone shows a similar pattern to the full data.

Table 1

Foreign Business as a Per cent of
Total for 16 Large US Companies, 1977

Company	Foreign sales	Foreign operating profits
Colgate-Palmolive	56	63
Gulf oil	55	...
Pfizer	53	64
ITT	51	52
IBM	50	45
Dow Chemical	45	35
Coca Cola	44	58
Xerox	44	35[a]
Johnson & Johnson	41	50
Ford Motor	35	44[a]
Standard Brands	34	35
Standard Oil (Ind)	25	27[a]
Du Pont	23	13
General Electric	21	22[a]
General Motors	21	11[a]
Caterpillar	19	10

a Net income.

Source: Business Week, April 24, 1978.
page 129.

Table 2

Sales by Majority owned Foreign Affiliates of 282 US Companies
($ bn)

	1966	1969	1971	1973	1974
Sales	95	150	200	300	450

Source: Chung, William K; Survey of Current Business
February 1977, page 29.

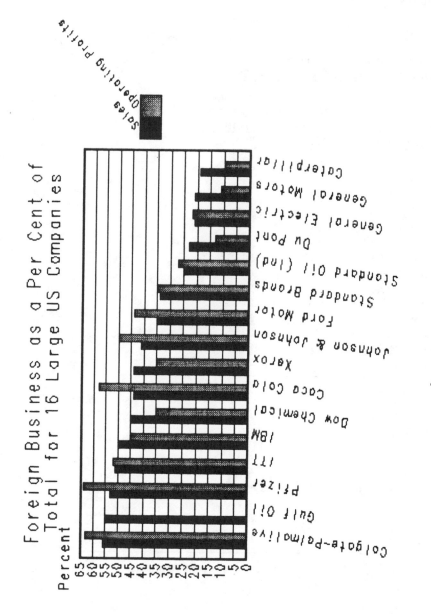

Foreign Business as a Per Cent of
Total for 16 Large US Companies

Percent

Sales Operating Profits

Company

Caterpillar
General Motors
General Electric
Du Pont
Standard Oil (Ind)
Standard Brands
Ford Motor
Johnson & Johnson
Xerox
Coca Cola
Dow Chemical
IBM
ITT
Pfizer
Gulf Oil
Colgate-Palmolive

65 60 55 50 45 40 35 30 25 20 15 10 5 0

Growth of Foreign Subsidiaries of US Companies

TOTAL SUBSIDIARIES

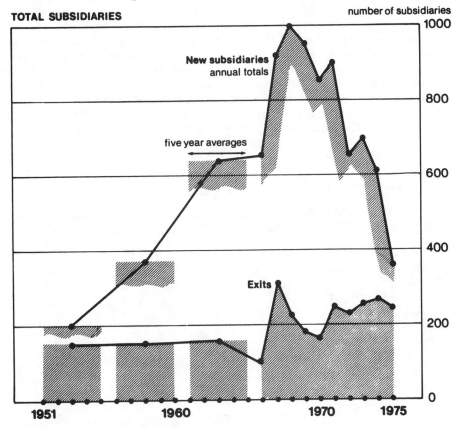

number of subsidiaries

Source: Harvard Multinational Enterprise Study

MANUFACTURING SUBSIDIARIES

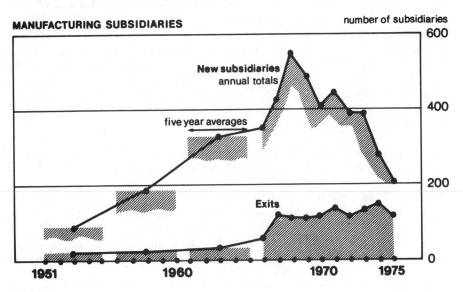

number of subsidiaries

Expropriation not the cause of corporate exits

Although the formation of new subsidiaries has slowed, the number of disinvestments has not fallen proportionately. This differing pattern indicates that diverse factors may be affecting these developments. One possibility is that the growth in the number of exits has resulted from governmental nationalisation or expropriations of subsidiaries. Certainly expropriations are well reported in the media and gain much attention; however, the increase in expropriations does not seem entirely to explain the exit phenomenon. Table 3 presents a breakdown by method of exit for the disinvestments which occurred. Although the number of expropriations has increased over the years to a high of 42 in 1975, the number of subsidiaries sold or liquidated has also been increasing.

Table 3

Patterns of Disinvestment

| | Method of exit | | | | |
	Sold	Liquidated	Expropriated	Unknown	Total
1951–55	40	52	1	23	116
1956–60	47	80	54	26	207
1961–65	82	157	24	53	316
1966	41	60	0	8	109
1967	167	151	3	8	329
1968	110	117	2	3	232
1969	125	78	3	1	207
1970	171	103	2	1	277
1971	146	124	3	1	274
1972	148	89	8	3	248
1973	147	124	9	0	280
1974	158	112	18	2	290
1975	133	92	42	0	267
1951–75	1,515	1,339	169	129	3,152

Source: Curhan, op cit, page 165.

Although part of the explanation for the disinvestment activity may be found in expropriations, the vast majority of exits still result from sales and liquidations. Some of these sales may have been "encouraged" by governmental pressure; nevertheless, most could probably be considered voluntary. In order to ascertain what factors might be causing these voluntary disinvestments, it would be well to review some theories concerning the initial international investment.

One of the earliest theories of direct foreign investment was developed by Hymer[1]. He stated that foreign investment occurs for two major reasons:

1. it is sometimes profitable to control enterprises in more than one country in order to remove competition between them;

2. some firms have advantages in a particular activity, and they may find it profitable to exploit these advantages by establishing foreign operations.

---

1 Hymer, Stephen H, The International Operations of National Firms: A Study of Direct Foreign Investment (Cambridge Mass: The MIT Press), 1976.

His investment model holds that foreign investment will occur only when there is some departure from the perfectly competitive market assumed in classical economic theory. Thus, he presupposed an oligopolistic industry structure as necessary for direct foreign investment. He indicated that a local firm always has some advantages over a foreign firm operating in the host economy. These advantages include better information about the economy, laws, politics, etc, immunity from discrimination against foreign firms, and less concern with exchange rate fluctuations. The foreign firm must possess some advantage over the local firm in order to enable it to compete in the local market. The foreign enterprise may have superior marketing skills, access to lower cost factors of production, a more efficient production function, economies of scale, or a differentiated product. The imperfect market for these factors would restrict the local firm from acquiring them and improving its competitive abilities.

Firms may also compete with one another in third country markets. If such international competition exists, it may be profitable to remove the element of competition and have a form of collusion. One type of collusion is the creation of cartels; however, US companies are effectively precluded from this avenue by antitrust laws. Mergers have therefore evolved as the most expeditious and effective method of reducing competition. In these cases the larger firm, typically the US company, emerges as dominant.

Motivations to foreign investment

Expanding on this concept of investment, a dynamic product life cycle theory was proposed by Vernon[1]. This model holds that as a product is developed, it will encounter several distinct stages during its life cycle. When a new product is first produced, it will normally be introduced in the home market of the innovating company. There are several reasons for this. First, since the product is new, there may be a need for improvements and alterations during its initial period of sales. Second, because it is an innovation, it will be relatively price inelastic, making low cost production less important than proximity to the market. As the product develops, foreign demand for the product will begin. This demand is initially met by exports from the home country to the foreign market. This increased volume will allow for expanding economies of scale in production resulting in lower production costs. Local firms in the foreign markets will be prevented from producing the product because of the high barriers to entry, high costs for production and distribution in the small local markets, and lack of technology for the production process.

As the demand for the product increases abroad, the size and appeal of these foreign markets will increase. When the technology becomes available, foreign competitors may begin to produce the product for their home market. This may be additionally encouraged by the foreign government imposing tariffs on the imported product. The resultant threat of competition from other manufacturers will encourage the original producer to begin manufacturing in the foreign market, the third stage of the cycle. Numerous studies have been undertaken to examine whether the motivation to invest abroad initially was voluntary or involuntary. Some have suggested that the impetus to foreign investment is competition in the marketplace.[2] They have argued that firms invest abroad to protect or obtain a market

1 Vernon, Raymond, Sovereignty at Bay (New York: Basic Books), 1971.   2 See Knickerbocker, F T, Oligopolistic Reaction and Multinational Enterprise (Boston, Mass: Divs. of Research, Grad. School of Business Admin Harvard Univ), 1973; Graham, E M, Oligopolistic Imitation and European Direct Investment in the United States, unpublished doctoral thesis, Harvard Business School, 1974; Moxon, R W, Offshore Production in the Less Developed Countries by American Electronic Companies, unpublished doctoral thesis, Harvard Business School, 1973; Stobaugh, R B et al, Nine Investments Abroad and Their Impact at Home (Boston, Mass: Div of Research, Harvard Business School), 1976.

position that would not otherwise be available if the firm did not produce abroad, and that foreign direct investment is in that sense involuntary. This assumption was accepted in the Reddaway Report (Effects of United Kingdom Direct Overseas Investment; Final Report. Cambridge University Press. 1968).

The proponents of the voluntary investment position argue that firms invest abroad to capitalise on a competitive advantage which they have over other firms.[1] Thus, the firms are not forced into the foreign investment, but rather elect to invest in order to capture an oligopolistic profit. Regardless of whether a company is forced by external competitive pressures to invest, or if the motivation is to capitalise on a competitive advantage, the end result in the foreign marketplace will be the same. The existence of some competitive advantage enables the foreign subsidiary to compete successfully in the foreign market. This competitive advantage could be a lower cost of capital, a trademark, marketing knowledge, a lower manufacturing cost based on economies of scale, better access to capital markets, superior managerial abilities, etc. Whatever advantages the firm possesses, it attempts to exploit them and maintain its position in the market.

Competition and disinvestment in mature industries

As the foreign market continues to develop, more competitors are thereby encouraged to enter the market; and the competitive advantage begins to erode. Other firms learn the technology of production; the market size expands to allow economies of scale to other firms; the marketing abilities of competitors increase; other firms gain access to the lower cost capital, etc. As these competitors increase their ability to compete, the foreign subsidiary loses its advantage, and its market share may decrease. A study by Stobaugh noted this decline of market power for US firms[2]. He found a gradual loss over time in the initially advantageous economic position of the USA within worldwide industries and subindustries.

The forces within the marketplace work to erode competitive advantages. At this stage in its life cycle, a product becomes a commodity, a non-differentiated product. The time frame in which this occurs depends upon the product. Some products have arrived at the commodity stage rapidly, for example petrochemicals, while other companies attempt to prolong the life of their products through upgrading management skill, product design changes, heavy advertising, and other methods. If a company is successful in these "holding actions", a product may never reach the commodity stage.

It is likely, however, that at some time the subsidiary's product will no longer have any competitive advantages over other products in the market. Accompanying this loss of differentiation is the loss of the "excess rent" or oligopolistic profit which the differentiation of competitive advantage allowed. With the decreased return for the subsidiary, the return for the parent multinational system also falls. At this senescent stage, Vernon contends that the firm has two courses of action: drop the product or hang on[3]. If the firm chooses to hang

---

1 See Caves, R E, "Causes of Direct Investment: Foreign Firms' Shares in Canadian and US Manufacturing Industries", The Review of Economics and Statistics, March 1974; Horst, T, "The Industrial Composition of US Exports and Subsidiary Sales to the Canadian Market", The American Economic Review, March 1972; Aliber, R Z, "A Theory of Direct Foreign Investment", in The Multinational Corporation, ed. Kindleberger, C P (Cambridge, Mass: MIT Press), 1970, Lee, C H, "A Stock Adjustment Analysis of Capital Movements: The United States – Canadian Case", Journal of Political Economy, July/August 1969. 2 Stobaugh, et al, op cit, page 213. 3 Vernon, Raymond, "The Location of Economic Activity", Economic Analysis and the Multinational Enterprise, edited by John H Dunning (London: George Allen and Unwin Ltd), 1974.

on, it will be faced with price competition and low profit margins leading to a lower return and perhaps a less than optimal system return. Given this alternative, many companies have chosen to drop out after their competitive advantages were eroded. Examples of industries in which US firms at one time had large foreign investments but have since withdrawn are electric power, life insurance, coffee plantations, and sugar plantations.[1]

Hypothesis for a disinvestment model

Based on the above model of economic behaviour, it can be said that:

as the competition in a market increases, the probability of the disinvestment of a particular subsidiary operating in that market will also increase.

Having developed a model of disinvestment, it is now possible to analyse the divestment activity which has occurred to determine whether it has followed the pattern suggested by the model.

According to the model, one would expect disinvestment to occur where a high level of competition exists. This would be in mature industries with products which are not easily differentiated, require a technology which is readily available, and have easily attained scale economies.

The manufacturing subsidiaries of the 187 US multinationals were segmented into 42 industrial classifications. The number of disinvestments was divided by the total number of subsidiaries established through 1975 to calculate a disinvestment percentage for each of these classifications. The results are shown in Table 4.

Table 4

Exits as a Percentage of Manufacturing Subsidiaries

Industry		Industry	
Textiles & apparel	41.5	Wood & furniture	17.1
Agric chemicals	32.5	Office mach & equipment	17.0
Leather	27.6	Metal cans	16.4
Elec transp equipment	26.9	Electronics	15.7
Beverages	26.5	Motor vehicles	15.0
Fabr plastics	25.8	Other chemicals	14.8
Other transp equipment	25.5	Glass	14.6
Industrial chemicals	23.8	Construction machinery	13.5
Plastics	23.0	Other electrical equipment	13.4
Miscellaneous	21.9	Other fabr metal	13.3
Radio & TV appliances	21.7	Other non-electrical mach	12.2
Food	20.7	Precision equipment	12.1
Electric light & wire	20.4	Cosmetics	11.6
Iron & steel	20.3	Abrasives	8.2
Specialist machinery	18.5	Drugs	7.8

(continued)

1 Stobaugh, Robert B. et al, "US Multinational Enterprises and the US Economy" in Bureau of International Commerce, US Department of Commerce, The Multinational Corporation, Vol 1 (Washington: Superintendent of Documents), 1972, page 26.

<u>Table 4</u> (continued)

<u>Exits as a Percentage of Manufacturing Subsidiaries</u>

Industry		Industry	
Communication	18.4	Printing	7.5
Other petroleum	18.4	Farm machinery	7.3
Paper	18.4	General machinery	5.9
Refined petroleum	17.9	Tobacco	3.3
Engines & turbines	17.8		
Non ferrous	17.7	Mean	17.5
Tyres	17.7		
Stone, clay, & cement	17.6		

Source: Harvard Multinational Enterprise Study.

As expected, the industries with mature, homogeneous products had the highest rates of disinvestment. In the textile industry, 41.5 per cent of the subsidiaries which were established were later divested. Other industries with high disinvestment rates were agricultural chemicals, leather products, electrical transportation equipment, and beverages. At the other extreme were tobacco, general machinery, farm machinery, printing, and drugs.

As in any type of data analysis, there may be other factors contributing to the disinvestment pattern. Some industries such as tobacco, leather products and farm machinery included relatively few subsidiaries, so the disinvestment rate could be easily biased by an unusual occurrence. However, a survey of the ranking of the industries confirms the pattern suggested by the disinvestment model. Those industries which are characterised by differentiated products and high technology have had relatively less disinvestment. The incidence of exits is higher in the more mature industries.

Purchasers of divested operations are not MNCs

The industry breakdown of disinvestments confirms the hypothesis that loss of competitive advantage leads to disinvestment. The disinvestment model suggests that local firms usually possess some advantages over foreign ones; therefore, one would expect that if a subsidiary were sold, it would be sold to a local firm. This is because of the higher value these subsidiaries would have to the local firms due to their competitive advantages. Unfortunately, the identity of buyers is not included in the Harvard study. However, a series of disinvestment case studies by Boddewyn yielded results which are compatible with this hypothesis[1]. Of the group of 40 subsidiaries studied, 27 were sold to local firms. Of the ten which were sold to foreign companies, he reported that most of the firms were already operating in the country. They were not using the acquisitions as a method of entry into the country.

Geographic spread of disinvestment

The model would lead one to expect a greater rate of disinvestment in more developed countries. This would occur for two reasons. First, in developed countries a higher level of competition would be likely to exist. A more developed economy would provide for greater scale economies and for the development of competitors. Second, the development of competitors would provide potential buyers for the sale of the subsidiary. In most cases, the sale of a subsidiary as a going concern will provide a greater income to the parent than would liquidation. Thus, the availability of buyers would facilitate the disinvestment of the subsidiary. The manufacturing subsidiaries of the 187 US multinational companies were segmented according to the location of operations. The percentage of disinvestments from the total subsidiaries established in each country was calculated. A summary of the divestment rates is shown in Table 5.

1 Boddewyn, J J, <u>International Divestment, A Survey of Corporate Experience</u> (New York: Business International), 1976.

Table 5

Divestment of Manufacturing Subsidiaries, 1950-75

Geographic area	Divestments as a % of total
Canada	39.5
Central America & Caribbean	28.6
South America	29.6
Europe	29.4
Belgium	28.8
France	32.5
Germany	27.2
Italy	32.0
Luxemburg	-
Netherlands	29.2
Denmark	31.0
Ireland	18.8
United Kingdom	34.5
Other	21.4
North Africa & Middle East	15.3
East & West Africa	7.2
South Asia	15.3
East Asia	13.6
South Dominions	23.1

Source: Harvard Multinational Enterprise Study.

As was to be expected, the disinvestment rate was higher in the developed countries of Europe and Canada. The less developed areas of Africa and Asia had relatively less disinvestment. The level of exits in Central America and the Caribbean and South America does not conform as closely to the disinvestment pattern as the other geographic areas. This could be due to the high level of expropriations in those areas. 73 per cent of the total expropriations for all areas occurred in these two regions. This may account for the higher than expected disinvestment rate in these two regions. Taking into account the unusual situation in Central and South America, the geographic distribution of disinvestments supports the pattern hypothesised by the product life cycle model.

Life cycle theory supports normal role for disinvestment

These data support the concept of the product life cycle model of foreign disinvestment. The stages of the life cycle for foreign subsidiaries are:

1.   introduction of a new product and production and sales in the home market;

2.   exporting of the product to meet foreign demand;

3.   establishment of foreign subsidiaries to produce and sell in foreign markets;

4.   growth of the foreign markets which fosters increased competition;

5.   disinvestment of the foreign subsidiary.

This model has several implications, for both businesses and the host country governments of foreign subsidiaries. From a business standpoint, the model indicates that there is a normal process of development of subsidiaries. Most businessmen are familiar with and have adapted to the product life cycle model as it pertains to individual products. They have learned to adjust to the stages of this life cycle. Management should similarly adapt to the life cycle stages of subsidiaries and become familiar with the implications of the stages. Managers should be aware that the falling profitability of a subsidiary, given its existing product range, may not be any more "correctable" than the profit level of a product which has passed its growth stage in the home market.

This means that managers should not view a decline in a subsidiary as a failure of management. Rather than an automatic reaction of pouring additional management talent into a senescent subsidiary, the best alternative would be to evaluate whether the subsidiary was in fact in a highly competitive market and if the firm would be better off divesting the subsidiary.

From the standpoint of governments, the model suggests that there may be alternatives to expropriations of foreign subsidiaries. Expropriations or nationalisations typically occur in mature industries where the technology of production and management capabilities are available outside the multinational systems. It is in these same industries where the greatest likelihood of voluntary disinvestment of subsidiaries occurs. Therefore, governments might be in a position to negotiate a mutually agreeable arrangement with the multinational company. A negotiated sale would be better for all parties concerned, and the model suggests that such arrangements are possible if the host governments are willing to allow for the subsidiaries to follow their life cycle.

The model has another important implication; disinvestment by multinational corporations is not a passing phenomenon. As new subsidiaries are established, they will enter into the life cycle. With the great number of subsidiaries established during the 1960s, there may be a significant number of subsidiaries already in or approaching the senescent stage of their product cycles. This portends continued disinvestment in the future, and business should prepare for its occurrence.

The Future of The International Oil Companies

The Pre-1970 Oil Order is Extinct
How Are The Oil Majors Facing New Political Pressures?

LOUIS TURNER[*]

No.4 1976

During the past three years the structure and organisation of the international petroleum industry has undergone vast changes. These have caused the multinational oil "majors" to lose their control over production and their influence on the price of crude oil, which, for more than two decades after the second world war, had been taken for granted as features of what were mainly vertically integrated businesses. The companies started to lose control over pricing when they crumbled in the face of pressures from producer governments in the Teheran-Tripoli negotiations of 1971. More recently, the process has accelerated, their upstream assets have been taken over in country after country, and now it needs only the final signing of the Aramco deal in Saudi Arabia for the pre-1973 order to be more or less formally extinct.

National oil companies such as Saudi Arabia's Petromin and Iran's NIOC are now increasing forces at the upstream end of the market. In 1975, such companies controlled 62 per cent of international oil production (i e non-communist and non-North American) against a mere 9 per cent twelve years earlier. Over the same period, the majors' share of crude production went down from 82 per cent to 30 per cent; of refining from 65 per cent to 47 per cent; and of marketing from 62 per cent to 45 per cent.

What is less obvious is that political pressures on the international companies have been simultaneously growing within the industrialised world. Countries as important as the UK (BNOC), Germany (Veba-Gelsenberg), France (Elf-Erap), Canada (Petro-Can) and in some ways Japan (JPDC) have all, over the last decade, been developing "national champions" which, whether state owned or not, have been seen as a way of countering the majors which have dominated the oil markets of the industrialised world for so long. Within Northern Europe, the development of North Sea hydrocarbons has meant that governments as traditionally friendly to the majors as those of the UK and the Netherlands have moved well away from the laissez-faire approach with which they previously handled oil matters. Within the USA, widespread distrust of the oil companies has been growing throughout the 1970s, first manifesting itself in the form of environmental resistance to industry proposals for offshore exploration and production, refineries and pipelines, but increasingly taking the form of demands for the divestiture of the companies, i e their breakup. Whether or not President Carter pursues his electioneering programme on horizontal divestiture (stripping them of their non-oil interests) it is clear that the old oil industry lobby within Congress is not the force of the past, and that some form of oil industry divestiture is now politically conceivable. The fact that this is so could be as significant as anything which Opec has been able to inflict on the industry. So, given the pressures from all sides, how will the traditional companies survive?

The emerging balance upstream

Although the old system of oil concessions has now been largely dismantled, the traditional companies have not been driven out of their historical upstream preserves. In most cases, the majors have managed to convert their old concessions into management or marketing contracts which, while not leaving them with the freedom or potential profitability of the former regime, still leave them with privileged entitlements to at least part of the crude which was formerly theirs and with commitments to continue many of the activities, such as exploration, which they had always carried out anyway.

[*] The author is a research fellow at the Royal Institute of International Affairs, and the arguments in this article are developed in Oil Companies in the International System, published by the RIIA Allen and Unwin, in 1978, London and Winchester, Mass.

The most important of such deals will be that between Saudi Arabia and the Aramco parents (Exxon, Texaco, Socal and Mobil). Informed reports suggest that these parents will continue lifting virtually all Aramco's oil production, even after the full 100 per cent takeover. Payment for operating the concern on behalf of the Saudi government will initially take the form of a 15 cents a barrel operating fee (payable even on that part of Aramco's production which the Saudis lift themselves) and an exploration fee of 6 cents a barrel. The companies are expected to continue exploring, putting up their own capital. In return, they will be rewarded for successful exploration by additional crude supply entitlements and a per barrel service fee which is directly related to the size of the new reserves which they identify.

The takeover deals being negotiated in Saudi Arabia have been preceded by similar arrangements in other parts of the oil world such as Venezuela, Kuwait and Qatar, with perhaps the most important distinction being the higher proportion of crude oil production being sold back to the former concessionaires in Saudi Arabia. The relatively tough Kuwaiti deals with ex-concessionaires BP and Gulf are basically straightforward oil supply contracts which, in contrast to the likely Aramco deal, do not call on the parent companies to perform a wider range of operational functions.

The success of state oil companies in making direct sales (Iran's NIOC is selling over a million barrels daily in the admittedly favourable markets ahead of the December 1976 Opec meeting) could tempt governments to rethink the proportion of crude oil production to be sold back to former producing companies. On the other hand, although there may be some pressure to adjust what might sometimes be seen as over generous terms, these new contractual arrangements seem to be free from many of the political objections directed against the old concessions system. The companies are now being visibly rewarded in direct proportion to their contribution to given countries' oil industries. As long as they provide superior technology, management or access to markets, they will be rewarded - if they contribute none of these, they will not. And the fact of the matter is that some of the national oil companies will continue to need the assured presence of the majors.

The managerial strengths (taken in the widest sense) of the oil companies should continue to give them a stake in the upstream end of the industry. One notes that, as explained above, the traditional companies have generally not been expelled from the countries with which they have hitherto been involved. Some governments have overcome quite extensive domestic opposition to do deals with the majors. The Venezuelan contracts, for instance, were only signed after considerable controversy. Other countries with traditional hostility to the oil companies, such as India, Brazil and Argentina, have all recently invited a limited number of them in to help explore for oil. Likewise, Norway is rethinking its original refusal to allow non-Norwegian companies to participate north of the 62nd parallel.

However, the future activities of the majors in the oil producing countries will also be of a rather different nature than in the past. The companies will in particular be encouraged to cooperate in high technology areas, such as offshore exploration and production, secondary and tertiary recovery on depleted fields, and chemical and natural gas processing.

In the meantime, the rapid growth of Opec economies offers the traditional companies the chance of taking a major stake in their industrialisation. Many of the relevant projects are not yet finalised, but Aramco is managing the construction of Saudi Arabia's gas gathering system, a project which is currently costed at between $16 and $20 bn, and which could well escalate higher. Mobil is involved in a number of enormous joint ventures with Petromin in Saudi Arabia, including a small lubes refinery, a crude oil pipeline project linked to a large export refinery, and a petrochemical exporting complex at Yanbu; these are all now entering the preliminary engineering stage. Socal is going into cable and wire manufacturing (with other companies) as part of Saudi Arabia's electrification programme. Gulf's real estate company has won a contract in Kuwait to expand and redevelop a community, and the

Kuwaiti government has joined this company in a jointly owned real estate company to develop throughout the Arab world. In Venezuela, BP, which was not a former concessionaire in that country, is combining with Venezuelan interests to propose a protein-from-oil plant.

The NOCs will continue to produce the bulk of crude

Superficially, it might appear that the greatest challenge to the majors will come from national oil companies such as NIOC (National Iranian Oil Company), which now ranks second in sales behind Shell in Fortune's list of non-American industrial companies. In some areas, it is true that the majors can do little about such competition. For instance, no international company will be able to stop such state oil companies from producing the bulk of the world's crude. And in shipping the majors would be unable to prevent those companies from increasing their stake in the tanker market, though the latter development is likely to cause more concern to the consumer country governments than to the majors (importing governments may have something to say from the security angle).

The battle becomes more of a genuine contest at the refining and marketing stages, because these are largely outside the jurisdiction of the producer governments. All the indications are that there will be a glut of refinery capacity throughout the world well into the 1980s, and on the face of it, the economics of export refineries are highly questionable.

Though the national oil companies may be wary about over investing, the likelihood is that pressures will build up on them to make a certain amount of what will basically be political investment in export refineries, which could pose problems for the majors and possibly the importing OECD governments. To the extent that such refining investments take place, the national oil companies will probably further erode the majors' share of the refining sector. Nevertheless in some cases, eg Mobil in Saudi Arabia, the majors will initially be supplying a large part of the managerial skills in operating the refineries, and undoubtedly taking a considerable responsibility for marketing. In return their proportionate share of financial commitment in these refining projects will be small – in the case of the Mobil/Petromin refinery Mobil is only putting up some 10 per cent of the capital.

Outside the immediate confines of the oil industry, the national oil companies should pose few problems for the large international oil companies. In any event, the state companies will be relatively inefficient, given that it takes time to develop the necessary depths of managerial expertise in societies which are short of skilled manpower. The most striking example of this has been Pertamina, which managed to run up debts of around $10 bn before corrective action was taken. Undoubtedly, such companies will learn, but even so there are other reasons for arguing that the national oil companies will coexist with, rather than re-place, the old majors. For although their politicians and some of their top managements may well have visions of taking these companies out into the international arena and competing head on with the traditional companies, the bulk of these state companies will be charged primarily with looking after the oil interests of their particular nation. It is possible that they will become more inward looking still and evolve into large industrial conglomerates within their parent economies, paying relatively little attention to foreign activities. For many, this route will appear to throw up considerably less in the way of both financial and political risks than competing in the international oil industry.

Although there may well be some regional cooperation between certain national oil companies, the experience of operating in many different situations under changing political and economic environments will, as well as their superior technology give a continuing competitive edge to the majors. Few of the indigenous markets catered for by the national oil companies will be large enough to permit this industrial learning process to take place within a single national economy.

Thus the likelihood is that the national oil companies and the majors will coexist. Neither is likely to be able to replace the other, and their roles will be predominantly complementary.

Operating environment in OECD countries

In retrospect, the years 1973-1976 may well be seen   as the high point in popular indignation expressed against the oil companies within the OECD world. There was already, prior to the 1973 oil embargo, some suspicion that the growing shortage of certain products was the result of oil company plotting, rather than a sign of a rapidly tightening oil market. Events during the embargo fed this suspicion, not because the companies behaved reprehensibly during it (for all the serious studies show they did their best to share the misery equally) but because no government had the detailed knowledge of the oil market to be sure that the companies really were behaving responsibly. The result was considerable misapprehension. The Japanese were convinced they had been hard done by. The Europeans believed the Germans were being favoured since that was the most profitable market; many pro-Israeli Americans believed the companies were allied with the Arab cause.

This clamour against the companies was strongest in the USA and culminated in the attempt to have them split up. As already mentioned, it is too soon to comment with authority on how far President Carter will push legislation, but it is already clear that the nature of the debate within Congress is changing from its initial concern with vertical divestiture (i e splitting production from refining) and moving towards horizontal divestiture, aimed at stopping oil companies from coming to dominate alternative energy developments such as coal or nuclear power. Viewed objectively, the industry's opponents do not have a particularly strong case: 13 oil companies with coal interests are likely to have only some 31 per cent of US coal production in 1985. Concentration would seem to be higher in uranium, where Exxon, Kerr-McGee and Conoco have 27 per cent of US production, and Getty, Exxon and a joint venture between Sohio and Reserve Oil have a proposed uranium milling capacity of 38 per cent of the total. Given that the combination of oil companies and nuclear energy combines two politically tendentious topics, horizontal divestiture might still well have a chance of enactment, though informed opinion at the time of writing guesses it will fail.

On the wider OECD level, the stock of the international oil companies seems to have gone up in official circles. This seems to have come about when the post-embargo inquiries showed that the companies had behaved responsibly, and when it became clear that the threat from Arab oil producers was far more serious than anything the companies might pose. Thus, when the International Energy Agency got down to business, it was virtually inevitable that its planned emergency allocation scheme should rest heavily on the cooperation of the oil companies. Around 16 companies are grouped in two bodies known as the Industry Advisory Board and the Industry Working Party, working with the IEA in developing a satisfactory allocation scheme as well as an information system about their pricing activities, which will allow governments to take a more informed position about the industry.

The fact that these companies are willing to cooperate to some extent in making their activities more "transparent" is going to make life both harder and easier for them within the OECD world. On the one hand, the fact that they are playing along with OECD governments should reduce some of the blind suspicion of their motives which existed amongst governments like the Italian and French prior to 1973. On the other hand, greater transparency of operation will tend to boost the trend toward price and profit controls on oil related activities, as will the idea that such companies cannot be allowed to make "excess" or "windfall" profits. OECD governments will also gain a greater knowledge on industry costs from the experience of their own state companies. It thus looks as though the companies engaged in the oil industry are entering an era in which they will increasingly be treated somewhat like utilities. This has its dangers, as the mismanagement of price controls in the US natural gas sector and in the Italian oil market have shown. On the other hand, the increasing emergence of the IEA as an international body which both sympathises with the needs of the companies and is starting to scrutinise the national energy policies of its members provides some assurance that governments will at least be forcibly reminded when over obsession with containing profit margins is likely to work against long term energy needs. In the process of implementing its November 1976 decision to evaluate member countries' energy policies against its overall targets for 1985, the IEA will identify those areas where price controls are unnecessarily prejudicing the future growth of supply.

There are signs, then, that the oil companies' life in the OECD world will become increasingly complex, though not necessarily impossible for them. A wide range of governments is now obviously much more alert to events in the industry than it was a decade ago. There is probably little the companies can do to stop governments increasingly regulating oil markets as these become more and more transparent. On the other hand, there are signs that the blind anti company sentiments which dominated some industrialised policy makers a year or two ago are now on the decline. The belief that intergovernmental deals will somehow offer cheaper and politically more acceptable oil than the oil companies could secure is now increasingly rare. Should the divestiture movement in the USA finally come to a halt within the next twelve months, then the oil companies might even start relaxing.

The majors now move towards diversification

The first result of the growth of conflicting pressures on the oil companies has been that they have become more profit conscious than they were in the days when success was primarily measured by how many barrels of crude each company could dispose of. They have now, for instance, become increasingly ready to divest themselves of unprofitable activities. BP and Shell both despaired of the Italian business environment and sold out during 1973 and 1974. Exxon similarly pulled out of India and the Philippines. During 1973, Gulf substantially pulled out of the German market. At the same time this growing concern with profitability has been given graphic expression by the decisions of Gulf, Conoco and Sun Oil to change their organisations from a geographic to a functional basis. In all companies, there is growing concern with identifying and monitoring profit centres.

Parallel to divestments have been considerable diversification efforts. The most obvious move has been into increasing their petrochemicals effort, with 6 per cent of Exxon's total sales now coming from chemicals, and 9 per cent of Shell's (only twelve companies in the world sell more chemicals than Shell). However, it is interesting to note that the kinds of bulk chemicals in which the oil companies have been strongest are exactly those which interest the Opec nations as they try to move into this industry themselves. With this sector of the industry also suffering from overcapacity in many areas, the majors are tending to move into more specialised chemicals, in which traditional chemical companies like Du Pont, Dow, ICI and Hoechst will undoubtedly prove formidable competitors.

A more recent approach has been to combine their strengths in the energy market with their general expertise in exploration and mining technology. Coupling this with the fact that new world oil reserve prospects are very much less than carboniferous fossil fuel reserves, many companies are now involved in coal on an increasingly global basis. Shell has a production sharing contract in Indonesia which should be producing coal within the next two years or so, after expenditure which could eventually total $1.2 bn. BP has recently bought a half interest in Australia's second largest exporter of black coals. Exxon is entering a coal exploration and development project with the Colombian government in an area every bit as inhospitable as those in which much of the world's oil has been found.

Similar considerations explain why various international companies are now heavily involved in the nuclear energy market, whether this involves uranium mining (Exxon and Conoco), fuel enrichment (Exxon), nuclear plant construction (Shell and, up to recently, Gulf). These projects have not been without their risks. General Atomics (the Shell-Gulf joint venture) has proved thoroughly disappointing as the market for nuclear reactors turned down over the last two or three years while General Atomics' development costs soared upward. The sums of money needed to win a leading place in this market are so great as to strain the resources of even the largest companies, and the financial rewards by no means assured. The oil companies are thus more cautious. Although a firm like Exxon is interested in entering the uranium enrichment field in the USA, it is unlikely to do so without some financial guarantees or assistance from the federal government. Similar considerations hold for companies like Shell, Conoco, Sunoco and Occidental which have been trying to get synthetic crude schemes off the drawing board. Shell Canada, for instance, has had to shelve a $3 bn tar sands project in the absence of the requested government equity capital or loan guarantees. This is not to say that the international oil companies will not eventually come to be active in this field, but it is clear that none of them have the resources to develop capital intensive industries such as this, which will not become economic until the international price of oil has risen to between $20 and $24 a barrel (Conoco estimates).

The one other attractive area of expansion is into the ocean. To start with, this has the attraction of being a high technology field in which, quite literally, technological progress is measured by the depths at which companies feel they can bring a hydrocarbons deposit onstream (Exxon currently holds the depth record for a production platform, which Shell should surpass in 1978). The technology is still developing fast (tension leg platforms, sea bed production techniques etc), and companies like BP are hoping to play an important role in the development of the Soviet Union's reserves in the Caspian Sea on the strength of their record in other seas of the world. The second attraction of the offshore arena is that the companies are moving into a part of the world which could well come under international, not national, jurisdiction. Of course, the exact outcome of the UN Law of the Seas conference still has to be determined, but developments in the oil companies' skills suggest that they will before long be able to operate outside the zones which are likely to be given to the coastal states for exploitation, thus escaping the attentions of rigid nationalists.

Technological expertise is their main strength

On the whole it is expected that international oil companies will survive by building on existing strengths, rather than by the kind of conglomerate style diversification exemplified by Mobil's takeover for Marcor, the US retailing company. The exact pattern of their future development, though, will depend on political events which will sometimes be beyond their control. For instance, diversification into alternative energy sources could be hit by a US decision to require oil companies to accept horizontal divestiture. Again, their future in the oceans will be affected by whatever international legal regime may emerge from the UN considerations.

What is clear, though, is that the majors will no longer be so distinct from smaller competitors in the oil industry. Some of the oil producing national oil companies will find ways of capitalising on their political hold over crude production and integrate downstream into the international arena, but this development will be slow. The majors may also be faced with some of the smaller companies coming together in more or less formal cooperative patterns (for instance, continental European companies like CFP, Elf, ENI, Petrofina and Veba have recently been taking common positions before the EEC Commission). OECD governments and international agencies will through the operation of their own state oil companies, and direct intervention, more closely control their domestic oil markets, though this does not imply increasingly unprofitable operations. The result will be a situation of considerable competitive flux, with politics playing an important role in defining the most appropriate strategy. The companies which will best survive will be those which build most thoroughly on their strengths and utilise their technological, marketing and general managerial expertise. There is every reason to suppose that the bulk of the international oil companies will succeed in adapting to these new circumstances.

166

Management Contracts:
Earning Profits from Fee Income In Place of Earnings on Equity

RICHARD ELLISON[•]   No.1 1976

In many developing countries nowadays, direct investment by foreign companies is actively discouraged. This can occur through "indigenisation" policies, whereby part of total owner- ship is transferred to local interests; through nationalisation; or as a consequence of administrative harassment or fiscal barriers. Often the same discouragement occurs through the mental processes of the companies' senior managements, when these consider investment in third world countries to be particularly risky. Moreover, in many such countries a reexamination of the balance of advantage of inward foreign direct investment has taken place in recent years, which in some cases has resulted in a decision that it is disadvantageous to the host country, at least in some industries. In some countries, too, there are physical as well as political limits to the amount of foreign direct investment that can be economically absorbed - as in some Middle Eastern countries. The need to provide infrastructure and personnel training may be seen to conflict with the expected mode of operation of multinational companies.

The management contract is increasingly seen as the basis on which such countries can work together with multinational companies. And if the third world is moving in this direc- tion away from encouragement of foreign equity ownership, adoption of management contracts has occurred widely among Comecon countries where previously multinational companies had been excluded altogether.

Indeed, so strong are the pressures against foreign direct investment, that the entire nature of multinational business may change radically in the next few decades. It is generally accepted that the multinational company is characterised by a huge and rapidly growing capital base which is used to earn a return in a large number of locations scattered around the world. Because this has been the pattern in the past does not mean that the multinational company will in future retain the same dimensions, capital growth rates, and methods of doing business. The question has already been asked whether such companies will become mobilisers of resources (manpower, technology, management) rather than mobilisers of capital.[1]

Various bodies, such as the UN Commission on the Transnational Corporation, are directing attention towards the alternatives to direct investment. As yet there has been little clarifi- cation of what these alternatives are, and how they are to be effectively operated. Licensing agreements and the outright sale of technical knowhow are common but do not satisfy all the requirements of the developing countries, especially the need for management and com- mercial expertise.

A multinational company can make available a whole range of both technical and managerial expertise to foreign enterprises in which it may or may not have a direct financial interest. Such arrangements can be flexible or tied to specific contract terms. Recent consultancy and research carried out in cooperation with some 14 UK based multinational companies has highlighted the increasing interest in the use of the management contract idea. The aim here is to outline a little more clearly the nature of such arrangements, together with some common problems and guidelines for overcoming them.

---

* At the time of writing of the University of Manchester Institute of Science and Technology.

1 Gabriel, Peter P, "From Capital Mobiliser to Management Seller" (Columbia Journal of World Business, March/April 1967).

Management contracts a strategy for expansion in their own right

One of the most important results of the current investigation has been to underline the trend among some firms towards using management contracts as a strategy in their own right. Companies can reap substantial benefits from their use especially if they set out actively to sell their stock of managerial skills and resources. The most successful companies are building an organisation framework specifically to exploit these opportunities, and there is increasing competition amongst companies for such contracts.

A further point has come out quite clearly, and has serious implications for multinational strategy. Although the research supports the advisability of short term contracts it would be a mistake to see this as limiting a company's long term opportunities in a particular country or market. The successful completion of a particular contract (success often being based upon the speed of completion and withdrawal) would in very many cases lead to opportunities for undertaking further contracts related to similar ventures, in the expansion or diversification phases of the local contract enterprise. Further, so competitive is the field becoming and so few are the companies which are experienced in operating such contracts, that successful operations in one country have often proved a decided advantage when opportunities arose in others. The world of management contract operations is still sufficiently sm il to be considered almost as a "club".

Management-only ventures are not confined to fields such as mining and construction which have traditionally included fixed lifetime project management contracts. Increasingly, they are being used for manufacturing and service industries. The companies in this study included those in consumer and industrial products, transportation and communications. The contracts are, of course, more common in the less developed countries, and are becoming an important feature in the Middle East where enormous sums are being earned by multinationals in this way. Differences between countries exist, especially with regard to the type of involvement with the local government. In the Middle East, for example, governments typically employ their own experts to monitor the activities of the managing company, and require strict specification of responsibilities and services to be provided in the contract terms. Such political and social factors will have implications for many aspects of the management contract relationship, affecting the question of equity participation, forms of payment, nature of the required skills, and the extent of control by the multinational over the contract venture.

The management contract defined

Under a management contract scheme, the managing (multinational) company undertakes the usual management functions, makes available a range of skills and resources, and trains local personnel. The contract covers payment to the managing company and (usually) the handing over of authority to trained locals after a certain period. There is a similarity to other methods of operating overseas such as joint ventures or licensing and technical service agreements; but the management contract is seen as being potentially much wider in scope. Confusion with other more limited contractual methods - such as licensing - can lead to quite inappropriate strategies being adopted.

A company may enter into a licensing agreement when the licensee does not possess a sufficient range of skills to cope with the new process and these have to be unexpectedly supplemented. And yet, a company can enter into a management contract arrangement without fully understanding the nature of the commitment, the suitability of its particular products and skills, the availability of managerial personnel or the capability of the receiving enterprise. The basic difference between the management contract and licensing is that the latter must rely upon an already functioning enterprise whilst the company using a management contract often must build the enterprise from scratch, relying not at all upon existing local expertise.

It is necessary, then, to look at the nature of the resources and skills provided. These have been listed as follows:[1]

    i.   human resources;

    ii.   procedures, standards, processes (technology, in a broad sense);

    iii.   corporate capabilities.

The first two categories are virtually self explanatory and they are normally provided under the other contractual arrangements referred to previously. They are nonetheless a significant part of the management contract, and it is important that a company defines the amount and nature of these resources it is willing or able to make available. Contracts can require anything from one or two key individuals up to several thousand for varying periods of time, raising implications for manpower planning, staffing, organisation and other policies.

A careful specification of the nature of the technology (procedures, standards and processes) must also be made by the company. Many companies have not formalised these elements or have done so in a way necessary only for their own internal uses, e g, accounts auditing. Numerous questions are raised, not the least of which is the suitability of the company's technology to a different environment. The basic requirement, however, is that the company must have a clear understanding of what, if anything, it has to sell, including intangible operating and marketing "knowhow" and experience. It is important that a proper price be placed upon these intangible assets.

Although a management contract incorporates many features similar to technical exchange agreements, together with similar "knowhow" for commercial, administrative and management procedures, what it is uniquely offering is "corporate capability". This is difficult to define but can include on the most simple level such elements as the large company's access to funds, general reputation, and worldwide procurement capability. More important is the fundamental distinction between the skills, knowledge, and capabilities of individuals and of these same individuals working within some type of organisation. A group develops, through working together over time, its own distinctive way of doing things. It is this almost indefinable skill which is such an important part of the management contract, for the aim is not simply to transfer it in the form of an existing multinational "team" but to transplant and reproduce it in local conditions to create a successful enterprise.

An important point should be mentioned here since it opens up a new range of possibilities for any company contemplating entering into such contractual arrangements. There are examples of several companies cooperating together in order to operate management contract ventures. This can be done when, perhaps, the scale of the contract venture is too large or where one company does not possess the full range of skills or resources required and these can be complemented by those of a partner. It is more usual to have only one of the companies taking overall responsibility for the operation of the contract, certain aspects being subcontracted to the second; although there are cases of full blown joint management ventures between companies.

Why companies use management contracts

A combination of factors influences companies to enter into management contracts and these are some of the most important:

---

1 Gabriel, Peter P, The International Transfer of Corporate Skills: Management Contracts in the Less Developed Countries (Harvard 1967).

i.   the management contract is the only method of involvement acceptable to the host governments;

ii.   the company wishes to protect an equity investment;

iii. the return from a direct investment would be too low;

iv.   the amount of capital required for a particular venture is too large for the company, or the host government would not want it to raise finance locally;

v.   the risk of investing is considered too high;

vi.   to secure a market for the company's products;

vii. to secure a source of raw materials for the company;

viii. to support a joint venture;

ix.   to support a licensing or technical knowhow agreement;

x.   where the company has a pool of underused resources or has incurred high expenditure on R & D;

xi.   as a deliberate and complementary part of a company's overall international strategy.

A distinction can be made between "offensive" and "defensive" reasons. In some cases a company has taken a positive ("offensive") decision to use a management contract, for example to earn an income or to secure a market, or in some cases to avoid some of the limitations imposed by statutory minority status. Another company has adopted the arrangement because a host government has acquired an interest in a subsidiary, or has prevented direct investment because the industry is seen as a key national resource which is kept under local "control". This is a "defensive" strategy and about half of the companies involved in our investigation could be placed in this category. Most of the remaining companies gave as their reason for operating management contracts that they wished to extend their international strategy – xi. above – a decision having been taken to exploit a profitable opportunity. These companies tended to be the more successful.

Contractual pitfalls are a major hazard

There are many different types of contract document which are used depending upon the nature of the particular situation. There are brief and general contract documents, and there are detailed and legalistic ones. The first type is often only three or four pages in length, and cases even exist where there is no formal contract at all. The brief contract outlines the purpose of the relationship and responsibilities of the two parties in general terms. The second type sometimes runs to several hundred pages, specifying in detail the obligations of the parties, often laying down how these are to be carried out. Circumstances may dictate otherwise, but the brief and general contract is often preferable since it can lead to better relationships. Disputes are settled in discussions regarding overall objectives, and of course national legislation, rather than by reference to legal interpretation of contractual details. There would, however, seem to be a tendency towards greater use of the legalistic contract resulting in part from the pressure of certain governments (especially in the Middle East) and the vivid imagination of most company lawyers. In most cases such a contract neither protects a company from government action nor ensures in itself a company's effective performance or goodwill.

The basis of remuneration

The remuneration package for operating the management contract can be one, or a mixture of, the following:

(a) fixed fee - a single annual amount determined in advance; or (b) fee contingent on profits, sales, or production; or (c) fees for the procurement of equipment or materials, often expressed as a percentage of the cost; or (d) fees based on the man hours logged by company personnel participating in running the contract venture.

The most common fee basis is one related to sales, and from experience this would also seem, in most circumstances, to be the most advisable method from the company's standpoint. Fixed fees are risky for a company in times of inflation and mistakes in calculating the amount or the cost of the resources provided can be disastrous. Many countries are now insisting on setting a fee fixed in advance but there are several instances of companies still securing contracts whilst refusing to accept this. A fee related to profits can cause serious problems if the consequent profit maximising objectives of the company conflict with the social and political objectives of the local enterprise or host government. Moreover, official policies may often adversely affect the profitability of the management contract venture.

Two further questions arise. First, should the salaries and direct expenses of personnel seconded to the contract venture (and those paying occasional visits) be met out of the fee, or be paid for separately by the local contract enterprise as a current expense? Normally the latter alternative is adopted, although individual practice does differ enormously. Secondly, how does a company establish what is an acceptable level (as distinct from basis) of payment for its services? Only a few companies have established guidelines for this but there is a great need for developing such guidelines, including particularly the true costs of central and operational management overhead. It would be possible to develop criteria for expected returns perhaps by treating the amounts expended by the company in operating such contracts as revenue expenditure, or by reference to an implicit capital commitment. The "opportunity cost" of the resources provided could also be incorporated into such a formula.

Some companies fail to give sufficient consideration to the tax treatment of such fee payments. The tax position of the local contract enterprise can, in the long term, be as important as that of the company itself. Consideration has to be given, for example, to whether the multinational managing company can incur a tax liability locally on its fee income.

Organisation, staffing and manpower planning

A company needs to adapt its organisation structure, internal relationships and control procedures in order to deal effectively with management contract opportunities and operations. In fact few companies are organised specifically to deal with management contracts. But there are a few examples of companies forming separate organisation units with such responsibilities. One company investigated had set up a subsidiary responsible for contract operations, which was expected to meet stringent performance standards in comparison with the group's other operating units. In other cases responsibility was variously shared between the main board directors, and the product or geographical divisions of a company. But even where divisions had the power to enter into management contracts, decisions were often pushed upwards to main board level. This was because the resources required to operate the management contract had to be provided from several line or functional departments outside a single product or geographical division. If internal mechanisms are normally employed to determine the allocation of resources and their cost such conflicts between different parts of the company are minimised.

The problems of manpower planning and staffing often do not appear as formidable as some multinational companies contend. Existing staff can be drafted in at short notice where the project has sufficient priority. Otherwise personnel can be employed on a short term basis. But this requires a special expertise as far as the company is concerned. The problems of absorbing personnel back into the company after completion of a contract, individual remuneration package, and the like, are not essentially different from those faced by an international company operating overseas subsidiaries. Few companies seem to meet special problems in this context. Indeed, the management contract operation has been mentioned as an opportunity for management development, providing interesting positions of responsibility for those who are not quite ready for such senior posts within the parent company.

A major difficulty, however, can be that of justifying the secondment of senior key executives to a contract operation, not owned directly by the company. This has various implications. The fee charged has to be worthwhile, as discussed above. In particular, the short term nature of the contract (which is usually the case) must be allowed for in calculating the fee. This is likely to prove acceptable to the host government if - as is usually the case - it places a high value upon a rapid transfer of management to its own nationals. Scarcity of key people tends to induce a company to complete a contract as quickly as possible. Rapid completion should ordinarily be seen by the company as a factor in the success of a contract venture, to be followed by the opening up of further possibilities. The commitment of scarce resources is vital to success in operating such management contracts. The use of only second best resources can lead to poor performance.

Control of the contract venture

Although no pattern of ownership exists between the managing enterprise and its local operation during the course of a contract, it normally has as much operational or day to day control as if it did. Such operational control leads to a significant influence over policy matters. The distribution of control between the company and the local partner (normally a government dominating the local board) can vary depending on various circumstances, such as the existence of any local expertise. The most serious problems arise when a company is not prepared for the local government or other partner to assume control over certain policy areas such as, commonly, pricing and personnel. It is therefore important for a company to understand the nature of the influence and control which the government wishes to exercise, before entering into the contract arrangement. Even though the company runs the contract enterprise in many ways as it would its own subsidiary it must be prepared to accept limits on its managerial freedom if that is part of the contract terms. Many companies operating management contracts as a second best alternative to investment, or as "defensive" replacements after losing complete control of a wholly owned subsidiary, find it difficult to accept these limits.

The authority or control exercised by a company rarely depends on such factors as the wording of a management contract, the proportion of equity held (if any), or representation on the board of the local venture. It is a far more subtle relationship, dependent in many ways upon the reputation, image and success of the company, and the host government's perceptions of these (not to mention the vagaries in the behaviour of host governments in many cases).

Training and the transfer of management to local nationals

In the majority of cases, the raison d'être of the management contract, as far as the local government is concerned, is that the company should train local personnel with a view to their assumption of complete responsibility in a short time. The most crucial problem of training is that company and government often differ as to their beliefs of how quickly this

172

and the transfer of responsibility can take place. Although some companies have experienced difficulties over these matters, the most important determinant of the speed of training appears to be the <u>attitude</u> of the company towards the process, rather than the techniques used. This attitude seems to be a product of the company's reasons for entering into management contracts. Those having the "defensive" reasons tend to see rapid training and transfer as an enormous problem and are hence constantly involved in disputes with the government concerned. Companies entering into the agreement for "offensive" reasons, accepting it as a short term relationship, do not generally have such problems and are able in many cases to change from using between 50 and 200 expatriates to virtually complete local management in a period of three to five years.

Factors influencing success in management contracts

In order to operate successfully and without constant conflicts it is vital that a company accepts the fixed lifetime of the management contract, at the same time appreciating the longer term opportunities which are often available. In many cases successful completion of one particular contract leads to further contracts being offered to the company, perhaps for a further expansion phase of the contract enterprise, a separate enterprise in the same country, or opportunities elsewhere in the world. Because there are relatively few companies experienced in operating management contracts their reputation becomes known and, therefore, although success is often measured on the speed of contract completion, this success tends not, in the long term, to diminish the company's revenue earning possibilities using this method. Companies established abroad for a long time often find it difficult to accept this philosophy (or else some of their employees do). This leads to what could be described as a "hanging on" syndrome, whereby there is an almost subconscious desire to retain complete control leading to a slower transfer of operations and conflicts with the local partner.

The holding of equity

In most cases, if a company holds a portion of the equity as well as a fee paying management contract, this tends to lead to such severe conflicts in the relationship between the two partners that the management contract arrangement virtually breaks down. It most often applies where the country concerned is, for example, one of the more nationalistic or left wing African states. The main problem is the inherent conflict between the profit maximising objectives of the company and the economic and social policies of the local government. It may well not apply where the local partner is not a government body but a commercial undertaking, since the basic objectives would tend to be similar. Hence, one of the most important questions to be considered when examining the advisability of equity participation is, apart from normal risk and return factors, the underlying objectives and likely policies of the other party contrasted with those of the company.

Conclusions

Unless special circumstances dictate otherwise, a company would in most cases be advised (as, with certain protections, would a foreign partner) to base the formal arrangement on a contract document which is as brief and as general as possible. Further, the period of time for which the contract is to run should be as short as possible. Between three and five years is the norm, with the possibility for renegotiation or mutual termination within the period built into it. The basis and amount of the fee, and also its fiscal treatment, must be considered carefully. Profit linking is generally to be avoided.

Whilst a company must be prepared to accept a great deal of responsibility for operations and generally control the contract enterprise in many ways as if it were a subsidiary, it must also accept certain limits to its power. These limits will depend upon the country of operation and may appear to interfere with efficiency. In most cases a company must accept training of local management as a prime responsibility and recognise that the speed of the process is one of the main bases of success, at least in the eyes of the host government partner. It is all too easy for a company to point to the difficulties of training, the lack of qualified locals, and the conflict between training and operating.

This brief statement sets out just some of the issues which are worth considering. No matter how important the details and the many facets of the operation of management contracts, the main obstacle to their successful use in many companies is an inappropriate overall philosophy, amounting to a prejudice against management without equity. Such contracts have to be seen as a major development in the future of international business. Then a company must accept that using this method it no longer owns and fully controls assets overseas but still provides the same commitment of resources and still earns a satisfactory return, if not into perpetuity.